T0146550

SAWADEE BUFFS

The Final Chapter of the Vietnam War

The Withdrawal

Colonel G. Alan Dugard

authorHOUSE®

AuthorHouse™
1663 Liberty Drive
Bloomington, IN 47403
www.authorhouse.com
Phone: 1 (800) 839-8640

Published by AuthorHouse 01/15/2020

ISBN: 978-1-5246-7004-7 (sc)
ISBN: 978-1-5246-7003-0 (e)

Library of Congress Control Number: 2017901491

Print information available on the last page.

Any people depicted in stock imagery provided by Thinkstock are models, and such images are being used for illustrative purposes only. Certain stock imagery © Thinkstock.

This book is printed on acid-free paper.

Because of the dynamic nature of the Internet, any web addresses or links contained in this book may have changed since publication and may no longer be valid. The views expressed in this work are solely those of the author and do not necessarily reflect the views of the publisher, and the publisher hereby disclaims any responsibility for them.

Dedicated to Rosemary Dugard,
The Keeper of History

"SAWADEE BUFFS" REVISED

"THE FINAL CHAPTER OF THE VIETNAM WAR-THE WITHDRAWL"

The Clock of Life is wound but once
And no one can tell just when the hands will stop
Or on what day or hour
Now is the only time we have
So, live it with a will
Don't wait until tomorrow
The hands may then be still

Unknown Author

FOREWORD

When you are a thirteen-year-old boy who has spent a lifetime believing his father is ten feet tall and bulletproof, there is little worry when he is summoned to war – no concern whatsoever that he will come home in one piece. It is a grand adventure, just like the many other adventures in the illustrious life of a man who punctuated my life as a child with tales of world travel, midnight bombing runs and piloting supersonic aircraft. Nothing to worry about.

Of course, this was the rationalization that got myself and my siblings through my Dad's year in Thailand in the waning days of the Vietnam War. I can honestly say we were never worried, but I do remember my mother's inability to hide her own fears on those nights when loneliness got the best of her. Unless you have been the child of a soldier or pilot, there is no way to describe the longing for the handwritten letters from thousands of miles away, the cherished (but once prohibitively expensive) long distance phone calls – and ultimately the homecoming. There is a letter in my files that my Dad wrote to me on my fourteenth birthday, exhorting me to step up in his absence. Even then, I knew the significance, and that I would cherish those words from a war zone decades later.

It has been forty years since my Dad returned safely. In that time, we have shared a vignette or two about the fall of Saigon or the Mayaquez incident, but very little about the dangers of being stationed in Southeast Asia during one of the most volatile ochs in world history. In his own words, it was an "historical adventure", just as I'd fooled myself into believing back in 1975.

But that year away from home was so much more.

In reading through these pages, I was instantly drawn back to that point in history. I could smell the air and feel the adrenaline. The writing is specific, the memories from so long ago amazingly vivid, sharpened by those long letters home – which still exist to this day. This is a tale of conflict and humanity; character and risk, confusion and loss. And, above all, unique. All great stories can be said to begin with the words "once upon a time" before the tale is unspooled, setting the stage for exciting twists and enchanting turns that are impossible to predict and long remembered. Those four simple words unlock a kingdom.

So, it is with the book you now hold in the palm of your hands.

If I may: "Once upon a time, there was a pilot. . ."

Martin Dugard
New York Times
Best Selling Author
February, 2017

PROLOGUE

Early in 1950 the United States sent American military advisors to assist the South Vietnamese Government in what was then called French-Indochina. U.S. involvement saw a surge in support of the South Vietnamese forces in the early 1960s resulting from an incident in the Gulf of Tonkin. War was declared against North Vietnam in 1962! American combat troops in that region reached an all-time high in 1968. The United States had established bases to support air operations in Thailand, Okinawa and Guam as well as in South Vietnam where fighter and bomber aircraft were stationed to fly missions to assist in the war. The missions flown during December1972 out of all these established bases was called "Linebacker II" and brought about a situation so dire for the North Vietnamese that they asked to discuss an end to the conflict. Peace talks were held in Paris and "The Paris Peace Accord" was signed in January 1973, supposedly ending the fighting and freeing our prisoners of war (POWs). The United States Congress then withdrew all financial support to the military which resulted in an inability to monitor this accord. Direct U. S. military involvement stopped totally in August 1973, leaving the South Vietnamese without the support necessary to sustain meaningful resistance to their northern adversary. The North Vietnamese, thus unopposed, and aware of the action by the United States Congress, renewed their military thrust against South Vietnam. This ended with the Communist forces of North Vietnam capturing the South Vietnamese government capital of Saigon on April 30th, 1975, signaling the end of the Vietnam War. The capitulation of support from the United States was interpreted by most that our military was no longer involved in Southeast Asia. In truth a large segment of the United States Air Force tactical and strategic forces remained in Thailand. For these combat forces the war was not over!

THE CALL

It was late on a March day in 1975, well after duty hours had expired at Mather AFB where I was the vice wing commander sitting in my office, when the direct line from 15th Air Force headquarters, located at March AFB rang. After the third ring I decided to answer the phone, thinking the wing commander had already gone home. As I picked it up I heard the voice of the wing commander, Colonel C. G. Smith, who had picked up with me, saying something to the individual on the other end of the line. It was Al Hawk the Government Service (GS) high level civilian in charge of personnel at 15th Air Force Headquarters at March AFB, who identified himself, although his voice was very familiar to anyone who was in the command. I put the phone down when I realized Curt Smith, the 320th Bomb Wing Commander at the same time had come on the line. Moments later Colonel Smith stood in front of me and told me that I was being reassigned. Initially I was surprised as I was just recently given the position as the 320th Bomb Wing Vice Commander. He told me that Al Hawk said I was in need of an isolated tour and a Southeast Asia assignment. My new assignment was to be the vice wing commander of the 307th Strategic Wing at U-Tapao AB in Thailand. I thought of the impact this would have on my family. My wife Rosemary had been through a great deal in the last two years as I had arrived on base at Mather AFB in Sacramento, California, as the newly appointed squadron commander only to be told that my new squadron, the 441st had deployed to Guam and that I was to follow them there as soon as possible. Within a week after arrival I was on my way to Guam, leaving Rosemary to move in to our on-base quarters. I remembered telling her it would only be for a short period of time, however I remained on the island with my squadron for six months, participating in the Linebacker II raids with all its effects on the families at Mather AFB.

This was something Rosemary was a principal in as she administered to the 441st squadron wives and families of the crews who were deployed and was instrumental in support for those who had lost husbands during that part of the Vietnam War.

I had an overseas return date due to my years of participation in the Nuclear Bomber Reflex program where crews were sent to bases in Spain, Morocco, and England to stand alert during the Cold War. These tours were only three weeks long, however they came at three to four week intervals, thus the time was cumulative and they did add up to give individuals unaccompanied tour credit. I had spent over ten years on that endless track, so my reflex days were well over the required time to establish that date. Knowing the Vietnam war was a factor that all pilots would have to take part in I had wanted to do my tour after I was to leave my SAC headquarters tour I had actually bartered with the Military Personnel people to get an assignment to OV-10s but was cut off by Lt. General P. K. Carlson, the 15th Air Force Commander, who wanted me to take a B-52 squadron in 15th Air Force. He had become familiar with me at the headquarters and was adamant that I come to his command. I was happy to oblige but knew the system and was only delaying the inevitable.

I returned from Guam in March 1973, well after the Eleven Day War and the Linebacker operation of the previous December. I had the good fortune of having been promoted to Colonel while there and subsequently being selected as the 320th Bomb Wing Director of Operations (DO), a role I dearly loved. The 441st B-52 crews and their aircraft had not yet returned from their deployment, having been held over for some mysterious reason. I did have the KC-135 squadron which was fully engaged in flying operations. My best friend Nevin (Ken) Chapman took my old position and was now the 441st squadron commander, however there were none of our aircraft on station, and despite the fact that operations in Vietnam had been terminated by the President there were no B-52s to fly. Nevin and I both collected our flying time in the KC-135 tanker aircraft. The B-52 crews would not return until the fall.

It was to be a great occasion when all finally returned home the following October and we were once again immersed in peacetime operations, fully engaged in the return to flying the Buff, an aircraft we were familiar with. In October with the return of crews and aircraft changes were being made to the staff as our wing commander Lawton Magee was reassigned and a new commander Colonel Curtis Smith took his place. It also had its effect on our vice wing commander, Colonel Bill Eveland, who was given a combat wing in one of the northern tier bases and I was selected to fill that opening. Nevin, who had been selected for Colonel in the last promotion cycle, was given the wing DO position and it was indeed a great situation and a very happy and prosperous wing environment. Rosemary was very involved introducing the new commander's wife to the wing wives and we all had a great outlook on life at the time. This new assignment would change everything, and I felt Rosemary would be devastated with the news!

As the new assignment was broken to her, I was surprised at her attitude. Even though she was very disappointed and obviously displeased, she threw herself into accepting the change. A lot would have to be done. I was given less than a month to make necessary arrangements and report to U-Tapao. It meant moving from our base quarters, as we could no longer live there and finding a suitable home in the area. All the Dugard children except the one-year old Mary were enrolled in local schools and moving off base in the local area would not affect them. It was no small task moving due to the limited time element. Fortunately, there were new home developments in the area that would accommodate Rosemary and our children, the five Ms, Martin, Matthew, Monique, Marc and Mary to live while I was gone. We found a suitable, just finished house in the nearby neighborhood, close to schools and the base facilities. A new house needs many things, but the emphasis would be on exterior amenities that were needed before moving in, such as lawns and fences. Some of the work could be done before I departed and we were obligated to leave the base therefore with a house barely livable, we moved into 2531 Stonehaven Drive. Some work could not be done prior to my departure due to the time of year (rain and cold weather, (It was the last days of March) and would have to wait until spring. When I left there was a nice fence that I had built around the back yard, but lots of dirt in front and back with no bushes, trees or flowers to be seen. Once again, I was leaving Rosemary to finish the move in more ways than I cared to think about.

The entire family came with me to Travis AFB on April 22nd, 1975, the day I left the mainland. I felt empty inside as I watched my older teen aged boys, my grade school daughter and young son look at the contract commercial aircraft I was about to leave on. I held my one year old daughter, Mary and talked to Rosemary about things such as how to get in touch with me during the trip, the places I would have to be and that I would let her know when I got to each stop on the long journey to Thailand. She was not happy, but she accepted this as the next step in our Air Force lives! Finally, I said goodbye to all of them, reluctantly crawled up the stairs to the aircraft and was led to a seat. I was a passenger who the Delta flight attendants treated very well due to my rank, but one with a very heavy heart. As we taxied out, I caught a last glimpse of my family standing on the tarmac, waving at the departing airplane. I know they felt worse than I did. I was departing on what would be an historic and adventurous trip to a country half-way around the world. A trip that I would later hold as one I was fortunate to have been a part of and to have experienced the historic events that would unfold in the next twelve months. It was a story I felt should be told as it had a great impact on this great country and could be said to be the beginning of the downward spiral our nation has undergone since the Vietnam War.

THE BRIEFINGS

With this assignment I was told I would have to spend time meeting and being briefed by the 3rd Air Division on Guam. The first stop, however, would be at PACAF (Pacific Air Force) headquarters at Hickam AFB on Oahu. The base at U-Tapao had a PACAF controlled Air Force base group, the 635th Combat Support Group. The base commander, the security police and other base amenities were under that command. The air operations to include maintenance and other support squadrons were under the Strategic Air Command. The 307th Strategic Wing had played a significant role in Vietnam as a major portion of the B-52 operations launched from there in support of the war. The previous wing commanders of the 307th were Air Force leaders and were known as such due to their efforts at U-Tapao RTAB, which was really a Thai Navy base. There were neither ships nor significant Thai aircraft, only a command element for the Thai Marines who were a segment for the security of the base. PACAF was a command that controlled all the bases in Southeast Asia and one that gave the impression that SAC was a minor contributor in the Vietnam War. This was something I had become very aware of during my Linebacker experience. I was rebuffed constantly when putting crews in for medals due to their role in the Linebacker raids over Hanoi and Haiphong. (PACAF didn't feel as we did about dodging SAMs in the most highly defended country in the world, nor did it affect them that there were aircraft being shot down nightly during the December raids). I had a brief meeting at PACAF headquarters discussing the interface between the two commands on site in Thailand. I was briefed that there was a significant presence on station of the Thai navy and though they had no role in our mission they had to be dealt with.

The next day I flew to Guam on the same commercial aircraft I was on yesterday, different stewardesses. Leaving Mather in the early spring, going through Hawaii and arriving in Guam I was reminded that there was a definite heat index I was going to experience as it was hot on Oahu and sweltering on Guam. I had spent a great deal of time there during the "Bullet Shot" missions, so should have been prepared, but I was not. My previous time on Guam I had run every day I wasn't flying, usually around the hottest part of the day and now the heat was hard to adjust to. It was very debilitating! I would spend the next few days in the company of General Minter, the 3rd Air Division commander, General Robert H. Gaughn, the Director of Operations and the intelligence section for briefings on the situation in Vietnam. The time there was to prepare me for what I would be confronted with on the base and the situation that was becoming more apparent and how it affects U-Tapao. There were explicit warnings that the situation was tenuous at best and that South Vietnam could be overrun at any time. My first meeting on April 24th was with General Gaughn, who I have had a history with and who gave me a knowing look and was quick to update me on basic news such as the evacuation of Americans and some Vietnamese from Saigon that was going on right now and Guam is their destination. C-141s have been taking refugees and families of Americans working in Saigon to Guam, where they are being housed at the Navy Base. It has become a bit tenuous as the C-141 crews say they are being shot at with small weapons on the approach and departure from Saigon. Many of the new arrivals are being put up temporarily on Anderson in the Tin City and the tents around the old concretes that I stayed in three years ago. I was informed that thirty tankers at UT have been placed on alert to support fighters from the up country in Thailand. if needed to get the Americans out of Saigon. The present force level at UT is thirty tankers and seventeen B-52Ds, by far the largest combat wing in the inventory.

Much of my time on Guam would be checking out in the D model B-52. Since I will be flying the "D", thus the need to a checkout program model while in Thailand I was told I would have to complete a series of Simulator rides, culminating in a check before I departed Guam. I had significant flying time in the B-52, however it was in the "G" model. The intelligence briefing took most of my time the next two days. I met with

General Minter the second day and he greeted me warmly and welcomed me to the legendary 8ᵗʰ Air Force. He was generous with information about my role and the fact that Colonel Calhoun, the present commander was anxiously awaiting my arrival as the previous vice commander had departed some time ago. I was very pleased that our meeting went well as I had previous dealings with him that were less than friendly. They had concerned personnel matters that I was involved in while at SAC (Strategic Air Command) headquarters as the Chief of the SAC Career Development Office. He seemed very pleased at my selection and he blessed my assignment as the new vice commander of the 307ᵗʰ while introducing me to other staff members. I was given a complete update on the situation at U-Tapao. It was most important to know how the effects of the impending fall of South Vietnam would affect the base. I was then briefed by the intelligence staff on the Thailand and more directly the U-Tapao role in the present events and the potential future events which were now imminent as the North Vietnamese army was rolling southward toward Saigon. They estimated that the North Vietnamese army could well reach Saigon in less than thirty days. Thailand would be affected and more specifically UT (as it was called) as it was the closest base to Saigon that could be reached by escaping aircraft. There was a Navy carrier in the vicinity in the South China Sea off the coast, but that could only be used by helicopters traversing to the capital and back. Could U-Tapao be used as a point of escape for refugees and escaping aircraft was my question and the answer was a resounding "yes". I was told that there was already a refugee camp for the Cambodians who had fled from the genocide perpetrated by the dictator, Pol Pot. The feeling was that U-Tapao would be the only escape location for exiting aircraft and crews and anyone fleeing Vietnamese territory.

There was no hope given to me by the briefers that there would be a change in the tide of war as it was unfolding. It was only a matter of time when the fall of South Vietnam would take place. It was obvious I would be involved in some significant history, but I was unaware or just very naive of how great an impact it would have on my life and on the future of the United States involvement in Southeast Asia. The briefings on Guam were very thorough and did prepare me somewhat for the situation I would be confronted with when I arrived at UT, but the human impact of those fleeing their homes was something no one could have anticipated. The briefings were over; my remaining time on Guam would be full days of "D" model simulator training. Flight checkouts would be accomplished in Thailand.

I left Guam later in the week on a deploying KC-135 taking part in the "Young Tiger" operations at UT. The aircraft was full of deploying bomber crews on their way to our mutual destination. No stewardesses in trim uniforms, only crew chiefs and a flight crew in green bags, no reclining seats, only jump seats, but at least a window looking forward over the vast expanse of the Pacific, which I had traversed many times on missions to Vietnam. The vision of the Philippines was imprinted in my memory as it seemed to rise out of the sea in a long series of islands, surface lights illuminating its coast. It appeared out of the darkness as it did on those missions to and from targets in Vietnam I had flown to before. The series of islands, usually with a thin cloud cover, were always something that impressed me with their beauty, especially with the red hues of the sun on early morning or evening flights that always seemed to enhance the scene as my aircraft passed by. It was my first actual flight that I didn't turn north into Vietnam and some designated targets, instead we were coursing around the edge of Cambodia, then entered into the Gulf of Thailand, darkness was everywhere, broken up by the small lights on the surface of the water below, signifying the flotilla of small fishing craft that were always there and the incredible display of stars illuminating the heavens. It was a moonless sky, there was no visible horizon, the lights below merging with the stars above. The sight of both the Southern Cross and the North Star at the same time was exhilarating and defined the heavens. In the many later flights out of UT it would become a common occurrence, but the first time to be able to see these two constellations at the same time was special. Finally, we made a turn more northerly and began our decent into U-Tapao air base and the appearance of a land mass punctuated by lead in lights to a long runway, signaled the beginning of this new and what would turn out to be an historical adventure.

U-TAPAO -APRIL 27TH, 1975

The many books about the mysterious far east, the land known as Siam was a world you only heard in fairy tales and now, I was here! Thailand seemed to be a mystery world I never imagined I would see, but it would unfold as a segment of my life that would be incomplete if I hadn't gone there. I had flown this route out of Guam many times going on sorties to Vietnam from Guam, but this time the heading we took would veer left, skirting the southern coast of Vietnam and Cambodia to the friendly bordering country of Thailand. Thailand was the only country in Southeast Asia that embraced the United States effort in Vietnam and has long been considered one of its staunchest Allies. I would learn a great deal about the country and its people in the next year, but I didn't know how much and how it would affect me. I had never been to U-Tapao during my previous time in Southeast Asia, despite its role in B-52 operations during the Vietnam War. All my missions had been from Guam, a twelve to fourteen-hour roundtrip depending on how far north our targets were. This flight was a non-eventful flight and was the beginning of a tour which had a significant effect on my life and my future in the Air Force. I noticed for the first time the features of a country emerging on all sides, green and the blue of the gulf of Thailand, merging into the sandy shores, seemed to give the image of peace and tranquility, but most of all I was stunned by the beauty that was unfolding. As we started our descent toward the land mass, I could make out our destination from the jump seat in the cockpit. The airfield was right on the coastline. On our final approach I noticed on the left side of the runway there was a rather distinctive hill and to the right of the runway there were revetments protecting a line of the tall-tail, signifying the all black B-52 Ds. A length of KC-135s appeared and a parked C-141 plus a couple of aircraft parked further down from the approach end by themselves. We had a smooth landing followed by a rollout to a taxiway halfway down the runway where we exited the runway.

My circadian rhythm was all out of wack and I felt I and the change in time were having an effect on my thought process. It was 2100 hours on a Saturday night when we landed. A follow me vehicle appeared to lead us to our taxi spot to an area in front of base operations and it signaled the end of a long and informative journey. It had taken almost a week and I was happy to finally be able to unpack my bags and settle into my new duty station. As the engines were shut down the cargo door opened, and a stair well was brought to the side of the aircraft. The first thing I was aware of was the intense, suffocating and surrounding heat. It seemed as if a blast furnace had been turned on. Could someone really live in this climate? The humidity was as high as the temperature! As the sweat rolled down from under my hat, I caught my first glimpse of a group of officers waiting on the tarmac. As I got to the bottom of the stairs a colonel with a nametag saying he was Calhoun came toward me with a big smile on his face. He enthusiastically welcomed me to UT, introduced me to some of the many staff members present, many of which I knew, John Thigpen, the director of Maintenance and Al Merrill, the Director of Intelligence, from SAC headquarters and ushered me to my vehicle, a four door Ford equipped with an UHF radio and other equipment befitting my vice commander position. He told me to follow him and he added quickly, "This country, once controlled by the British government, traffic flows on the opposite side of the street from the United States, so don't let your mind wander to your old driving habits". He led me to Base Operations to orient our location, we then turned left away from base operations two short blocks to the 307 Strategic Wing headquarters, the command section for me to report to tomorrow for in-processing. I followed his vehicle down a few streets away from the flight line to what was to be my home for the next year. It hardly took enough time to get the air-conditioning in the car to get to a comfortable level. We drove only a short distance and entry was made into an area with a series of identical residences used as housing for officers assigned for their tour in Southeast Asia. We drove down a pebble stone U-shaped drive to the bottom of the U and stopped in front of one of the units. It was marked with the numbers 3226. It was a stationary mobile home, enclosed by a high fence. There was a high gate, hiding an enclosed garden like area, I could see that the mobile home was not very mobile as it had no wheels attached and instead it was bolstered with a foundation. I was told it was the only quarters with a bathtub on the base. Inside the gate was a rather large area beset with trees and bushes. I used the key given to me by Calhoun and took a two-step entry into a small living room. It was adequately furnished with even a small, maybe a sixteen-inch TV. Thankfully the air conditioner was on as it was reported that it was "only" 85 degrees, but the humidity must have been in the nineties. Wayne bid me adieu and said that standup briefing was at 0730 hrs in the morning and he would see me then. The quarters had a small kitchen, a bathroom, with the tub and two small bedrooms. A window air conditioner worked diligently in one of the bedrooms. I decided not to waste any time, dropped my bags, got out of my dripping flight suit, took a shower and jumped into bed. Sleep came quickly and so did morning.

THE HEADQUARTERS
COMMAND SECTION

The next morning, I awoke early and unsuccessfully tried to go back to sleep, however I finally got up and went out for a morning run. Unaware of the hazards or the roads I was taking I was careful to note what I had passed as I was just going to do a 180 and go back the same route. I was totally wet after a hundred yards. It was 0600 hours and it seemed to be already around 90 degrees, but I knew better. I finished the run and went inside to cool down and shower. After a quick look around to take in the new scenery I left my new abode and wended my way back to the flight line took a left, paying close attention to get in the left lane and soon sighted the 307th Headquarters sign. I parked my car in the space which signaled it was for the vice commander and saw Wayne getting out of his vehicle. I joined "Alfa", as wing commanders are known as, (I would be "Bravo") to go inside the air- conditioned building. A small entry led into an office room with two desks, one occupied by Captain Lee Steinegan, the executive officer and the other by Sergeant Tom White, the wing clerk and to the side another desk occupied by a rather tall, pretty and well-endowed female who Colonel Calhoun introduced me to as the command section secretary, Billie Strecker. She smiled sweetly, stepped out from behind her desk and shook my hand. She was taller than me and had the personality of a person who knows who they are. She wore rimless glasses, had flowing brown hair, high cheek bones and a smile as big as a house. Billie had been the wing secretary for a number of years and was conversant in the Thai language, knew everything and everybody and was to be the source of information and background of the area, the customs, culture and those I needed to be aware of during my time in country. It turns out that Billie had been a "Playboy Bunny" in her other life and she had the assets to prove it. She was also intelligent, resourceful

12

and very capable in her duties. She would be my entry into Thailand and the reason for any success I would enjoy during my tenure. I learned quickly to listen intently to her about meetings and social affairs with the Thais and their thoughts and actions. She would tell me who to trust and who not to. I would find her efficiency and knowledge to be the cornerstone of my time in this hot and humid country. Without it I would be totally out of synch with the environment, the people and the mission that was to unfold.

Sergeant White showed me to my office which was next to the commander's and gave me some introductory information and papers I needed to fill out for my security clearance and badge. For many years going to a new duty station I would have to go from office to office to complete all these requirements necessary to access information and be admitted to locations needed to perform my duties. The Sunday (yes Sunday as every day was a work-day) abbreviated morning briefing started with the same information I had received two days earlier with some updates about the situation in Saigon. The weather said the monsoon season was upon us and that heavy rain was very likely for the next few days, hopefully it would not interfere with events that could happen at any time. The flight schedule for today was very heavy with tanker support for the up-country fighters and bomber sorties, sort of saber rattling to the Vietnamese border. Once the standup briefing (that's what they wre called) I went back to my office to confront the paperwork already on my desk. Billie walked in as the security police, intelligence and personnel representatives were completing all my required access papers, to include taking my security badge photo, my military drivers license, and gave me a cool glass of water. She informed me that there was a farewell party for one of the officers that night at the Thai officers club and she felt it might be a good time to meet some of the staff. She gave me the time and the location of the club and said she would let one of the squadron commanders know I would be there to introduce me around. She would not be going, as she had other plans for the evening. Everything was completed in about an hour.

My new security badge would admit me to all the highly classified security areas on the base to include the vault and crypto area. U-Tapao was the gathering station for all the classified information, which was garnered in Southeast Asia, to include the present status of events in Vietnam. Much of this information was "down-linked" from high altitude U-2 missions, sending photos and intercepted communications from the advancing North

Vietnamese forces in South Vietnam. This was relayed from the intelligence gathering station located at Korat, a base in the far northern reaches of Thailand. The crypto area called Rammasun was one step above all other intelligence material gathered and entry to that area was very selective. The first duty day had passed quickly and it was now late in my first day, and I had a lot of unfinished business in my quarters. I needed to unpack my bags and look for something to eat. Calhoun had left the office so I told Billie I would return after I unpacked. I found myself retracing my path to my "Hootch". The flight line was close at hand so I took a slight deviation to look at the revetments, which were numerous, but now showing the after effects of the U.S. retreat from the war, thanks to congress and their plethora of peacenik representatives who never fought a war or better, yet did not have a responsible bone in their bodies. I counted sixteen B-52s, a long way from the number on station during the Linebacker II raids of December 1972, somewhere in the neighborhood of fifty-five. I had been told we were now flying routine training missions to maintain crew currency, but also to remind the Thais that we were still there, watching their back. I wondered aloud whether even that number of B-52s would be around very long. There were thirty KC-135s by my count, a number that I would remember for the extent of my tour. Two of the tankers were taxing out to the runway and I could hear power units ramping up in the revetments, meaning the B-52 were going to be going off soon.

The tankers would be used extensively during my time and I would in fact exit on one of the last of the "Young Tiger" force devoted to supporting the Vietnam War. It was hot, humid and very quiet as I turned off the flight line and headed back to my quarters. I parked and went into my new home to find this diminutive women, maybe 5 feet tall, standing in the middle of the living room with a cloth in her hands. She introduced herself as Lum thien, bowing respectfully with the name Wayne said last night was that of my maid. She was dressed to work and had a smile across her small round face. She bowed gently from the waist and saluted me with the traditional "Wai", (hands in a prayer-like position) held above her head, a sign of respect for someone she felt inferior to and uttered the first "Sawadee Cup" I was to hear in Thailand. "Sawadee" is both a greeting and a farewell and "Ca or Cup" indicates female or male when addressing a person. She referred to me as "Bot", her pronunciation for boss. She spoke decent English, most of which she had garnered from doing the quarters for a long line of Air Force officers who had lived in this horseshoe of "homes" provided for those who directed the war in Vietnam from UT. She then escorted me through the rest of the unit. She also told me where to place my dirty clothes and to leave any mess I made as she would clean up for me. She seemed pleased with her work preparing the unit for me and pointed out such amenities as closets and drawers. The kitchen had a refrigerator, stove and oven, all the necessities for life in the tropics! The one thing that really pleased me was the fact that in the late morning heat my new abode was very comfortable, cool and clean and Lum thien would make sure of the clean part and I was hoping the cool would continue. I repeated Sawadee, with a respectful Wai to Lum thien and proceeded to go into the bedroom and finally unpack the rest of my clothes and placed them in drawers and hung my uniforms in the closet with my flight suits. It seemed strange, but I wasn't going to be leaving soon so neatly arranged my clothes in a familiar pattern I have used for years.

The trailer was well situated as it seemed to be in the center of all the activity, Gym and Chapel and close to the Officers-Club. I wandered around the outside, gazing in the front and the back and noticed a path toward the gym and the chapel. Satisfied, I left to return to the office, where Wayne had reappeared and wanted to take me for a tour of the base. We piled into his car and he took me first to the beach area and showed me the Cambodian camp and told me there were 1400 people in the camp. Pol-Pot had done a number on these people and they were safe now but were prevented from wandering outside their camp perimeter. Throughout the base there were Thai Marines in bunkers and towers with manned Marines overlooking the flight line. In the revetments some of the B-52s were cocked with conventional weapons and ready to be launched if the need should arise if an insurgent force came into Thai territory. It was obvious that there was an atmosphere of war everywhere. Sappers had tried to penetrate this and other bases in Thailand, as the war was coming to a close. Later in the day tanker crews were placed on cockpit alert for fighter support in the event they were needed to support the Vietnamese with-drawl. The tour didn't take too long as off the flight line there was little to see except the enclave of shops and a small commissary just a couple of klicks from the chapel.

SINGHAI BEER

At the time of my arrival at UT there had been no change in the number of active bases in Thailand in addition to this one. There were four fighter bases up country which included the fighters at the previously mentioned intelligence gathering base at Korat RTAB. This information about current activities in Vietnam was downloaded and forwarded to assess the threats that were apparent in Vietnam and its surroundings. Most of this information was gathered by the U-2 contingent based at UT. The Operations Officer was an individual who would become a life-long friend, Lieutenant Colonel Jerry Sinclair. The U-2s would launch from U-Tapao twice a day and fly missions over both north and south Vietnam, gathering signal, photo and verbal intelligence and downloading instant activities and information to our crypto network for immediate dissemination to gathering centers. There were at any time two to three reconnaissance birds (U-2s) and four crews on temporary duty on base. The crews rotated much like the B-52 and KC-135 crews in country. (It was the way SAC did their business 179 days was the maximum in-country time to preclude an overseas return date. It was a never-ending cycle for the crews). The U-2 launch time was at 0615 hours (6:15 am) every morning and 1815 hours (6:15 pm) every evening without change or exception during my eleven plus months in Thailand, however special missions were sometimes flown at the direction from a higher level. My count of aircraft was confirmed in later information given to me as there were just sixteen B-52s and the temporary assigned crews to man them and a full super squadron of thirty KC-135s and thirty-six crews to man them. The 135 crews supported not only the "peacetime" B-52 training, but also all the necessary "Young Tiger" missions in support of the fighter squadrons as well as the B-52 sorties in Southeast Asia. The permanent party officer staff in the 307th Strategic Wing was small. There was the command staff, which included intelligence, maintenance and operations personnel and command post controllers, and it totaled about thirty- eight. The enlisted staff was relatively large as there were three separate squadrons in maintenance alone. In addition, the PACAF base commander had the security police squadron and other base function personnel as well as his own staff which were on full year, tours. Permanent party individuals were there for an isolated and unaccompanied (without family) tour. The crews and some squadron staff were all on Temporary Duty (TDY). The normal TDY tour was for 179 days, therefore the faces changed, but the mission did not. Aircraft were rotated on a need basis from the CONUS bases. In addition, there was a contingent of navy reconnaissance aircraft and crews. They had their own ramp which was at the far end of the base and the personnel were seldom seen as they flew their missions and were not an integral part of our daily life and work. I did not have any daily communication with any of the Navy personnel and in-fact no contact. Their mission was mostly into the gulf areas, tracking other country vessels, mostly Chinese. Of course there was the Thai Navy, who had their own functions to include a large Marine force and they were under the command of a Thai Navy captain, named Vichit, who will be an ally and an adversary of sorts in the future as he had his own mission and it was at times in opposition to ours.

I returned to my quarters and prepared to spend my first full night in Thailand. I showered and put on a clean civilian outfit with the heat and humidity in mind and got in my Air Force vehicle and ventured out on the base streets. Billie had given me instructions on how to find the Thai officers club which was a relatively short trip to the base entrance and the Thai Officer club was to the left of the departure gate. It was now about 1800 hours and the sun was still pushing out hot rays even though it was close to setting. The country is at 10 degrees north latitude, so being that close to the equator days were always close to the same length as night, twelve hours. The heat does not go away. Nights, the temperature might go down to the mid-seventies, however the humidity stays in the nineties and that is in the winter. It was now the end of March and summer was coming. I parked my car and walked into the club. The first room was open, with the exception of a bar on the right wall, complete with a bartender. There were a few people at the bar, a mixture of men dressed in what I thought were Thai navy uniforms and others in civilian attire. I saw what looked like an American and asked him where the Sawadee party was and he pointed to a set of double doors and said he was going there. He introduced himself as Lt. Colonel Yaryan, a member of the B-52 contingent. He told me if I wanted a drink, I would have to get it at the bar as they did not have any in the party room. I introduced myself and headed to the bar to get a drink. I asked the bartender what kind of beer they had, and he named two or three Thai beers and I asked for one those he named, a "Singhai". He asked a strange question wanting to know if I wanted a bottle or a half a bottle. I drink beer and naturally asked for the bottle. He took out a "Bottle" that look like it was a quart size, opened it and gave it to me in exchange for an American dollar as I didn't have the Thai equivalent 20 bot. I followed Colonel Yaryan into the party and found approximately thirty individuals, no females in fairly, sedate conversation, no loud noise, but very light banter. Colonel Yaryan introduced me around and led me to the departing officer, who worked in scheduling and was leaving tomorrow on a redeploying tanker whose crew was replaced by the one that brought me from the Philippines. He had completed his year and was very happy to be going home. He seemed to portray a feeling of pity for me as I was just arriving in country. I was then engaged in conversation with others who had been at UT for varying time frames, all looking to the possibility of going home early due to the possible B-52 drawdown. This was something already being discussed at the higher echelons of command. The role of the B-52 would be non-existent if there was no conflict in Vietnam. The B-52s had not been allowed to assist the south Vietnamese almost since the end of Linebacker II. Why were they still here? Ask someone at the highest level and I'm sure they would tell you it was all political.

The conversations never rose above a sort of mumbling of time left before going home. With that they welcomed me to the wing and asked the obvious questions of where I was last stationed and other pertinent questions about life in the states. One looked casually at my bottle of beer and asked about the size and I imparted the question I was asked. All laughed as they then told me of the ingredients in the beer and that it was very powerful, having been brewed in Thailand and fermented with formaldehyde. I had only had a couple of sucks on the bottle and I thought it tasted really good, so sort of played down the effect of a foreign beer. It was not an enduring type of party, so after about an hour, having finished my bottle and eaten the meager snacks that were available I made my amends, wished the departing staff member good luck and left the club. I easily found my way back to my abode, drank in the coolness and found the main bedroom with a bed turned down by Lam Tien and ready for my now very weary body. I felt a bit inebriated, but not seriously and the ride back to my quarters had been without incident, even driving on the right side (the English had influenced the Thais greatly in their time in Asia) of the road. I had a "hot line" phone next to my bed so picked it up and asked the command post if they would do me a favor and give me a call at 0600. They acknowledged the call and said that they would make sure I would get a wakeup call in the morning. It was about 1000 hours now so I might get into tune with the time change if I got a good night sleep.

I didn't need the call as I awoke at about 0500 with a stabbing pain in the middle of my forehead. It was like someone had thrust an ice pick between my eyes and left it there. Getting out of bed was a nightmare, but I had to get up and solve the pain. I found the bathroom and looked for my Dopp kit where my bottle of ibuprofen was. Finding it, I quickly took out three pills and threw them into my mouth and washed them down with water. I went back to my bed and waited for the pain to dissipate. About forty-five minutes later I was able to get up, answer the command post call telling me it was 0600, shower, and dress, find my car and drive to the headquarters. I walked in and found a smiling Billie at her desk. It was 0700 hours, so I was a bit surprised she was in so early. Coffee was brewing and she asked how the party was and so I related my tale of the "bottle" and she laughed and said she should have warned me about Thai beer. She said nobody buys the "bottle" and merely sips the half. A lesson learned and probably the reason I switched to gin or an American beer as a preferred drink in any Thai establishment in my tenure there. Billie asked how I liked my coffee and I responded "black", to her delight. She brought me a cup and since no one else was in the command area yet she sat down and asked about my family and other data about me. It was then I found out about her and her experiences, not only in Thailand, but her time as a "Playboy Bunny". She had come from Kansas and when finished with school was selected as a bunny and spent about a year doing it. She took the civil service exam for working for the government, looking for adventure and she had opted to put in for foreign duty and was assigned to U-Tapao. She had been here for over five years and loved it. There were other opportunities in other places, but she kept asking to extend her stay. I would learn that she was a friend to everyone and was highly popular with the Thai business establishments on base. I finished my coffee and decided I would check out the command post and the Special Security Office (SSO). Billie directed me to the command post, and I went to the outer door rang the bell and waited for a response. Entry was of course very restricted, and I was hoping someone would recognize me from yesterday's introductions. The door buzzed open and I walked in to find the duty controller talking to Lt. Colonel Yaryan, who had stopped by to check on B-52 launches for the day. I was introduced to the duty contingent and was given my second cup of coffee. It was no different than any other command post, so I was familiar with the surroundings and apparent common equipment. I set about getting familiar with the operations of the bomber and tanker sorties being flown that day. One ominous item I noted was the NOTAM (notice to airmen) that stated the possibility of the influx of friendly aircraft from Vietnam due to the situation there. I asked about it and the duty controller said they had been advised that UT was on alert to accept all aircraft from Vietnam in the event there was an evacuation of personnel and aircraft. It was basically what I had been briefed on my many briefings my trip to UT. I was curious about the SSO and so I thought I would visit the location but did not want to go unannounced so went back and asked Billie to give them a call. As she was doing so Colonel Calhoun came in and said he would introduce me to the secure area. Entry to the confines was strictly controlled and entry was maintained through a fenced in area outside of the headquarters. There was a twenty-foot narrow, single file length of barbed wire lane to a guard in a small minimally widened enclosure who checked our badges and allowed us to pass to another twenty-foot corridor to the entry door. Colonel Calhoun showed his badge through the one-way window and the door opened to a small enclosed space where we entered, and Colonel Calhoun announced I was the new vice commander. The door behind us closed and was secured. Through another secure door I showed my badge, the door was buzzed open and we both entered the high-level secure area.

I was introduced around and noticed there were some in civilian attire as well as others in uniform. There was voice input that was being monitored and other information being disseminated and gathered as I watched the busy enclave doing their job. This intelligence area was very active, and it was obvious that the vocal information was not only being received but was also being passed to other agencies that were in the intelligence chain. We were then briefed by the senior duty officer that the North Vietnamese army had made a breakthrough along the coast of South Vietnam and were progressing rapidly towards Saigon. Estimates were that they would reach the city before tomorrow. A startling update and one that called for some coordinated action on the base. With this information we left the SSO and headed back to the office.

A standard morning standup (all senior staff would meet each day for current input for the command section where no one was in a standing position, except the briefer.) was scheduled. We entered the command briefing room to see a group of officers milling around and when seeing us they snapped to attention. I was introduced to those who had not yet met me and a weather briefing ensued. It was to be hot, high in the low nineties and humid, close to 90 percent, with a possibility of thunderstorms later in the day. I would find that this was almost the standard briefing for the weather in Thailand. Highs were always in the 90s and humidity the same. The lows were generally in the mid-70s, even in December. Today the low would be 83 degrees, as the monsoon season was upon us. This was followed by the intelligence briefing. The briefing officer stood and pointed to a map of Southeast Asia. Highlighted was South Vietnam and the major proceeded to tell the story we had just heard in the SSO, showing the position of the NVA. They had overrun Hue, a city famous for stopping the NVA about four and a half years ago with the assistance of B-52s sorties flown in support of the Marines on the ground; something I had been involved in. The area surrounding Saigon was shown and the main roads into the city were briefed as ideal avenues for an advancing army. Colonel Calhoun then asked the base commander, Colonel Hal Austin, who ordinarily did not attend this meeting but was asked to come based on the role he would play, if his base resources were prepared for refugees. The answer was an affirmative and stated they had prepared an area across the inlet from an established refugee camp now in being, housing

Cambodians, who escaped the Pol-Pot regime. Arriving Vietnamese would be placed there before being processed and later sent to the Philippines. The rest of the staff members were given assignments for the imminent fall of Saigon, which would signal the victory that North Vietnam had pursued for the last fifteen years. They would now control the fertile south with all its farming benefits. Little did we imagine at the time what we would experience in the next twenty four hours or maybe less, who knows as we had abandoned the south Vietnamese and left them to fend for themselves, a policy the United States would in the future continually use to the detriment of those we leave behind.

As one who had participated in the Linebacker raids, sometimes known as the "Eleven Day War", I was very aware of the fact that North Vietnam was defeated and had no capacity to wage war on December 29th, 1972. I was privy to the daily BDA (bomb damage assessment) photos downlinked from SR-71 aircraft after each night's B-52 raids. By this date it showed very railroad yard was destroyed, every airport was neutralized and the port at Haiphong was blocked to shipping leaving and arriving. Raids on the 30th met with zero resistance as there were no missiles left to fire and no ammunition left to load and most of all no way to get resupplied. Knowing they were on the brink of total defeat they asked the United States to return to the table in Paris, which we did and agreed to measures that would lead to their capability to rebuild their capacity to wage war. Of course, at that time we were happy because they released our prisoners of war, but it stopped there. The tragedy of our nation took place when a clueless congress (and an encouraging media dedicated to end the war) cut off funding to our efforts in Vietnam and left South Vietnam to sure defeat. Now, today we were faced with the results of that historical blunder, the fall of the south to the communist regime to the north.

THE BASE

I decided I would try to familiarize myself with the base, one that I had been briefed as belonging to Thailand, but paid for and maintained by the United States and I had been reminded by Calhoun that we were tenants on a Thai Navy base. It was under the overall command of Admiral Samut whose command office was located at Sattahip, the massive Navy base about ten kilometers down the road. He was not resident on the U-Tapao base proper. The Thai Navy commander on station was Captain Vichit, an individual I would get very involved with in my future dealings on the base. My drive with Wayne yesterday was quick and I wanted to see for myself places other than the flight line and the road to the Thai O' Club, which was also the road to exit the facility. The U.S. section of the base was basically adjacent to the flight line, two to three blocks deep with the ordinary base facilities, but with a commercial Thai flair. There was a post office, and I stopped to secure a post office mail-box, Box 1532. I would learn later it was a stopping off place for some retired veterans who had married Thai women and settled in the vicinity of the base or at least close to the Pattya region south of Bangkok. A bowling alley was rather apparent as was the base movie and of course a chapel. There were Thai shops selling jewelry and other Thai goods, such as traditional clothing, cloths, carvings, trinkets and other simple items. One such store was almost next door, but across the street to the command center and another was in the same complex as the Officers Club. There were also a few located in the Base Exchange area. The maintenance area was by far the largest in terms of structures and included a DC hanger capable of major work on the B-52s and the KC-135s. Along every road on both sides there were deep culverts, some more severe than others. I would learn that these were sometimes filled with rainwater which would be deep enough to swim in as when it rained it was not a drizzle, it poured! When the monsoons came the culverts flowed over, always flowing toward the ocean. The water was permanent in some of the deeper culverts and any body of water was referred to as a Klong, whether it was in lake form or a stream or water in a culvert. Near the maintenance area, across one of the culverts I saw a rectangular chain link area about 20-30 feet long standing alone. I thought it looked a lot like a cage of some sort and mused at what could be inside. I would ask Billie later. I would stop by the base chapel later hoping to see the former base chaplain from Mather, Father Saulnier, who was assigned here a couple of months ago. He was a favorite Catholic priest and it would be good to see him again. I worked my way to the main road into the base and found that it basically separated the base in what was the U.S. side and what is the Thai side. Interestingly the Thai side was a small town in addition to the military presence. It was not a town that was inhabited with Thai military dependents, this was a small place inhabited by ordinary citizens. I would have to say it was not the best environment or the most desirable place on the base. It did need a good rain to wash away the stink from some of the deep culverts where the water had dried up! I drove again past the main gate and noted the Air Force security guards and their Thai counterpart Marines checking the entry opening to incoming pedestrians. I also saw a large number of taxis waiting outside the gate and it dawned on me that there were no private autos for the military personnel on the base. Transportation off base was only available commercially.

I thought I would stop by the base commissary and get some food as I needed to have some necessary supplies available in my quarters. The obvious place to eat was the U.S.A.F. officer's club, but there were some other establishments on base for light meals, one such served hamburgers, which I later found out were really water buffalo burgers, not bad either, however the meat was a bit darker. The bowling alley also had light meals. I stopped at the commissary and bought the necessary items to supplement my other options on base and returned to my "Hootch" (trailer) to put them in my refrigerator. I found Lum thien cleaning and picking up some dirty clothes I left. She bowed and delivered another Wai and said, "Hello Bot". We came to an agreement on her salary for her taking care of my quarters and doing my laundry. I would pay her twenty dollars a month, which was the standard amount for maid service. I found out that she had a daughter who was going to school in Bangkok. There were no schools after the fourth grade in the immediate area and the money she made was basically to allow her daughter to continue her education. Bangkok was seventy kilometers north of U-Tapao so her daughter had to board as well as go to school, an expense not many of the locals could afford. She had five other clients, so our fee was enough for her to allow her daughter to continue her education. It was a moment of pride when she talked of her daughter and her ongoing endeavors in Bangkok. Our conversation covered many aspects of living in my new quarters including some words of caution. She told me not to leave valuables out as the "steely boys" would take whatever I left of value. It was apparent that she had little ability to stop any entry they attempted. I assured her I didn't bring anything of value and would carry my wallet when I left my "Hootch". There was no secure way to really lock up the trailer as the flimsy locks on the doors would easily give way. She was happy with my response and she assured me she would watch over my new home and take good care of it and as time would tell she was a God send. Left alone I looked around and felt a bit lonely and depressed. I would be away from my family and destined to live in this trailer for the next year. I felt terribly isolated.

Suddenly there was a knock on the door. I couldn't imagine who it might be, but thinking it was some kind of a messenger, I opened the door to find a diminutive individual with grey hair fastened and pulled straight back in a pony tail, very thick glasses, barefoot and a wide grin looking up at me. A bit taken back I asked what I could do for him and he started talking to me in excellent English, giving me his name, Manas Manat and telling me he was there to assist me in whatever way he could. He addressed me by name and title and seemed most aware of why I was in Thailand. The conversation went nowhere as he said he merely wanted to introduce himself and as quickly as he appeared, he was gone. I thought someone must have given him my name. This was to be my first, but certainly not the last meeting with this very interesting man.

I left to return to the headquarters and found virtually no one there except Billie. I asked about the character who showed up at my door, who I identified to her and she laughed and told me that Manas Manat was an individual very much a part of the base lore and she would fill me in when I had more time. Billie said everyone had gone to the SSO, so thought I would see what had changed. I made my way through the maze of sentries and holding positions and pressed the buzzer for entry. I displayed my new line badge and the responding buzz opened the door and I entered. Most everyone was huddled around the chief intelligence officer who was reading the latest information on the advance of the NVA (North Vietnamese Army). After digesting the message, he said it was apparent that Saigon would be under siege that night. Colonel Calhoun determined there was nothing we could do right now as preparations for any UT fallout had been made. We dispersed from the SSO and went back to the headquarters. Billie was clearing her desk in preparation of going to her quarters and I said goodnight as she was leaving the office. I decided I would try to set up my office and went about unpacking the few items I had brought with me from Mather. Placing pictures and other personal items in and on my desk, I noted that a nameplate had been placed on my desk. It was good to know who I was! It was pouring rain outside and I was told it was the hottest day of the year at 97 degrees. I hesitated to go out into the rain, but with this activity completed I decided to leave and get something to eat and felt the Officers Club was my best bet. I dashed the few feet to my car and swung into the seat, shut the door and looked at my watch. It was late and despite the quick leap for my car I was soaked. It was a five-minute drive to the club. I found a parking slot in front with the designation for the 307th SW Vice Commander and pulled in. I noted the Thai shops around the club, one, in particular caught my eye, a jewelry shop with the name "Johnny's Gems", as it was still open and a couple of familiar faces from my evening at the Thai O Club were walking out. I said hello and casually asked if they bought out the store as we ran to the door to avoid complete saturation from the rain that seemed to be going sideways. They laughed and we all went into the officer's club, took off and shook our wet hats to avoid the wing bell from singing out free beer to all. They went right into the dining area, which was not too busy, but I decided I needed something to drink first. I found the bar and asked what kind of beer they had and was pleased to hear "San Miguel", a familiar Philippine beer that I used to stock the squadron rest area with on Guam during my stay there. I would buy it by the case, and it worked out to about five cents a bottle. It was for sale in the crew lounge for fifteen cents on the honor system. It turned out they also had some American beer such as Bud and Miller but chose the former and sat down. The beer tasted great. After last night I would not repeat my thirst desires and had just the one twelve-ounce bottle and went into the dining area and sat down and noted a group wearing orange flight suits at one of the tables. I could make out that they were part of the U-2 (99th SRS) squadron on temporary duty in Thailand and they acknowledged my presence with a wave which I returned with a smile. One of the individuals had been at last night's going away party and we had talked briefly about their activity. They usually launched two birds a day and they would do all their intelligence gathering over the regions to the west, gathering signal, communication and photo information which would be instantly down linked to that gathering station in northern Thailand and then distributed to other stations for assessment. I had heard the 0615 launch of the U-2 this morning recovering from last night's Thai beer episode as you could not miss the sound of this aircraft taking off. I thought then that much of the intelligence we were getting was probably from that early flight. There would be another such flight to update the situation. As I was eating an old friend from B-58 days, Larry Duval walked in. He was working in and out of Saigon, directing C-130 operations evacuating people out of the area. He had flown numerous flights into the beleaguered city and had another flight tonight. He said it was very chaotic and thought this would be the last of them. We talked while we ate and then he excused himself. I told him to watch his "six" and he chomped on his cigar and said he would. I proceeded to eat my dinner and left to catch some sleep as the time change and the beer made me very sleepy.

ADJUSTMENT

It had been a long night and I was ready for some shuteye. I had been up since five this morning had only coffee and something, they called a doughnut, but didn't look like it or taste like it. It was now mid-afternoon, but my body was not sure what time it was as I had gone through multiple time zones in the last week. I decided to tough it out and try to wait for a proper time to sleep in this new country. I had tried this ruse on my body previously as when in B-47s at Pease AFB in New Hampshire the crews would fly to Spain and England to pull nuclear alert. We would take off around 2100 hours (9:00 PM) on a Tuesday night and fly about a seven hour mission, with an in-flight refueling, to one of the two countries, landing about 1000 hours (10 am) on Wednesday morning, debrief and go to quarters, but not assuming alert status until the next morning, Thursday. First you could go to sleep immediately after debriefing which meant waking in the early evening and stumbling through the night. Staying up, plodding through the day, eat an early supper and going to bed was an alternative. Quite frankly neither worked well, but I preferred to stay up, maybe even go to the gym, but never find a cozy corner to rest. Despite all attempts, day one on alert was always a foggy day. Now, after my first two days in Thailand I was in the mood for some rest and was feeling the need to get some rack time. It was obvious that I had experienced a significant time change for the days seemed like nights and the nights were like days. In fact, it was just about a twelve-hour time change. In addition, the driving on the wrong side of the road to go in the right direction was also something I was trying to get used to. When crossing the street, look in the wrong direction or you might get run over. All of this combined with the heat index of well over ninety degrees had me hoping I would adjust soon. I finally decided to just go to bed and hope things evened out shortly. I returned to my quarters to find Lum thien still working the bedroom and so I decided to go to the burger joint to get a burger and something to drink. The Water Buffalo burger wasn't too bad. The meat a bit darker and the juice cool and refreshing so I sat and rehashed the day. What a change in events. I had been on some of the last raids against the North Vietnamese and in fact was sitting on the hammerhead on Guam, with Major Glenn Robinson, known as Robbie, in a fully bomb laden B-52G ready to launch on my third mission over the north when Robbie's crew was told to taxi back to his parking slot. I had accepted a dare from Robbie to ride in the jump seat with his crew on this mission and happily I was saved from that experience. A truce had been declared by the North Vietnamese due to the fact that they had run out of supplies and had no defense capability as a result of our eleven days of bombing their railroads, airdromes and blocking the entrance to Haiphong, their major seaport for resupply. The previous two nights our bombers had experienced no opposition as the NVA were out of the resources to wage war.

Incredibly, we backed off and let them off the hook. As I had said before, their position was indefensible as they had no means to resupply, no means to defend themselves and no capability to continue with the war. I had seen the BDA (bomb damage assessment) for our many night raids and it was obvious they were totally frozen in place. Now, a scant three years later the NVA were about to take over the south and the innocent people of Vietnam were taking whatever means they could to get out of the way of the juggernaut from the north. Interestingly enough years later, I became friends with a retired Marine Colonel named Al Rebock who was a prime force in the evacuation of the US Embassy in Saigon. We discovered some thirty years after the fact that Al and I had been on the two ends of that horrific day, his was the evacuation of personnel from the embassy and its environs and mine, their recovery at UT. Colonel Al Rebock was one of the last to leave the embassy in Saigon.

I returned to the trailer and for the first time noted that I had a fruit bearing banana tree and a pineapple "bush" in my front yard. The fence around my yard was high enough to prevent anyone from seeing what was going on in this fairly good-sized space. I t was mostly grass with a few small bushes and flowers scattered around the landlocked trailer. It was hot, but there was a decent amount of shade and a couple of wooden chairs that seemed worthy of using, so I went inside, pulled out a San Miguel beer I had picked up from the commissary and came back and plunked myself into a chair after carefully examining the underside for possible non friendly spiders and spreading a towel to save me a splinter or two. I knew that drinking a beer would surely hasten a much-needed sleep, and I was about to succumb when the gate rattled and then opened to one of my new neighbors, Lieutenant Colonel Yaryan, the staff senior officer for the B-52 crews. He was a permanent party on base and was also the squadron commander for the temporary duty (TDY) crews. We exchanged pleasantries and then he asked me if I would like to get in some "Buff" flying time. I was current in the B-52 G and had completed the simulator check in the "D" model on Guam on my way here. I had also flown the KC-135 as I used the tanker for flying time at Mather while awaiting the return of the B-52Gs from Guam, but never actually checked out formally before I left Mather AFB. It would be a good way to pass the time and to become familiar with the crews, so said I would love to. All the local flights were flown under peace time rules and so it was basically good relaxing stick time, actually in the Buff, wheel time! I would learn later that much of the refueling was done over the Laotian Border, not a friendly place. I would have to see what kind of schedule I would be on and check with Calhoun to see what the situation would allow but was sure at sometime soon I would be able to get off the ground. All the B-52s on U-Tapao were the "D" model, one type I didn't have much time in but they were essentially the same aircraft, just system and engine differences. There didn't seem to be any mission for them now, so most flights were to maintain currency for the crews and would be somewhat short in duration, more than likely with a token offload from a tanker and some Touch and Go's in the pattern.

We decided we would work on the time tomorrow and he left to eat dinner. I was now a bit hungry myself, but too tired to eat and the sun was sinking rapidly in the west, as night comes quickly at ten degrees north of the equator, so decided I had delayed long enough and entered my air conditioned trailer to hit the sack. What would tomorrow bring? I was sure there will be more ramifications in the aftermath of today, but I felt nothing could match it for drama and it was surely an interesting start to my year tour in Thailand!

THE FALL OF SAIGON

Sleep didn't last too long as my hotline phone rang at about 0200 hours. The command post said that I was wanted in the Command Post immediately. I quickly dressed, throwing on a flight suit and proceeded to the command post and was met by Colonel Calhoun and Colonel Dan Egbert, the Director of Operations, who I met for the first time. Evidently the situation to the west had accelerated and Saigon was under siege and events were cascading towards the total occupation of the city. The United States Embassy in Saigon was being evacuated. We could expect escaping aircraft coming our way at first light. Over coffee we decided that Colonel Calhoun was going to be in the command post, Colonel Egbert in the tower and I would monitor the ramp for receiving and parking of the incoming aircraft. I would be in communication in my vehicle to both the CP and the tower over a common channel. I could also listen to tower communications on another ground control frequency to assess parking needs and ramp locations. I would need a map of the ramp and the parking areas that would be involved. The SAC ramp, (the revetment area) as it was known would not be used for the incoming resources and parking of any incoming aircraft would be closed to beyond the Navy area. My hand-held brick was silent for the time being, but I knew it would light up soon.

INCOMING AIRCRAFT

Recovered South Vietnamese Aircraft

Driving out I was taken in by the silence around me. There were no power units belting out their song, no aircraft moving about and right now at about 0530 hours no discernible movement on the tarmac. I passed by the U-2 hanger and could see activity that signaled preparations for what I thought was their launch at 0615. I was but shouldn't have been surprised to see it taxiing out, with its accompanying small truck, to the end of the runway. The accompanying vehicle placed itself on the side of the right wing to start roll and would pick up the outrigger takeoff gear which fall off as the long U bird wing lifts to a flight condition. The wingspan of the U bird is long and drooping until it attains lift. Without the temporary outriggers, slight deviations on the sensitive control column of the U-2 would result in the outer edge of the wing to scrape the runway until it accepts lift and flies on its own. Without any delay it blasted down the runway, nose rising to almost the vertical and rocketed into the dark. The flaming tail disappearing into the night. Obviously, it was to play a part in this exercise that was about to unfold. I watched with admitted envy the U-2 power up and lift off almost immediately. (Later, I would enjoy a flight in the U bird. It is an astonishing aircraft and the only one that I know of that the wing tips are the first to fly and the last to stop flying. Most aircraft lift starts at the wing root and works out to the tips.) At the end of the runway where I sat the reconnaissance bird must have already risen to 3-4 thousand feet as I watched the torch tail coming out of its powerful engine. It was very impressive and that's coming from a B-58 pilot whose climb speed was 425 knots and initial angle of attack was 15 to 25 degrees. The roar subsided and I sat with my radio on and my eyes glued to the approach end. Daylight is very predictable in Thailand as it sits ten degrees north of the Equator; therefore, sunrise and sunset are virtually the same no matter what season you are in. There were a constant twelve-hour days and nights plus or minus a few minutes throughout the year! I positioned myself on the hammerhead on the far end of the runway just as the sun started to rise. I could feel the cool air coming through my vehicle as I had the front windows open but knew that as soon as that sun broke the horizon, heat would build quickly. The sun now had peeked over the ramp; a golden hue overtook the mountains to the left of the runway looking to the east. This particular "mountain" really only a dominant hill, I was told was known as "Buddha Mountain". It was a landmark that identified U-Tapao and its environs to anyone who was ever stationed there. The sun's rising became obvious as the top of the "Buddha Mountain" was now aglow in its rays and with it the heat was now becoming obvious. I was tempted to turn on the AC and take a spin down the taxiway, but felt I needed to address my phobia about heat and "cool it". I left the windows open and picked up a sweet scent of morning. The tower would be the first to know if aircraft were approaching so I waited for their call. However, the silence was not interrupted by a call from the tower; there was no morning dew to worry about, visibility was clear and unlimited, it was now pristine enough to take in the anything on final. I strained to see if I could pick up anything on final.

It wasn't long before I saw what appeared to be an engine exhaust far out on the approach to the south and then heard the tower call that they had seen an aircraft on final. There had been no radio contact! As it got closer the form was that of a fighter aircraft and then it was apparent it was an F-5, a Thai fighter version of a T-38, a two pilot training aircraft, configured for guns with a single pilot position. It touched down and rolled to a stop and was met by a "Follow-Me" vehicle after it turned off the runway to be taken to the main ramp area. I was curious about the aircraft and was going to go with it when my eye caught yet another aircraft on final and then another turned an overhead close behind it in a pitchout. It was then obvious that the line was just forming of incoming aircraft. There was no way I could leave right now! There were aircraft on downwind as well as on final and some were turning downwind onto base and then to final. It was apparent that some of the aircraft were making radio contact with the tower, but many were not and that could be a very big problem. The "Follow-Me's" were overwhelmed with the F-5s There was at least one occasion that aircraft passed each other on the runway going in the opposite direction. As they exited the runway they just went to where the first aircraft had gone. Suddenly, there was every kind of South Vietnamese military aircraft now overwhelming our capacity to park them, but park them we did and basically by type of aircraft.

This was until two F-5s on final actually made a transmission in with a call sign and announced, "hot guns". I was asked to place these aircraft into an area that had been designated for that purpose and being unfamiliar with the airdrome I had to be directed to where it was. Finally with a flight line map and tower help I became the "follow-Me" and escorted the two aircraft to the appropriate parking area, parked my car and got out and was joined by a group of weapon specialists from the MMS (Munitions Maintenance Squadron) group. The aircraft were parked and chalked, and the lead aircraft cockpit opened with its pilot exiting the aircraft. I walked toward him and noticed he had the rank of a Lieutenant Colonel and his name tag had a two-letter name "Si". I shook his hand and he started telling me in perfect English about his prepared launch from Ton Son Nuit in Saigon. He had a four-ship cell that was launching to attack the approaching NVA (North Vietnamese Army), when tanks appeared on the airdrome. He and his flight quickly taxied to the hammerhead for launch, but as he and the number two took the active a tank blocked the runway access for the other two aircraft. He and his wing man launched as they were being fired upon, fully armed and made passes at the advancing army forces. He saw the two blocked aircraft overrun with NVA soldiers and the two pilots were dragged from their aircraft. He said he witnessed that the two were forced down and that their hands were chopped off by the soldiers. After expending all his ammo and rockets he and his wing man came to UT, which had been designated by his superiors as the recovery base. He was the wing commander of the outfit and had forty-one aircraft in his wing. He saw two other aircraft of his group hit by rockets and exploded before departure. Twenty-five or six of his group survived the fall of Saigon. Colonel Si, learning I had been in Guam recently, expressed concern over his wife and seven children, none of which speak English. They had been evacuated to Guam a week ago. I assured him they were being well taken care of and related that living conditions were good. A flight line bus pulled up and the two of them departed the area, along with other pilots of the F-5s who had gathered around us. I never saw them again or did any other 307th staff member. I'm sure some of the attached "Intelligence" people debriefed them before departure. I wondered about Larry Duval as I saw a series of C-130s land, and he was not among them. I found out later he got out and flew directly to Okinawa with his last load of Americans and some Vietnamese employees at the embassy.

The landings continued for another four-hour period, maybe more, as I lost track of time. I saw that the first aircraft that landed and some of those following had more than a single pilot. The single engine, single pilot F-5 had the assistant crew chief, the crew chief and sitting on top of them the pilot, no chutes, no helmet, just three individuals getting out of town. One type of aircraft, The A-1-E with a normal three-man crew, had nine individuals jammed in and to top it off there were over ten of those aircraft that arrived. Parking them became a major problem as aas soon as they

35

stopped the aircraft individuals were exiting and walking aimlessly on the ramp. Finally, a bus arrived, and a contingent of security police established order, herding them into the now awaiting bus. My conversations with the tower were ongoing and at random I would be asked to help direct the traffic on the ramp. One aircraft that must have been in a hurry to get out of "Dodge", arrived with its tail lock still in place. C-130s arrived loaded with pilots, wives, children, soldiers, many wounded and all feeling lucky to be alive. A few Caribou aircraft arrived loaded with wives and children. I personally escorted two "Gooney Birds" (C-47s) to the ramp and watched the doors open to three tall (yes, I said tall) South Vietnamese Marines who were covered with bandoleers and hand grenades standing in the entrance door. They disgorged themselves of their weapons and started down the steps and were followed by refugees. Men, women and children, someone put the count at ninety-seven, an incredible number for an aircraft that normally carried forty to fifty people. Busses lined up to take them away and slowly things were grinding to a halt.

I was told that Saigon had taken over a thousand rockets. It was reported that C-47s had crashed on takeoff loaded with people and a SA-7 hit on a departing C-119 resulting in its crashing just off the runway. One non-military, with no markings DC-3 landed, came to park, shut down his engines as his tires went flat. A very interesting thing happened amid all the action as there was a team of airmen armed with paint guns painting over the South Vietnam marking on each aircraft as fast as the engines were shut down.

There was an ending to the turmoil, busses had conveyed all forms of people away, I realized that all the personnel in view were wearing Air Force fatigues and that vehicle traffic was confined to the familiar "bread trucks", normally on the ramp. I ventured out and could not see any sign of another aircraft on final approach on what was now a very hot and steamy day when suddenly my radio blared out that another aircraft was on final. I looked out and saw something, but it was not distinguishable. Whatever it was it was not a fast mover. Slowly it took form and at last I recognized a two reciprocal engine C-45. It touched down at the approach end of the runway and could have turned off at the first taxiway from the runway, but I was being told to take it to the Navy ramp and to park it heading into the revetment. It was, of course a "tail dragger" and slowly "essed" (most who have never flown a tail dragger would not know what it means, but in order to have visibility forward and to see where you were going, you had to move the aircraft nose left to right in order to see forward through a side window as the nose of the aircraft was above your sight line straight ahead). It moved down the runway, until it was even with the Navy area, turned and made its way to the ramp. An airman jumped out of a follow-me vehicle and guided this late arrival to its designated location. It was well clear of any other aircraft parking area and there were no Navy aircraft on-station, so this vacant area was selected for a reason. Parking with the nose right next to the Navy revetment, the engines stopped and there was a short pause and the door aft of the wing opened and two individuals, dressed in white shirts and black pants emerged. They both had on wheel hats and upon hitting the hot tarmac they turned, took off their hats, threw them into the airplane, closed the door and walked up to me and gave me a set of keys, and said "it's all yours". It was a short conversation and he did tell me that on takeoff he witnessed hostile forces with a number of AK-47s pointed at him from the side of the runway as he dodged debris and bodies on his takeoff roll. He didn't divulge where he had taken off from, nor did I ask him, but it wasn't anywhere close to Saigon. He saluted me and sauntered off, never to be seen again. I stared at that aircraft for another minute or so, inspected the fuselage for bullet holes, saw none and wondered how they had managed to get out of an undisclosed location.

That C-45 was still in that spot when I left almost a year later. I learned or surmised later that it was an "Air America" aircraft, better known as a covert CIA aircraft and a couple of pilots who were more than likely retired military who were recruited to fly missions in Vietnam. They probably had a home base likely in another area but had been in the process of closing some mission for some covert reason and were caught in the rapid fall of the country. Being a "slow-mover", they were passed by the other aircraft or had taken a land route to recover at UT. That takeoff from his departure location must have been the longest in his career. I had flown that aircraft once, when stationed in Roswell, New Mexico, as I needed to get flying time to be paid my flight pay. You had to get four hours/month and my aircraft at the time, the B-47 were all deployed to England and as I was new to the base, I had to get my time from base flight. Another second lieutenant and I were told to meet at base ops and we would be met by a Lieutenant Colonel, whose name I don't remember, who would provide us a flight to Albuquerque and then to Las Vegas, returning later that day. He allowed the two of us to take turns and to act as co-pilots in the right seat, explaining what to do and when to do it and gave us time on the controls. There was no auto-pilot that I recall so we would hand fly, which was a "piece of cake" for us as we had always flown without any artificial means. He was impressed that we could hold altitude and heading, so much so that he said he would let us each get a landing and takeoff. I was in the seat when we were to land at Nellis AFB in Las Vegas. He talked me down final, dropping the gear and milking the flaps. As round-out approached, he tried to help me with cutting the power and lifting the nose. I touched down and then saw the tower pass by, as I glanced over to the tower at the controller level, about forty feet above the runway. He quickly added power for our go-around. It was apparent that I needed more instruction on landings! He did give me another chance, with better results and I did get my needed flying time, but never flew the aircraft again.

I had a neighbor in New Hampshire who had signed a very lucrative contract for a five-year commitment for a job with Air America. It would match his Air Force retirement pay as well as pay him big bucks for the five years. He left his family in their New Hampshire house and they were still there when I left a year later, but I never saw him again. I turned to return to my car, grateful that it had air conditioning as I was feeling the effects of being involved with the action on the ramp. It was obvious I had not acclimated to the heat and humidity. It was very hot, and the tarmac had picked up and stored the heat. The soles of my shoes were burning, and the sun was merciless. My shirt and t-shirt were drenched, and my hat was dripping down my back. I was thinking a good rain was what was needed but fortunately it had not rained this day so far and the visibility was very good. It could have been a very dire day if it had.

I took in the scene on the ramp and it was staggering. Over seventy-three aircraft had arrived from South Vietnam and no telling how many people were on board those aircraft. Powers to be behind the scene were already working to remove the F-5s from the ramp as it was reported that the North Vietnam government was declaring that they were trophies of war and had to be returned to them. The activity for these aircraft and the personnel who came in them was already in motion. I was finally convinced that there would be no additional aircraft coming into the UT Air Base so told the tower I would do a runway check, rolled up my windows and sprinted to the beach end of the runway. I was cleared on and drove the length of this12,200 foot,300 feet wide highway, built originally as a Japanese airdrome in WW II and then expanded to accommodate B-52s and their mission in Vietnam. I found no debris and cleared at the far end and drove down the ramp past the now quiet and strangely peaceful display of multiple aircraft, parked in a semblance of order. Driving by the large DC hanger I saw the crowd of refugees being processed and children standing looking blankly at the scene around them. It would take months to sort out what to do with all the planes, but that was above my pay grade and duty classification. It was a task for PACAF, the Embassy people and their Washington counterparts to take care of. Many of the older aircraft would still be there when I left a year later, most would have been pirated for spare parts and were mere shells with landing gear, but only the F-5s would be gone within days, actually within hours, despite the demand of North Vietnam that they were war rewards and they should have them. Those twenty-five or six aircraft were airlifted by an equipped helicopter to a U.S. Navy carrier, USS Long Beach, brought to the area for the purpose of removing them.

With the tumult of the day behind me, I returned to the command section. Colonel Calhoun had not experienced the flight line activity as he had been confined to the Command Post for the duration of the morning events and therefore was unaware of the real trauma of the individuals who arrived or the chaos that had occurred on the ramp. He asked how things had gone and I replied that the ramp was full, and someone would have a difficult time managing those who arrived on the various aircraft. He indicated we (the 307th Strategic Wing) were not involved and he would prove to be right as luckily for us, PACAF through the base commander, Colonel Hal Austin, would be responsible for all the interaction that would be needed for the refugees. This was only the beginning and It would prove to be a nightmare that I would unfortunately become involved in somewhat over the months to come. The 307th SW day was over as flying our sorties had been cancelled long ago.

THE AFTERMATH

I awoke very early the next morning and decided to take a morning run. It was 0530 hours and obviously a smart move to escape the heat. I slowly got ready as darkness turned to a wonderful dawn. As I opened my gate, I heard the booming sound of the U-2 launching. It was exactly 0615 hours. I started out the horseshoe driveway and picked up one of the roads going by the airmen barracks, then by the base hospital. It was actually cool this morning and as the sun became more obvious and I turned a corner I noticed an object to the side of the road, which suddenly rose and identified itself as a snake. I arched left only to see it slowly slip down to a slither position, going away from me. I would learn that the cobra was very prevalent in the area. As they rose up, they were in a striking move, however they were limited by the length of their body above ground and would fall that length to strike, missing a strike they would have to reestablish that position, but would not go forward. I was also told later to just avoid that length and I would be fine. It sounded like a good plan however I would give them a wide berth as I would grow accustomed to seeing many of them on my morning runs. They loved the warm surface of the road! I returned to the trailer after about a forty-minute run, showered, grabbed a banana off the tree outside and headed to the flight line and the 307th headquarters building. Billie and Sergeant White were busy working at their desks. Billie rose and followed me into the vice commander's office, with a pot of coffee and asked how I liked my coffee. Telling her I drank it black she smiled behind her pretty, rimless glasses and poured me a cup into a mug I hadn't seen before. She had obviously picked one up somewhere and I would learn over time she was a most generous and giving person. Billie gave me a sheet showing my schedule for the day. Mostly I was to meet staff members I had not seen since my arrival, but also some Thai officers, including one Captain Vichit of the Thai Navy, the commander of the Thai forces on base. I asked for some background information on him and was told our Deputy Commander for Intelligence, Colonel Hal Morrow would come over before the meeting and fill me in.

I had met some of the officers in the 307th in the last two days, but outside of a couple like Lt. Colonel Yaryan, I had not spent any time with them. I went to the command post just to see what basically I could find out about yesterday's operation. I was buzzed in through the double doors and was surprised to see a captain I knew from my time on Guam, Ron Steffin. We exchanged pleasantries and he showed me around the CP, which of course was very like the many I had experienced in the past. I did note on the aircraft board the listing of the B-52s on station. I counted seventeen, a rather large number when you consider that with the state of Vietnam presently and that by congressional order, the bombing of Cambodia ceased on August 15, 1973, it would seem that this show of force was meaningless under the present constraints placed upon the remaining forces in Southeast Asia. There were three fighter wings, plus OV-10s in other bases in Thailand, along with our thirty tankers at UT. Our government had already abandoned Vietnam, how long would it retain forces in this part of the world? The crews I'm sure would rather spend their time flying missions at home, not playing the part of a political pawn in SEA. I would never understand the hesitation that the Pentagon thinking seemed to be enveloped in, both now and in the return of aircraft from Guam after the peace talks in Paris and the return of our POWs.

I returned to the office to find Colonel Morrow waiting in the outer area and invited him in. He gave me some basic info on the Thai command structure, telling me that Captain Vichit worked for Admiral Samut, whose headquarters was separated by a few kilometers east of the base. There was a very thin Thai officer force on the base and the enlisted was mainly navy security personnel, tough Thai Marines and clerical staff. He informed me that they would stand security positions with our Air Police at the gates to the base and on patrol. He didn't have too much information on Vichit other than the normal overview handout and that he was seldom seen outside his office, but he did enjoy social affairs which were plentiful. I thanked him and he departed. Billie came in and asked if she could add some information on Vichit. She had been in-country through six or seven wing commanders and knew the Thai commander as well as anyone. She proceeded to tell me not to trust him as he was very stealthy and devious, and she felt he was behind many of the thefts of equipment on the base. I felt prepared to meet this Thai Navy captain.

It was a very formal meeting with the captain later that day and as we talked, I felt he had little regard for me or the United States Air Force. After a brief exchange of pleasantries, we shook hands and he departed. There would be many more meetings with the Thai Navy commander, some pleasant and some more formal and not all under pleasant circumstances. I left the office to see how the ramp had weathered the onslaught of yesterday's action and drove out to the area by the DC hanger. The revetments were full of B-52s and the Tanker aircraft were parked in a row in the Tanker area which stretched almost half-way down the runway. There wasn't any obvious activity in the SAC area, however it was apparent the F-5s, which had been parked just adjacent to this part of the ramp had been secretly moved from the base. I had counted twenty-five or six arriving in the early hours of yesterday. Today there were none that I could see. I was told later of the aircraft carrier "Long Beach" steaming into a position about three miles off-shore had received the F-5s last night, each airlifted by helicopter to the flight deck. One was dropped accidently before reaching the carrier but was recovered later and moved to the carrier. The C-130s were in the process of leaving today for Clark AB in the Philippines. I drove further down the ramp and noticed many of the other aircraft, the C-7 Caribou, A1-Es and the C-119s had been moved to the north end of the ramp, closer to the navy area and farther away from public scrutiny and there was a lot of activity surrounding them. Some additional aircraft had arrived later last night, not from Saigon, but from the bases on the outer islands and remote locations. The two-engine Air America aircraft had not been moved and was still nosed into the revetment by the Navy operations building.

I exited the north end and went back to the SAC area and passed by the large cage by the maintenance area. There were a few people standing by the cage so being curious pulled into the parking area to see what was in the enclosure. I walked over to see a seemingly empty cage, until I noticed the longest slithering object I had ever seen moving out of a water pan that stretched almost the length of the enclosure. I was to find out later this was "Pete", a Burmese reticulated python. History had it that Pete was found on the ramp with a brother or sister at a very young age, three to four feet in length, in the late 1960s. A cage was built to house the two snakes, one eventually dying from some malady, however Pete survived and grew. It was estimated Pete was over twenty-four feet long presently and all said he was a very docile snake, who was fed a chicken once a week. There was a story that he was blind in one eye due to having a meal of a duck and the duck took umbrage at being eaten and pecked Pete in the eye. I would find out much later this was not true. Mesmerized by the size, I looked once again at the cage which was made out of chain link fencing, easily thirty feet long, barren except for a pan filled with water probably twenty-five feet long and wide and deep enough to accommodate Pete. The cage was probably ten to twelve feet wide, totally enclosed, with a small door on one end. Pete did seem to be very placid and not unhappy about his state in life. It seemed everyone was waiting for the feeding that was to take place this morning. Not wanting to wait around for today's victim, I would make sure I would make the next feeding. I wandered back to the office and told Billie of my finding. She laughed and said, "you haven't seen "Iron Mike" yet?" Of course, I wondered who that might be. The story was that somewhere along the line an ape of some origin was found injured and was nursed back to health by the base Vet. (Yes, they did have one on station). When his recovery period ended none seemed to know what to do with him; the ape seemed happy in captivity, so they decided to make him a mascot of sorts. He was well fed and housed in a spacious cage and had lots of attention. He had grown older and was mostly happy, but could get agitated if driven by taunting, which some of the younger generation of airmen could do from time to time. If agitated, watch out as he would throw things at the perpetrator. If there was nothing handy, he would defecate in his paw, wind up and chuck that, so be kind to Mike or suffer the consequences.

Billie asked me if I had a moment to discuss something and I said sure, fire away. She asked if I had seen the jewelry shop adjacent to the Officer's club and I said yes, I had gone by it yesterday evening. The proprietor was an individual named Johnny Su and he has been in that location since the arrival of the Air Force. It seems the base commander or some other base authority (maybe Vichit) wanted to evict him as Johnny also had the shop by the Base Exchange. Whoever it was said he wanted to share the wealth and let another individual have that shop. Billie felt that wasn't fair as Johnny had worked hard to establish that location and at one time in the past agreed to open it to make it more accessible to the crews passing through U-Tapao and had built it into a thriving business. I had known the base commander, Hal Austin previously at SAC Headquarters and felt I could talk to him and told her that when I saw him, I would bring it up. He was now, of course a PACAF individual and he had very little dealings with SAC. On reflection I'm sure it was his people that were painting the South Vietnamese aircraft yesterday on orders from higher up. When I mentioned it Wayne said that he was unaware of that activity. Interesting that the information was not shared on things that matter. Why the secrecy?

Hal's world was generally confined to the security of the base and to the maintenance of the confines and buildings on the base. Much of that seemed to melt into the SAC mission as the Air Police guarded our aircraft and the base chaplain tended to the entire flock. The hospital was for everyone and so the Base Commander was someone who had responsibility, but the functions of the base were shared by many. The SAC wing was a tenant on his base, and even though SAC had the mission, the Base Commander was in control of the workings of the base and its functions. SAC had all the aircraft, the maintenance and the personnel who supported that mission. It would be a strange position for me to take and I was beginning to see that there seemed to be a lack of trust in having the present wing commander, Colonel Calhoun, handle this situation. Unlike the usual status of an Air Force installation where one command had both functions this split in authority presented major drawbacks. How to deal with Hal Austin would be something I would have to assess and select the right time to address the background surrounding the eviction. My previous dealings with him would tell me it would not be easy to infringe on his authority or his decisions.

Colonel Calhoun was off station to some affair and I was left with the "brick". As I was about to leave the command center, I was informed that the tankers that were deployed to UT as part of an exercise called "Frequent Wind" were to be sent back to Okinawa. The takeoff briefing would take place tomorrow morning for those crews. The "exercise" was really to support, if needed, fighters involved if launched for the Vietnam tragedy.

The morning briefing forecast rain arrived, and it was coming down in buckets as I approached my car. I had no raincoat, but it probably would not have helped as the humidity was such that the rain seemed refreshing and the wind was pushing the drops sideways! Now,in the midst of my twelfth day with this steady rain coming down, I was called and asked to go to the runway at the five-thousand foot marker as a transient T-39 had skidded off the runway. As I got to the scene, the pilot and a group of others were standing on the tarmac, looking at the aircraft. I bypassed the pilot and others and walked onto the grassy, wet accident scene. I approached the aircraft as a fire truck and a group of others were discussing the situation. There was no indication that that the PACAF people were going to become involved as they were notified by the command post of the incident and said to inform the 307th of the problem. I was the first operations type to arrive and those around indicated there was no after problem with the aircraft. Having a considerable amount of flying time in the T-39, It appeared to me that the pilot after touchdown on the wet runway had begun to hydroplane and floated to the edge of the runway and "hit the binders". One gear caught the edge of the runway grass and sheared the left truck and pan-caked into the median between the runway and the taxiway. Other than the gear and doing some minor damage to the belly and horizontal stabilizer there was not much else that looked damaged. I went to the pilot and his passengers (The T-39 has two pilot positions and six passenger seats) and counting affirmed that they had a full capacity on the aircraft. I watched them entering a flight line bus, approaching him I told the pilot I would see him in base ops. When talking to him fifteen minutes later my assessment was verified when he told me he was in a skid and couldn't control the airplane and it just went off the runway. I asked him if he used the brakes and he admitted he did. Of course, this is a cardinal sin when in a hydroplane situation. By this time others from Base Operations had arrived and were inquiring about the accident and the circumstances surrounding what had happened. After some discussion it was determined that I was the only one on the base that had flying time in the aircraft. It was not a SAC crew or aircraft, in fact the pilot was from PACAF, but for the time being I was going to have to convene an accident board. PACAF would ultimately be the final authority on the cause of the accident. I discussed it with the 307th Flying Safety Officer later that day and together we prepared a statement of cause but did not attribute it at this time to weather or pilot error, but, listed both as contributing factors. The primary cause was later changed by PACAF to pilot error and cited limited flying time and lack of experience in the T-39. They did cite weather and runway conditions as a contributing cause. The aircraft was removed from its position with our "Cherry Picker" crane, placed on one of our 307th large flatbed trucks, brought into our DC hanger, where repairs were made by our maintenance personnel. It flew out of UT a week later.

The Undersecretary of State, Christopher Plummer, visited on Day 16. He didn't seem interested in anything operational. He expressed some enthusiasm about the airplanes that recovered here, mostly the C-47s and the A1-E hogs which were being cannibalized for parts as we watched. He might have absorbed the immensity of what had transpired, but I didn't think so as he quickly departed the base without any comment about or questions of the final day of Saigon. I don't think he gained a thing from his trip and was merely filling a need to say he had visited the base after the action had taken place during the loss of South Vietnam. Sycophants like him were the problem in our relationship with the Thai Government as all the local English papers spill vitriol against America on their editorial pages, to the point that you would think the United States did not have a friend in the world. His departure back to Bangkok on a T-39 was followed closely by Wayne leaving on a departing, redeploying tanker for an overdue break from the activity here.

With Wayne gone I would need some intelligence information to carry me if asked. An SSO briefing was given to me on how to treat highly classified material and the consequences of divulging any information from them. After receiving the briefing, I was cleared to see documents that truly astounded me, one being a night-by-night report on "Linebacker II", which was chilling to say the least. Looking at nights I flew I now know the meaning of "Fate is the Hunter". As a single B-52G on a mission over Hanoi it was easy to not pick up the big picture, suddenly the small memories of those nights and the close encounters with a mélange of SAM firings brought into focus how close the close calls actually were.

As I set about to familiarize myself with the workings of the 307th, I began to visit the various maintenance squadrons, the first being the Organizational Maintenance Squadron" (OMS). Huge! Over five hundred personnel were assigned and this was followed by trips to the Field Maintenance Squadron (FMS) and the Munitions Maintenance Squadron (MMS). There was a total of over twelve hundred in the three squadrons as they dwarfed the Operational staff of less than a hundred permanent personnel assigned. But of course, we had the large bomber and tanker temporary duty crews and staff which number over three to four hundred officers and enlisted.

THE VOLATILE ENVIRONMENT

Life on and off the base was full of dangerous activity. The Thai naval personnel were a threat to anything of value. What they did during the day was one of protecting the base proper, but what they did off duty and perhaps also on duty was something totally different. There were many incidents during my year in Thailand that would indicate that Captain Vichit ran a theft ring of the highest level and as the days for the US presence in this country grew shorter, the threat grew exponentially. While off base, the first suspect level would have to be the cab drivers. They are everywhere and as essential as they are to being able to travel around the territory and as true to their word they were on pickups at the golf course, they were the source of a great many of the problems that plagued the livelihood of the airmen on the base. Vulnerable Airmen were often taken advantage of, money and personal items disappeared from inebriated individuals returning to the base. They were also a great conduit for the drug traffic in the area surrounding the base. If they were not a provider, they could get it for you, whether soft or hard drugs. The heroin traffic in Thailand provided the purest form of the drug and our addict level was one we worried about daily. Many of the GIs would purposely be caught to delay their return to the US as when they are detained for drug-possession they would have to remain in the country for an additional six months and this would allow them to continue their addictive habit. The cabbies were prone to taking advantage of anyone who was having difficulties as they were thieves who will steal anything and everything. Items would appear on the black market in Bangkok almost instantly after being reported stolen. The dollar loss was staggering, and it was a daily thing.

On my thirteenth day in country I was asked to come to a luncheon with some Thai officials in the local area. I would accompany our top

Security NCOIC (Non-Commissioned Officer in Charge). When I arrived, I found that the "officials" were local police, Thai Marine officers, local bar owners and one grand "Madam". The local police were small in stature, tough looking, never smiled and carried the biggest guns on their hip. The marines were taller, even tougher looking with a gun positioned like they were going to take part in a "fast draw" competition. The Madam, about fifty was dressed to the teeth, but in good taste and not gaudy at all. She was well endowed, somewhat attractive and acted very demure, but looks and action can be deceiving! The bar owners ran the gamut, ranging from well-dressed to seedy, seemingly smarter than the average bear, most spoke two languages and they were big in their muscular appearance. They were definitely not the average Thai in size or in action and they looked like they were their own bouncers. The bar owners entered the luncheon as a group and didn't seem to be packing a gun and I felt they didn't feel they needed one if the occasion arose. I was ushered to a seat and as I sat down two of the bar owners sat on either side of me. Both were from Newland, the small town right outside of the base main gate. The discussion immediately turned to the many incidents that happen to the GIs from the base, robberies, beatings, fights and others. I had been briefed in detail on the many recent incidents that had occurred off-base locally so was prepared to ask questions and give alternatives unless some action was taken. They gave me some cures to preclude the incidents, a possible solution to the on-going situation to preclude making these small hamlets "off limits", which would kill their business. Most of their cures would not be accepted by civilized Americans but were perfectly normal to the Thais who felt an eye-for-an-eye was the best philosophy. An argument broke out between base officials and the locals about GIs escorting Thai women on the base as their guests. The locals felt that the GI entertainment should be off base and not at the Airmen or NCO Club. It got very heated but ultimately a cool atmosphere took over. The "Madam" had been in the middle of it and according to the interpreter she was being accused by Captain Vichit of a not-so-pure life. It sure broke up the day and would lead to other occasions that I experienced off base with our NCOIC Chief Master Sergeant McLaren.

As it turned out as I returned to the base, I was informed there had been an incident with a young sergeant who was shot when he resisted a thief who tried to take his camera then ultimately ran off with it. All this happened in broad daylight! It was another case of we have what they want. Fortunately, the sergeant would recover, but had to be sent to Clark AB in the Philippines. The thief was not found which is very normal.

With this incident fresh in my mind I would take a tour of the local towns the next night with Chief McLaren. As it was the normal town patrol, it was an eye opener as an area not twenty yards from the gate was termed "more dangerous than Harlem" at night. Little groups of Filthy, people were bartering for goods, probably drugs? Cabs everywhere, with drivers in groups eying you as you left the base in a Security Police vehicle. We traveled through Sattahip, not much better, but cleaner and safer and it had an abundance of shops. Going further east from the gate you went through Bonchon and then hit Newland, both were very GI oriented and visited. These are establishments that are dependent on the GI business. Bonchon was also a domicile for some married GIs and others with "Teelocks", the name for unmarried women living (shaking up) with a GI. The bump in the road called

Newland has a plethora of nightclubs, most of which are very nice, some are "dives" and all have girls, bands and they attract big crowds of airmen from the base. Newland is very safe as the businesses do not tolerate fights or unruly people as their bread and butter depends on how well the GIs accept them. It also has a security police patrol in and around the area. All the owners, including my new friends from the luncheon, met me warmly, very much like royalty and as they walked me around, they assured me they ran good clean places. I was the diminutive figure walking with Chief McLaren and these tough bar owners eliciting stares from the crowds in every establishment. I did not see the usually tough looking natives, but many young, pretty, Thai women sitting with off-duty airmen, dancing and having a good time. The Chief told me that the drug traffic stays away from the Bonchon-Newland area as the bar owners control it with an iron fist. Drug traffic Thais caught here seemed to disappear if they are discovered. Even the cab drivers are careful not to get involved here. I was impressed with the candor and the obvious feeling of security here. After more than two hours walking through the many places I had seen enough and told the assembled owners that I felt the areas of the two cities were places were a good place for homesick airmen to spend an evening.

They responded in numerous "Wai's" and the Chief and I then travelled down the road to Sattaheep, known locally for the temple located there and a jewelry store that was popular with the incoming crews, but also with a number of bars that are also frequented by the crews. We drove through the town and the chief and I walked to one of the brightly lit taverns. Unlike Newland it was very quiet. We talked to the owner for a couple of minutes, telling him it was a trip to familiarize me with the area. He seemed a bit relieved and offered us a drink, which we refused. We left and walked further down the street and finally turned back to our Air Police vehicle and returned to the base.

THE RATS

The following day I remarked to Billie about my trip the previous night and though she had never ventured to the areas she had heard through her sources that the owners were more than interested in making it a place that airmen could spend time without fear of being taken for a ride. Each day came with new surprises and more information. Having the highest security clearance gave me opportunities to keep up with the latest in the saga of Vietnam and the triumph of the North Vietnamese. It was a tragedy of our time and one that made me wonder about all my crews who flew during the "Linebacker II" raids, and especially my crews who didn't return. That war was over! It is amazing how a victory can be turned into a catastrophe due to a spineless congress and an overpowering media. Enough, I thought to myself. I was getting weary again and left to go back to my quarters and eat some supper, then study some material relative to our relationship with the Embassy and the MAAG in Bangkok, which Wayne had given me. He alluded to the fact that he didn't think he would be here very long as he had a friend in the headquarters that would push him into a wing at home. He felt I would be the one long-term that would handle these functions. I would go over them tonight after I ate, in order to be able to brief some of the aspects of the role SAC would play in the coming months of what would be a drawdown in our mission. I had bought a few items to eat and had a full-service kitchen, to include a microwave oven, so it seemed easier to eat there, rather than going to the club for a meal every day. I had found some good looking thick-cut pork chops at the commissary and served them with apple sauce and some canned green beans. I settled in after eating, lying on the sofa, sucking on a beer and reading the reports I had been handed and at the same time fingering the TV set. I was attempting to find something on the limited programming of the very small set in my first try at watching it when I heard a sound in the kitchen. I hadn't washed the dishes yet, but thought a dish had settled in the sink, so went back to reading the report I had brought with me. But then again, a distinct sound, a bit more obvious than the last one, so I got up and looked around the corner only to see a large, gray rat, finishing off the remnants that I had left. I was about ten feet away and somewhat startled and not knowing exactly what to do I slowly started to walk toward it. It looked up and didn't move from its feast. The only weapon I could see was a broom leaning against the wall. I grabbed at it and continued my stroll towards the rat. He was still not impressed with my presence but started to move toward the kitchen wall away from the sink. When I was in striking distance he dove through a small hole in the corner of the wall and disappeared. Somewhat chagrined I cleaned the dishes and the sink telling myself that I would tell Lum thien in the morning and see about getting a trap or two to get rid of this sudden menace to my lifestyle.

I have always hated rats and have had close encounters as a young teenager. My dad raised chickens and rabbits in our large backyard and kept the area extremely clean. The rabbit pens were on raised stakes and the chickens were fenced in with laying hens above the yard in a raised enclosure. The calm environs were suddenly disturbed by the baby chicks and rabbits being attacked by rats. The culprit area was a neighbor who had an extremely dirty rundown barn and enclosures, all ignored by the owner. This went on despite my dad's appeal to the neighbor. Losing bunnies and chicks then led to a hen being attacked and killed. My dad had tried every legal maneuver, but politics being what they were the board of health said they would look into it. After a week of more losses, my buddy and I took matters into our own hands and armed with baseball bats, found the rat nests in the floor of the old barn and swung away. They seemed very lethargic and didn't scurry about, but after some damage we retreated and went home. The next day the neighbor told my dad he had put out rat poison yesterday, thus the reason for the drugged rats. I didn't tell my dad of our mission and the rat problem did go away. Now my immediate problem was to rid my "home" of the kitchen rat.

I purchased two rat traps the next day and told Lum thien of the problem. The next night I ate my dinner and left enough in the kitchen sink to attract my rat. I set one of my traps, baited it with peanut butter and went into the next room. I became engrossed in a book I was reading, when suddenly I heard the snap of the trap. I jumped up turned the corner, and saw my adversary, caught in the middle of his body, dragging the trap, step-clop, step-clop, step-clop to his escape route. He arrived only to find that his encased body and the trap would not fit in the hole. I arrived at the same time with my weapon-of-the-day, a hammer I had discovered in a drawer earlier in the day and quickly dispatched one rat. Pleased with my conquest I took a shovel from outside and carried the rat through the gate to the area near where I had parked my staff car, I released the trap and dropped the carcass in front of my trailer. If a jungle predator doesn't finish it off Lum thien would dispose of the rat when she came to clean my living quarters the next morning.

When I started my morning run, I noticed the rat was still where I left it and hadn't been carried off by night prowlers. I've been told snakes are not interested in any type of carrion. Returning to my place I showered and dressed and stopped by the club for a cup of coffee and a sweet roll. The operations officer of the U-2 outfit, Jerry Sinclair was finishing his breakfast as he had supervised the launch of his bird earlier. I told him my rat tale and he thought that was very funny, saying he had not had a problem, but heard others had. I liked Jerry and his candor, and we would become good friends after our extended tours were over, but other events in the next few months would give us tales to spin for years to come. Arriving at the office I told the story of the rat, who couldn't be killed in a trap to anyone who cared to listen, starting with Billie and anyone who happened through the command section, but I forgot soon after as we were to meet an incoming KC-135 bringing in some new officers to our little world and then I was to meet with the Base Commander and would discuss the problem of Johnny Su, the jeweler.

The Tanker landed with replacements, mostly of maintenance officers and a command post controller. They were welcomed to the heated environs of U-Tapao and carted off to find their quarters. I hustled over to the Base Commanders office, hoping to talk to Colonel Austin and found out he had suddenly been reassigned due to some Vietnamese refugee handling problems. He had been summarily fired. I would learn later that in the process of dispatching that crowd some of the fleeing refugees had been forced against their will onto the C-141s to the Philippines. He was not taking visitors at the time, so I left. I hadn't solved Billie's Johnny Su problem, but was pleased to tell her it was probably resolved without any effort on my part and told her not to worry about Johnny Su as the guy who was taking away his shop was no longer a player on station. Johnny Su was the least of his problems. I found out later he was not the source of the problem for Johnny, it went much deeper! XXXXXXX

One of the tanker permanent party officers, Major Pat Richmond was waiting for me when I returned. He was the chief of Tanker Operations, a very personable individual, with a ready laugh and a man with a question. He wanted to know if I played golf and of course I said I did. It seems that the Thai Admiral Samut was a golfer and had a course located out in the jungle not far from the base which we could use. He asked if I had clubs and indeed I did, as I had brought them on the hope if nothing else I could work on my game. The fact is I was told there would be opportunities to play by others who had been to UT before! He and another permanent party officer, Major Karl Kaufman, who was a mission planner in the B-52 operation, went out on a regular basis to play the course. Pat explained that to get there you could go to the main gate of the base and catch a cab and bargain with the driver to take you to the admiral's course and pick you up at a pre-designated time after you played. I was not too certain of the pickup, but if that was how it was done, I would give it a try. The price for the round trip was somewhere between five hundred and six hundred baht, (five or six dollars). The price of a round of golf was about the same and for another five hundred baht you could get a caddie, which was a good idea as there were no carts and the temperatures were always in the nineties with the humidity the same. I told them I was game and so we set a date to play the next Saturday. This would become a pleasant way to pass some time and I might even improve my game.

When I returned to my trailer home at the end of the day Lum thien was pleased I had caught the rat and cautioned me there might be more. I heard her warning so set my trap again that night and did catch another rat, but that was not the end of it as over the next week I had killed nine rats, none as big or tough as the first one and all deposited in front of my trailer to be disposed of by Lum thien. As a matter of course I did not have a problem for the rest of my tour, but a legend was born, a family of rats had been eradicated. You could say I ended the rat menace with my deadly trap and my handy hammer.

PLAYING GOLF IN THAILAND

Karl, Kathy, Colonel Dugard and caddies

Going to the base main gate was an adventure as there is a joint security arrangement with the Thai Navy so there are two guards on what would prove to be a seemingly porous gate. There are many cabs waiting outside to include small Baht busses, people selling all sorts of wares and food. Off duty airmen were looking for a ride into one of the small villages that were attractive to them and now Air Force officers looking to engage a cab for a two-way ride to and back for a golf game. As I said before I was a bit apprehensive that the cab driver would take our money and not pick us up five hours after dropping us off and you had to give him the money before he would agree to the trip to and from the golf course. Yet, for the entire time I spent there and the many times I played golf at Admiral Samut's course, there was never a time that the cab driver failed to show up for the return trip. Also to be noted always at the proscribed time. Being used to the type of golf course that I had played in the past and I have played golf in many places around the world to include Spain and Ireland, Thailand's course was the most unique. It had a "club house" which was no more than a place open to the elements with a corrugated tin roof and a place to pay your fees and hire a caddie (which you were insane not to) and buy a cool drink. I never saw alcohol on sale, of course if you drank one of the Thai beers you wouldn't make it past your first swing. There was a rack to place your shoes on after changing into golf shoes and you hoped they would be there when you returned. The word "foursome" does not apply here as you will find groups of players, surrounded by caddies and a gallery that observes them, calling out 'dit ma" on good shots or mumbling "ma di" on bad ones. "Six-somes or Seven-somes" were common. The caddies all had numbers on their yellow, long sleeved and pants uniforms and there were no names given or uttered. It was sixty-three and any other number they were designated with. Not being conversant in the language was not a problem as they knew enough English to acknowledge you wanted a caddie and they knew how to follow a ball. The caddies would seldom go into the rough (jungle) to retrieve a ball but would point to where it left the fairway. Usually a new ball was in order.

For the first two months I played the first hole, (which was later changed) with a first tee that was aimed at a mystery area, as in front of you were huge mounds of dirt, mostly round at the top, which I was to discover later was an old elephant burying ground. Due to the fact that elephants are vegetarian, most of the mounds had bushes at the top from the seeds in the elephants when they died. Hitting around these mounds was an adventure as no matter where your first drive went you seemed to be stymied for your second. After hitting your drive, you went in the direction of your hit since you could not see where the ball landed. Once you got to the green, assuming you made it, (this is where you need a caddie for the first time) you had to putt on an undulating area where your path to the hole could be interrupted by any number of slithery objects, known as snakes which the caddie would quickly clear away. Going along a narrow path to the second tee, you discovered that you were indeed in the jungle as fairways were surrounded by foliage and a thick, deep rough. By now, a group of young boys would be tracking you, watching your swing and following the flight of the ball. If it went right or left into the deep foliage, they would get your ball for you at the mere cost of five baht (a nickel). I t was a bargain as going into that dense area was not what I really wanted to do. It became apparent that the course, all eighteen holes was carved out of the jungle. There was one large beautiful lake that was at the beginning of the eighteen. Then the jungle took over. The caddies knew every nook and cranny of the course and would direct you from time to time to avoid certain hazards that could occur on the jungle paths. You would find a refreshing "Fanta" and Ice at almost every hole and it was necessary for the intake of one to stay hydrated.

By the time you get to the ninth hole you were as far away from the first tee box as you could get. It was at this point that most of the sounds of the jungle would intensify. I was told most of the noise was from baboons, but it could have been from other kinds of meat-eating wild beasts as I didn't know the difference. Working your way back to the start was as much a chore as going out. One of the oddities of the course was the fact that I never saw a mowing machine of any kind and yet the fairways were of relatively short grass. I don't think they had a maintenance group either, as it was just an area carved out to please the Thai Navy brass and we were just fortunate enough to be able to play there.

When it rained there were very few refuges for cover. Those that were there had four bamboo poles stuck in the ground and a thatch roof over it. Amazingly, they worked very well despite that they were only about four feet wide and maybe five feet long and no siding. I discovered once again that when the rain came in Thailand it came in a deluge and it came straight down. The biggest damage when undercover was to your lower body as the drops were so intense that the rebound off the ground came up two feet and drowned you from the ankles to the knees. Another obstacle on the course was of course the cobras. They were plentiful but they were also obvious. If you got too close, they would rise-up showing the head and about half of their body, causing you to go in a different direction. The young boys following you would sometimes play with them like they were a wayward mouse. They would throw a mongoose, which were also plentiful on the course at the snake to see if they would engage in a fight, which they often did. The mongoose always won! The course was known as "Plutaluang Golf Course" and it was supposedly measured at 6749 yards, however I'm sure it was at least 7000. There were interesting holes such as the one shaped as an eight in that there was a large area to drive in, however your second shot had to go through this very narrow opening, maybe ten to twelve yards wide, into another large expanse and finished at the hole which had dense foliage around the sides and the back of the green. Fortunately to its credit it was a par five, 406 yards long. The unique elephant hole did change after our initial playing rounds and they improved the club house as a new starting tee. It was still open air but had a permanent roof and there was an open bar, where you could buy soft drinks and some other pleasant cool drinks, but no water. It was also an elevated tee to a rather short hole. It was a par four, only 340 yards, but if you drove over two hundred and twenty yards you were in a large (twenty yards wide) klong (pond). Of course, your second shot had to be over the klong to a green surrounded by water. I forgot to mention that if you went into the klong on your drive, the ball would be given back to you by an individual who was constantly in the water up to his neck who we named the "Klong Monster". He wore a pork-pie hat and would only be seen if he retrieved a ball. He was tanned and would rise over the edge of the water, hat secure and the ball in his hand. Obviously, there was a charge for his services, five baht! (nickel). After the change in the first hole, the hole of the elephant mounds disappeared and was never used. Maybe the Admiral got tired of the stymied second shot! One of the other interesting decisions you had was that It became common to hire two caddies, one to carry your bag and the other as a fore caddie, going out before you hit your drive off the tee to mark your ball. They were generally teen-aged girls. I don't remember any boy caddies, only little boys that would gladly retrieve your ball from the jungle for the customary five baht. The girl caddies would occasionally smile, but for the most part they spoke no English and were not surprised or emotional on your effort or your shot. They always wore yellow baggy suits that seemed very hot in an area where heat was a way of life. Pat Richmond, Karl Kaufman and I played golf probably once a week. We would have a fourth on some days, but not always. Pat was a very good golfer and Karl, left-handed was not far behind and we always had a good time, but best of all it broke the monotony of the tour when times seemed to drag. We would laugh a lot and shared some good moments on that course in the jungle. On one day in early August as we played a seven-foot water viper slithered across the grass. They are very poisonous and are to be avoided. We watched him slide into some brush at the side of the fairway. Our two young female caddies were going to chase it for a dinner until we urged them to back off. The sounds of the wild was in our ears and the threat of wildlife was not far away, but outside of cobras, slithering vipers and the Mongoose, we saw basically nothing else.

The Krate which we had been warned to avoid was a deadly little green snake, tattooed in alternating green shades, never showed on the course. They were one-step snakes who did not have fangs, instead knawing teeth. We would see them later and other places. I'm sure we were seen by some of those who made those outrageous sounds, but they were more scared of those buffoons with sticks in their hands and we were too dumb to care. As Winston Churchill said, "Golf is a game played by fools with sticks designed by the devil". On most occasions as we finished our round, hot and sweaty, our driver would be waiting for us. We would buy a round of cool drinks, including one for the driver, but barely could finish them on the short ride back to the base gate.

THE MONSOON WEATHER, RUNNING AND OTHER EXERCISE OPTIONS

I was told before I arrived about the rainy season. U-Tapao does have a climate and an atmosphere that induces precipitation due to the high humidity and heat. Late afternoons the buildup of towering cumulus clouds could be seen building and you knew it will only be a short period of time before they move in and dump significant amounts of rain, with accompanying thunder and lightning. Usually, it will dissipate during the early night hours and the following morning will dawn cloudless and somewhat cool, only around 75 degrees. In this discussion about rain there was a mention of the monsoons that pass through the greater belt of Southeast Asia, to include Thailand. They mention that the spring monsoon happens in April and the fall monsoon, sometime in October. What they didn't mention was the severity and the duration of each of these seasonal passages. As this semi-annual front moves through, it will last for weeks and the rain is fierce at times. Umbrellas don't suffice as the rain hits the ground so hard it will bounce up to your waist. Shelter of some sort is needed. Periodically it will let up enough to move about and then without as much as the bang of thunder it will commence again. The three to four feet deep ditches (Klongs) on each side of the streets on base will fill up with water and flow so swiftly to deeper culverts that you could be swept away if you fell in. The monsoonal formation becomes part of the yearly life-style, as the natives anticipate and prepare for the coming of the rain. This is not to say they pile up sand bags or dig moats around there flimsy homes, most of which have thatched roofs and open siding, but you can see their efforts to bolster up the roof and move items from the underside of their raised floor to keep them dry.

The passage ends as suddenly as it started. The movement is from south to north in April and north to south in October. Playing golf can be a difficult task, but it can be done, as long as you know you will have an extra-long day in order to finish eighteen holes. Base life goes on and aircraft fly their assigned missions. I never put on a raincoat during my year, (it was too sweltering hot) but I did get very wet on many occasions.

There was one thing about Thailand that everyone must accept and that is it was going to rain. Umbrellas were useless as the bounce of the water as it hit the ground would insure you would not stay dry. Combine the rain with the humidity when it was in the nineties and you had what is known as an uncomfortable situation. In one day on the base they recorded five inches of rain, not necessarily an anomaly it was reported. The month of May average for rainfall is nine inches, by the fifth of May we had received eight inches. A woman in San Antonio once described how she coped with such weather when she said "I go from my air- conditioned house to my air-conditioned car to my air conditioned office", which seemed to fit many of those assigned here, but some of us had other routines. Despite the fact that monsoons go through Thailand twice a year, once going north and once going south, it doesn't seem to affect daily life. The rains come and the roadside ditches fill with water, and they flow like raging rivers into the larger and deeper klongs going out to the gulf. In the metal trailer, it sounds like the walls and roof will collapse and crush you. The rains stop and the humidity is enough to evoke more moisture than what the rain brought. And then the heat! I don't remember many days above the low nineties, but the combination was fierce. It was always a pleasure to go into an air-conditioned building, however many of the Thai businesses were more open air and not comfortable at all. I remember that in December (you know –winter) the highs would still hit the eighties and the lows would go all the way down to the low seventies. I saw with my own eyes, the natives wearing overcoat type clothing and burning fires to keep warm during the "winter" mornings, while the non-natives (me) were reveling in the cool weather. Running in the heat was insane therefore my routine four miles was done at dawn as the U-2 took to the sky and the sun just peeking over the horizon with the temperature in the low to mid- seventies. It was a pleasant time and the beauty of the red dawns was not only beautiful, but consistent. It was hard on shoes as the humidity was still high and the shoes would squish as they filled with water, both from sweat and rain.

There were other forms of exercise available to all of those stationed at the U-Tapao Royal Thai Navy Base. The base gym was almost adjacent to the officer's trailers and there was a direct path to the gym from where I lived. Adjacent to the gym were two tennis courts and two four-wall handball courts. You can only imagine the heat in one of those handball courts during the day! However, I did find a handball player or two who would gut it out. Paddleball opponents were available, and I did play when I had to, but preferred handball. In the gym there was a basketball court, and a squash court. The gym was not air conditioned. The other options for conditioning on the base was to ride a bike which many chose to do, however there was a problem associated with bike riding and that was to make sure it was not stolen. Also, there was only so much you could see riding a bike on the base and to go off the base on a bike was a high form of stupidity. The "steely boys" as Lam tien called them were very active and a bike left unattended would disappear before you could count to ten. One sure way to keep your bike was to make it so unattractive that those who were the culprits were revolted by the sight of the bike. One of my staff, Major Trent Martin had such a bike. It had no fenders, no kick stand, the seat rotated, and it was covered in mud and other debris. Trent didn't even have a lock for the bike, and it was nothing to find it thrown in a heap outside his quarters and it would remain there even with fierce rain. Everyone else would take their bike indoors at night and when going to some location, intricate locks were installed in the hopes of delaying the attempt at snatching their valuable mode of transportation, however this was not always effective.

There was one notorious theft of a bike that occurred that caused a great deal of consternation and that happened to our chaplain, Father Saulnier. He rode his bike everywhere and had a sign on the rack in back that said, "God Squad". It disappeared one day from in front of the chapel. I received a call from the Base Provost Marshall that the good priest had reported his bike was taken out of its rack in front of the chapel. I told him to get a hold of his counterpart in Thai security and tell him that this bike was to be found and returned ASAP. I contacted the Thai Commander's office and reiterated that statement as it was a sacred bike and the culprit would suffer greatly if it was not returned. It was back in the chapel bike rack in fifteen minutes and there was never a repeat problem.

Thievery was a way of life on the base. Nothing was secure form the theft gangs and their leaders. They were identified as the Thai Navy enlisted and one of their leaders was none other than Captain Vichit. There were some egregious thefts that took place and I will detail them as we go forward. The Thai village on base was not involved for the most part, however they had free reign of the base and on occasion would be seen scurrying back to that side of the base on an almost new bike. The Thai Navy personnel were much more adept as they would put the bikes in a disappearing official Thai security vehicle, take them to one of the local villages and sell them. Lum thien was constantly protecting me as she told me not to hide a door key outside the trailer as the "steely boys" would find it. She found the first key I placed outside and said anyone could find the key if she did. I never tried again! She will not allow anyone in the trailers she works in and there does seem to be a code that exists that they don't jeopardize her job by coming in while she is in the area. She was a sweet lady, totally honest and I'm sure she would have resisted any attempt to violate her trailers or her trust.

THE ROUTINE

Base life fell into place and it was one filled with the gathering of information on the aftermath of the fall of Saigon. There was a thought and some saber rattling that Thailand was in peril of invasion. Our security was expanded on the perimeter fence which consisted of miles of two iron Link fences, topped with barbed wire, side by side which had about a ten- yard area between them that was patrolled day and night by one of our Air Police and one of their Thai Navy counterparts. There were reports of "sapper" teams infiltrating the country in an attempt to do crippling damage to the base. It was becoming a time to stay alert to those who came on base and what they were doing there however, it is hard when half the base is a town and the residents come and go as they please. The security of the main gate did improve, and it was obvious as nothing vehicular could come on the base without a thorough search. As we found out later, vehicles leaving the base were not stopped. An interim base commander arrived, Colonel Bob Janka, sent from the OV-10 base up north. We had a lot in common as we would discover. Our official meetings were short and fulfilling and he became a tennis opponent on a frequent basis when both of us could muster a common break in our schedule.

Our flight schedule did not change as the U-2s were very involved in a meaningful mission, launching two birds a day, one at 0615 and another at 1815 hours. Other flights were at HHQ request and the constant rotation of aircraft. It was strange as we were still changing out B-52 crews and the constant stream of new KC-135 crews and aircraft was a part of our daily life. Fifteen of the tankers had been redeployed after our major fall of Saigon exercise was finished. The B-52s and the remaining KC-135s were flying routine missions to fill monthly flying requirements, but it was an active schedule as the tankers were supporting the many fighters from up country, including the F-111 Wing. I managed to get a couple of B52-D flights during the first couple of months, but flying time was scarce and the crews needed their seat time. I did manage to stay current and then a funny thing happened. Colonel Calhoun went to Guam on business and then home to the CONUS on leave and I was left with the wing and the problems that were occurring. I was grounded from off-base activity as well as getting a flight or two until he returned or someone was cleared to carry the brick. It was supposed to be for a short period of time, however the absence seemed to expand by the day. I heard he had spent some time in the headquarters at Offutt, talking about a follow-on assignment, but there were not too many people who were knowledgeable about his whereabouts. The comical aspect of his absence came from Manas Manat, the mystery visitor who was now coming by the office to see me and spend some time talking about himself and his background on a recurring basis. He seemed to know more about Calhoun than anybody else on the base. He imparted that the good Colonel would only come back to pack his belongings and complete six months in-country to get credit for an overseas, remote tour. I was skeptical but had nothing else to hang my hat on. The word spread quickly within the wing and slowly it was obvious to all I was handling all of the day-to-day activities and had sole passion of the brick, which meant I not only couldn't fly, but I couldn't go anywhere as there was no one else to take command in the SAC scheme of things, that meant no golf until this was resolved.

My immediate commander at the 3rd Air Division on Guam was General Minter, with General Gaughn as his second in command, a sometimes gruff individual who I indicated was very involved in the Vietnamese refugee problem that I had seen as I passed through Guam on my way to starting this tour. He was a former squadron commander during my first days in the Air Force in Roswell New Mexico. It was reported that General Minter was to be reassigned shortly to the Pentagon. AS it turned out within days he was replaced by General Tom Rew. He was a new one star and my wing commander when I was stationed in Guam during the "Bullet Shot" days. General Rew was a very mild-mannered, studious man, whose calm demeanor during our Linebacker II raids was a significant influence on the crews who were under a great deal of stress from the constant flights into North Vietnam. He flew on day one during

Linebacker in the jump seat and went to Hanoi in the lead aircraft with my good friend Larry (Robbie) Robinson (an eventful experience according to Larry).

I was asking 3rd AD for approval to let Colonel Merril take the radio on occasion so I could get an occasional flight and leave the base to play golf. In the meantime, Manas became the source of a great deal of information and seemed to have a direct line to some sort of intelligence gathering that we could not tap into or understand. On the flip side, I was now gathering information on Manas from base sources, other than Billie. I found out a great deal of background on this mysterious man. He was here during the occupation of the Japanese during WW II and had been a worker when they were building the airfield that we are now using at U-Tapao. The story I heard was that he worked for them during the day and killed them at night (those are his words). I was also told he was an informant for the OSS, the precursor to the CIA and would provide intelligence information to submarines when they came close on to the shores of the Gulf of Thailand near the base. It was also said that his back had been broken and that he was paralyzed from the waist down but recovered, and also that he had lost his sight, but in his words, he willed his sight to return. Some myth, some fiction, but after knowing him there is no doubt that he has some source of energy that most would like to possess. I believe!

Finally, after some knee-bending pleading I received approval from the 3rd Air Division that I could use others to relieve me from the radio if I remained local. Golf was now back on the burner which was a relief for up to this time I had no other place I could go off base to relax and off I went to stroll in the jungle. I was still the vice commander of the 307th Strategic Wing, but for all intents and purposes, I would be the commander in practice and responsibility. This would only change when I was formally given command in the near future, a role I was told would happen with the departure of Wayne, who we discovered through official sources was now going to be given the command of the wing at Seymore Johnson AFB in North Carolina. He still had to return in order to complete his six months. Only Manas could tell us when that would be!

THE MAYAGUEZ

On the twelfth of May at 0900Z, we were informed of the capture of the United States freighter, the Mayaguez. Our role at that time was not yet determined but we were waiting for our country's response to this act of piracy by the Cambodian government. On the 13th of May, briefings were given by our chief of combat intelligence, Captain Alan Geer on the sequence of events and the present situation. Captain Geer was prepared to take the lead in disseminating intelligence data and the nature of response passed to us as our SSO was the source of all gathered intelligence and became the center of activity. Despite the fact that we had current information, that other in-country locations did not have, command problems took over. The bureaucracy of command structure was an ever-present problem and PACAF wanted to run the railroad from their headquarters in Hawaii.

We were informed that U-Tapao would be the central base of operation, however there was no coordination with us on what we were supposed to furnish as the operating base. C-141s from Kadena AFB in Okinawa were to bring in a Marine task force and they were to be housed and fed at U-Tapao. The original number was ten thousand marines. Incredible! Fortunately, the number was pared down. The new number was a moderate force of 230 marines. The 635th Combat Support Group (PACAF) was to be responsible for this force and had to find a place to house them. The only hanger available was the U-2 hanger, which entailed taking our two birds out of the hanger, providing a cover for them to avoid satellite detection and then finding enough cots, blankets, and food to take care of this force. The separate service problem was overshadowed by the commanders of PACAF, as they were not keeping our SSO and our intelligence personnel aware of what was going on. At the same time, up-country helicopters were to be sent to U-Tapao as the staging position to transport the marines to and from any battle arena area. Captain Geer informed me that the boat was believed to be at a Cambodian wharf. We had been briefed later by our intelligence sources it was indeed the place where the Mayaguez was docked. In all over twenty Air Force helicopters were dispatched with crews to our base from locations up country. Once again, the PACAF hierarchy kept us out of the loop. The 635th was notified, but the SAC command was not. We were told after the fact that we were to supply interrogation teams needed to debrief crews and survivors that had been picked up from a sunken Cambodian Gunboat, however there was no coordination with our command section or our chief of intelligence to carry this out. This was an initial indication of the poor direction and control, typifying the Mayaguez operation. OPREPs (official reporting information of events transmissions) bypassed our intelligence and were being sent instead to PACAF, through U-Dorn AB up-country. All tasking was being sent without coordination with the 307th Strategic Wing and yet the wing's KC-135s were being tasked to support fighter operations in support of the effort on May 14 and May 15. Also, space had to be provided for the Marines and parking for twenty helicopters and again no channel requests were made for this support. There was no request for the U-2s to assist in the search for the boat and they were not tasked to provide recon for this effort.

U-Tapao AB was getting very busy! Helicopters were arriving from up country PACAF bases, C-141s were landing from Okinawa, disgorging marines and taking off again without refueling. Our SSO intelligence information was receiving reports that the Cambodian troop strength was significant, and their armament was very current on an island off the Cambodian coast called Koh Tang. The report had the captive tanker docked and the crew was being held for ransom on that island. The first Frags (mission requirements) were received. We scheduled pre-takeoff briefings for our tanker force in support of the upcoming response to the Cambodian government's action of piracy. Early in the morning of the 13th the Marine Commander, Lt. Colonel Hopkins, the force operative, wanted clarification on the specific type of area "denial agent" to be deployed during the Mayaguez operation as his troops had only white gas mask filters which were adaptable to the CBU-19/30 mask only. A secure call to command headquarters confirmed that only that mask would be necessary.

I also informed Lt Colonel Hopkins of the possibility of increased troop strength and high-level weapons on Koh Tang Island. He felt he would wait until his commander would arrive later as his immediate superior was scheduled to arrive that night to assume command of the Marine forces.

All of the "intelligence" information was coming through our SSO so I was aware of all the action taking place on the ramp, however there was no PACAF interface with me on the use of their resources and how it would affect the overall operation. Interestingly I was asked to meet the incoming Marine Commander that night. I met him late that evening when he arrived and drove him to his temporary quarters. I gave him the same information that I had passed to Lt. Colonel Hopkins that morning, but his response was a nod of the head. He was a gruff, non-communicative colonel, dressed in combat fatigues who I envisioned as one who was born a marine and had not any use for anyone who was not a marine. I opened the door to his temporary quarters as he lurched by me, grabbed the key and turned to close the door. I wished him well in the upcoming endeavor, but don't believe I got a response as the door closed.

A little after midnight I was called to the SSO. They were in receipt of a highly classified secure message from PACAF command channels with the latest intelligence estimates containing information that had severe ramifications for the events which were already very much underway. After reading the message, it was imperative that I deliver it to the Marine force commander before any further helicopter deployment took place into UT. I had dropped him off only an hour earlier and knew he was more than likely not going to be very happy to be awakened. I knew he had a long day and more on his mind about the events before him, but I had to catch him before any firm decisions were made. I drove immediately to his quarters and woke him up. He arrived at the door in his skivvies and a marine green shirt. He was a bit surprised, but amiable. I told him I had a message of interest that he needed to be aware of. He told me to read it to him as I sensed he did not have his glasses with him, and he had worn them when I took him to his quarters. I read the entire message and felt a sense of relief as I did. The essence of the message indicated that the Mayaguez crew was no longer on Kho Tang Island, which told me that there was no reason to invade this island. It also divulged that the island was being defended by a crack, Cambodian regiment with advanced weaponry. I waited for his reply as the wheels were in motion to start the briefings for crews and it was obvious the marines were being prepared for combat. He looked blankly at me and then said, "My orders are to attack the island; we're attacking the island". Stunned I said I would take him to the SSO, and he could get clarification and ask for further guidance on a secure line. He refused and said he had his orders and they were to take the island. I argued with him that there was no reason to try to take the island as there was no one there except a highly skilled defensive force. He brushed me off and closed the door. I drove to the SSO and made sure that it was known the message was delivered.

Later in the early morning of the 14th of May the 307th staff had been working throughout the last twenty-four hours on the "frag orders" for the tankers. It was obvious we were going to involve all our crews and at least fifteen KC-135s. Crew briefings were done in large groups with four crews launching at the crack of dawn and four follow-up aircraft placed on a "demand call" ready on the ramp to relieve the tankers in the air. Other crews were confined to quarters and were to be prepared to be ready to launch as the need arose. The aircraft in the air would orbit on a designated location and await the call to pass gas. Sort of a new "Young Tiger", the name used for the tanker force supporting aircraft during the Vietnam War.

Well before sunrise on May 15 our 307th tankers were taking off to support fighters from Udorn, Takli and Korat ABs in their support of the helicopters taking marines to Koh Tang Island. The sun rose during this splendor of activity, only to be interrupted by the U-2 launch at 0615 hours. From the time I left the Marine Commander and during the ensuing hours, the 307th intelligence office was not informed of when the attack operation would start or consulted on operation planning. I later learned that the invading force assaulted the target area at 0645 hrs. There had been no attempt by higher headquarters to coordinate fighter support with the Jolly Greens from our intelligence sources. The 307th was completely in the dark for this ongoing operation. The use of the helicopters from UT, loaded with marines were launching continuously as the sun rose and the heat took over the base functions. The fighters from the up-country bases were deployed to the areas close to where the ship was berthed, Sihanookville, not surrounding the landing of the Marines to suppress the firepower of the defenders of the Island. (This island had no tactical interest as neither the crew or the ship were being held there). Helicopter crews were going to the island unsupported.

Mission (intelligence) debriefings would be in order when they returned, however the crews who were able to return were not brought to the debriefing area and instead turned around without imparting intelligence data. To quote our chief of intelligence "Aircrew debriefings are conducted for two reasons. First and foremost is to acquire information on the area threat environment for subsequent missions, thereby protecting not only the personnel involved, but also the aircraft. Secondly, debriefings are conducted to provide high-level agencies with timely information from the operations area." The comment was made in the after-action report that "by not directing aircrews to debriefing sessions upon their return to U-Tapao, Mayaquez operations planners effectively kept their crews uninformed of the threat situation".

Brigidier General Baxter the 13th Advon Commander, was sent to U-Tapao to coordinate the action and despite repeated attempts to update him through our intelligence directorate to brief him on the hostile environment on Koh Tang Island, he rebuffed us. Unfortunately, the complete and factual reporting was disregarded. Information was consistently volunteered by team members to the Special Operations Group however it was consistently met with a "so what" attitude by Colonel Anders, the 56 SOW (Special Operations Wing) Commander. There was a request to upload two B-52s with full bomb loads and prepare to launch and strike the airfield and the port of Sihanookville, where the docked cargo ship was moored. This was later cancelled. The 307th tanker crews flew in support of the Mayaguez operation throughout the day until all activity was terminated by 1400 hours local time and debriefings of our tanker crews were accomplished by our intelligence office after the last aircraft landed and with the final OPREP sent off.

What were the ultimate results of this disastrous day? There was the loss of three USAF CH-53C helicopters from extreme gunfire while attempting to insert troops on an island of no consequence, one helicopter crew unaccounted for and twenty helicopters badly damaged. Some of badly damaged were able to return to U-Tapao and others barely able to land on a carrier stationed close to the island. The marine landing force was unable to get beyond the beach area and a total of eighteen USAF and Marine personnel were subsequently listed as missing in action (MIA). This was added to the marines and Air Force crewmembers who had abandoned their helicopters and lost their lives on the island and whose bodies were recovered. It was reported later that a total of forty-one individuals lost their lives in the operation. It was reported that the retreat to evacuate the island was so confused and the opposition so intense that two, maybe three marines were abandoned and left to fend for themselves. (This was later verified as one marine was reported executed on the 25th of May by the Cambodians).

The wrap up of the operation was presented to the participating crews on the 16th of May and to the wing staff a few hours later by Captain Geer. Eight of the nine helicopters in the island assault had been shot down or were no longer operational. Only five, three from the initial group and two others "In-reserve", were left able to conduct operations.

About forty KC-135 combat sorties were flown in response to the Mayaguez operation. They provided refueling for the fighters engaged in the support of the operation and covering the ship itself. It was early during this time that the crew of the ship was released. The invasion of Koh Tang was insane! Fighters were in the air continuously for over twenty-four hours. The tanker force furnished refueling for twenty straight hours. Twenty of the 307th tanker force crews were involved. Specific "frag orders" directed the tankers to fly continuous orbits in the Gulf of Siam, unlike previous locations, calling for the tanker crews to adapt to the needs of the fighter sorties. It ended as fast as it began! Someone somewhere came to their senses as the assault of the island was a disaster and the losses were inexcusable. The forced with-drawl of the marines from the island was made and what was left of the helicopter force arrived and departed. The two B-52s were downloaded of their bombs and the crews were told they would not fly. The entire Marine force was gone from U-Tapao that day as once again the C-141s arrived, loaded their human cargo and left, barely shutting down engines, along with their inept command structure.

The events of those three days seemed surreal after the fact. The 307th personnel and crews did what they had to do and wanted to do more but the vast chasm between the Marine Command, PACAF and us and more important, the divide between PACAF commanders on our base and our wing was one that could have caused lives to be lost and valuable machinery to be destroyed. Perhaps sound intelligence briefings, a command decision to not invade an island for no reason and some coordination of effort would have saved those Air Force crew members and marines lost on Kho-Tang. As it turned out the crew of the Mayaguez had been released from another island before the assault on Koh Tang had begun and were placed on a fishing Trawler and picked up almost immediately by a U.S. Navy destroyer.

I was very disappointed in the PACAF attitude, but it was one I experienced before during the Linebacker II missions in Vietnam when I was sending in recommendations for citations for crews who had been subjected to difficult and hazardous flights over the six pack area, only to have them downgraded by PACAF. They just couldn't get it through their heads that we are one Air Force and that flying a B-52 over Hanoi and evading SAMS was no different than flying a Thud or an F-4 over the same area, dodging AAA, maybe more so as we were at an altitude that was very vulnerable. The awards given to the B-52 crews were out of proportion to those given to the Tactical Air Command crews who richly deserved them. In spending time with many of those who flew the Linebacker raids with PACAF in B-66s, F-4s and F-111s, they felt the B-52s and their crews were most deserving of any credit they could get for their heroic acts. We all were called "River Rats" for having flown over Hanoi, facing the most formidable defenses in the world. I'm very proud to be a "River Rat" and feel I earned that distinction.

For some reason, my operation report, which was critical of PACAF and Marine "Activities" was suppressed at some level. General Baxter, the ADVON commander criticized our intelligence for not giving him up-to-date information, but when confronted with the many references to attempted contact, he backed off and later apologized. As an aftermath to this comedy of errors, the Cambodian Gunboat who precipitated the Mayaguez capture and the ensuing events' pulled into the deep water port at Sattahip and surrendered indicating they had not consulted the Khmer leadership before their action and felt they would be punished severely for their attack if they returned to Kom Pong Som. A postscript to this tragic event came in the form of a message from the Commander in Chief Strategic Air Command (CINCSAC) who forwarded a message from the Secretary of Defense (SECDEF) which read "Recent weeks have seen United States Military Forces called upon to perform some of the most difficult and unique assignments in our nation's history: Again, as in previous weeks, I am pleased to express my admiration, respect and gratitude to Air Force, Marine Corps and Navy personnel for the successful completion of a highly professional military operation, our military reaction to the piracy of the Mayaguez was a reaffirmation of the principal of peaceful ocean transit, this nation and the entire civilized world can be grateful for the skill shown by military forces in gaining the release of the Mayaguez, its crew and, by doing so, guaranteeing freedom of the seas; my highest commendation to all who participated in this operation". James Schlesinger, Secretary of Defense. Other messages from the various levels of command were also received with similarly laudatory comments. If they only knew the truth!

In a conversation with Father Saulnier the day after the marines were gone he told me he spent time talking to the marines that had been sent to UT for the morning attack and they told them of being loaded on the incoming C-141s and sitting on the floor, locking legs for the flight from Okinawa. He found them calm and uncomplaining. He later was to visit some of the injured, some severe at the base hospital before they were evacuated to the Philippines.

Some years later, when I responded to a glowing article in one of the service magazines on the Mayaguez rescue operation, providing them with documented information which gave a factual account of what happened and refuted their claim that there was no intelligence on the Koh Tang defense I was informed they would not publish my response as it was a dead issue and there would be no further comments allowed. Someone, somewhere, realized it was a tragic fiasco and has put a lid on the truth!

RELIEF FROM THE BRICK

A good friend of mine Chuck Pheiffer from my B-47 days in New Hampshire, in fact a bachelor I shared a house with, in York, Maine, arrived in UT on the courier from U-Dorn. It turns out he was in his last days at the up-country base and heard I was here and was on station on business and called me. Colonel Al Merrill, our present Director of Intelligence, was a friend of his and arranged a meeting of officers to coordinate the latest intelligence situation presently driving events in the country. Colonel Pfeiffer was a very talented radar-navigator and was considered the model for officers in his position. He was an interesting guy, who, as long as I lived with him, had only one aim and that was to be the best he could be. It was good to see him, and we agreed to hire a cab and go to Pattya for dinner tomorrow night.

The new Director of Operations Colonel Denis O'Brien was arriving tomorrow to replace the already departed Dan Egbert. Al Merrill and I would go to meet him and welcome him to Thailand and the 307th Strategic Wing. No sooner had he landed and was in his new home that I took him to the Operations Center and gave him a briefing on what had happened in the preceding couple of weeks and told him to bone up on Tanker-Fighter operations as that would be what we were all about. Like me, he was a bomber guy, so tankers were new to him. It was a "down" day so all he had to do was answer the phone and quell uprisings. Confident that he was well versed on needed responses I gave him the "brick". I informed 3rd Air Division I would be off station for a few hours and then scooped up Chuck Pfeiffer and Al, went to the gate and grabbed a cab for the trip to Pattya Beach.

It was a good diversion from the base actions of the past few days. The ride on the two lane road was the next thing to a horror show as oncoming cars seem to be on a collision course with the vehicle you are in, but do go to their side of the road before they collide and I had to keep remembering that travel was opposite from what I'm used to. Chuck and Al seemed more used to it than I, but I didn't yell out too often. The many dirt roads in Pattya seemed out of place as the hotels reminded me of Miami Beach and the restaurants were gourmet. The decor was great and the food outstanding. We ate at "Dolf Rics" who is German, speaks like a Brit, plays classical music and writes a "Gourmet" column for the Bangkok Press. The food was spectacular and after our meal we wandered through the streets, finding many of the areas were in direct contrast to the glitzy hotels and restaurants. There were some interesting bars but didn't choose to take them on. Instead we decided to head back to the base. The ride back in total darkness was more terrifying than the one coming to Pattya. There seemed to be more traffic and mostly cabs, and trucks and they had a habit of turning off their lights until another car was seen? They had some idea in their heads that it saved their car batteries? Our return driver was very adept at avoiding the oncoming head-on traffic. Fortunately, we arrived safely and got back to our trailers. I wrote in my memory book that Pattya was a place to go to. A few days later a good friend of mine from B-58 days, Bill Gilmore appeared in civilian attire, informed me he had retired and now lived in Thailand. He was on a visit to pick up his mail and happened by the to the on-base USO facility and in our conversation informed me he lived in Pattya. He had married a Thai and she owned a sizable amount of land on the beach. He said I should visit him and told him I would next time I went that way.

BOBBY JANKA

The replacement base commander, Colonel Bob Janka and I seemed to have great deal in common as he and I look each other in the eye (both five foot six), both Catholic and very sports oriented. We both have Irish wives and many children he has six and me with five. We play sports in the same fashion, hard and we want to win. Our tennis game is even, and it makes it fun to play him. Everyone thinks we have had a long relationship. But our career paths to our present positions are totally different, he, being a fighter guy and all my background is in bombers. We now have the same maid and live next door to each other. Lam tien often mixes our clothes and has started to number them as "Bot Three" and "Bot Four". We often still get the other's clothes but are quick to meet to get them in the right drawers. He is a former "Thunderbird" F-4 jock and a great guy who stabilized the inner workings of the base when he came on in an interim basis. He always says, "If you need a friend, Call LBJ (Little Bobby Janka). During the Mayaguez situation he was the FNG (fn new guy) and was sort of pushed to the side. We often discussed the sequence of events and he was very upset with the series of events and the lack of coordination that occurred. He would be in my ear constantly on events as they happened. He was a joy to have around, despite the fact he was a PACAF "weenie".

THE CAMBODIAN
REFUGEE REQUEST

Shortly after our Sunday drive-by of the Cambodian Camp, a group of Cambodians came forward to Colonel Janka, the interim base commander, with a request. A significant number of the interned members wanted to return to Cambodia, a country they fled from some months prior to my arrival. It was at a time when the dictator, Pol Pot, was conducting a well-publicized genocide of those who he felt did not belong in his regime. The elderly men and women were being killed or left to die. Cholera was rampant and many of the city dwellers were forced into the jungles to fend for themselves, most eventually dying of starvation or disease. It had been a blood bath where thousands of people were killed, with many fleeing across the river to the safety of Thailand. Thailand was the only bordering country that was not deemed hostile to those leaving the country and not involved in active war against others. Vietnam and Laos were not welcoming any foreign intrusions into their country and it was not safe to even try.

It seemed odd that some would want to leave the safety of the camp, however you could sympathize with their desire to leave the confines of what was a prison as they could not leave the camp to travel freely, nor did the Thai government want them as permanent residents. Their future was obviously a clouded one as the only path to some form of life was through the United States government and resettlement to that distant land. Even though there was an active refugee program the time delay was significant. The fall of Saigon and the overwhelming number of Vietnamese that were now asking for asylum made for a formidable barrier to their hope of leaving the camp. Colonel Janka really had no choice but to grant their request as it was their country of origin and a return to that place was something that could not be refused.

A convoy was set up to take them to a border crossing about ninety kilometers from the base. It would consist of a couple of flatbed trucks where some ninety-eight individuals would be transported to the border, accompanied by a small security detail and a translator and some of the senior camp officials. Not all were military as embassy staff were needed to assist in the crossing. Upon arriving at the border crossing, they were met by a contingent of Cambodian officials standing on the narrow pedestrian bridge. After a brief exchange of papers, photos taken by the press and some other limited conversation at the bridge that curved across the river into a dense jungle, the refugees were taken off the flatbed trucks, their names checked as they proceeded to the crossing point, single file to the bridge, where two or three were started at a time and as they disappeared about the mid-point of the bridge, the next two or three would start their journey back to their country. This continued until all of them had crossed the bridge. The team that formed the official party overseeing the return, satisfied that all had been returned, then headed back to U-T. Upon arrival they indicated to Colonel Janka that all went without incident.

Within a day or two, reading the Bangkok Press, English Edition, there was a story on the front page about the finding of three Cambodian men who had survived the systematic beheading of those who were returning to Cambodia. According to the story, and not any official account, as the groups of those crossing the bridge came to the end of the bridge, they were led down a path where they were killed by Pol Pot's army personnel. Evidently these men were warned somehow of their impending fate and jumped off the bridge into the river below and were rescued at some point down river. It was not known how many others might have jumped in, but these three gave a terrifying account of their experience to the paper. Being a tenant on the base, PACAF Pacific Air Forces felt no need to give us an official report or any other information about the incident and in fact there was no follow on to the story in the Bangkok paper. It was obvious that this entire happening was not to be discussed as when brought up to any of the base officials they had no comment. Even my tennis partner friend said it was a subject he couldn't discuss, but did say it did occur and it was not a rumor.

On day 84 since I left my family on the tarmac at Travis AFB I took a ride to the beach with a newly arrived officer and found the Vietnamese camp gone and the Cambodian camp down to around 350 people, or at least that is what I was told. Most of the remainder of the refugees were told they would leave for the United States within the next two weeks, a wind-down that would signal the end of the refugee crisis of the Vietnam War as far as Thailand is concerned.

IDENTIFYING THE THREAT

The political climate (not weather) in the area was becoming quite difficult. Many factors were contributing to the situation. The average Thai citizenry does not participate in the political process, nor do most of these surrounding the base care as it is all about staying alive. Most are very indifferent to the political process as the reality is that the Thai military are in control and they are the predominate force in the country. They oversee all the government process, the weaponry and as such are the dominant power. The citizens' isolation and indifference from any process of government lend itself to the little need for a highly structured political system. For this reason, the ordinary Thai citizen pays little attention to government matters. Laotian and Cambodian refugees were a problem as they were living in camps much like the one at UT, financed by the Thai government, but under the control of the United Nations.

Intelligence sources were frequently indicating that Communist insurgency was on the upswing in south Thailand and that the under siege Malaysian Communist party was a significant part of the problem and the remnants of that group was using Thailand as a sanctuary. Also, Muslim separatists and a wave of banditry were both on the upswing. Theft was going beyond the basic thievery of a bike as thieves were looking for anything sellable, such as copper wire and other necessities for the simple operations of a base, such as electricity and water. Banks of lights over the ramp have been known to be burglarized during the night. Our "Charlie Tower" was burglarized with the window air conditioner being stolen leading to very hot launch supervision by the DO staff. There definitely was something going on within the base.

The security police are a function of the base commander as it is a PACAF function. The Base Commander, LBJ and I have met over some of the problems, but he seems unable to do much as he says his security police unit is stretched out. The involvement of the Thai marine security force is also part of the problem. Despite that patrols are a joint effort and are conducted with true scrutiny, it stops there. The Thai marines are very capable of being engaged in thievery and in fact they are the principle problem. On base they are not subject to search and they use whatever means necessary to secret things of value, such as bikes and other small items. There are two sides to this situation as off-base the local merchants and small towns off base depend on the base personnel for their livelihood and as such take the side of the base personnel being here. They stop at no means to protect the GI as he is their livelihood. Even minor thievery is dealt with severely if discovered.

The biggest danger is a radical Thai, carrying a gun, because they don't care who you are or what you do! It is interesting to note that there are counter contracts let out on those who harass the American military. The wing security liaison, CM/Sgt McLaren reported that in Bonchong Province, about five kilometers from the base they found a Thai, with his throat cut and a message attached to wit "Leave the GIs alone". Apparently, a contract was let out by local merchants on those who insist on harassing the base military. He was the fifth known victim, but the first I heard of.

I am in awe of the different lifestyle and mores of this strange country. The local natives live very simple lives. They live off the land in skimpy bungalows or huts and raise enough food for themselves and not much more. I watched as one such family prepared their breakfast. The husband waded out into a marshy klong and had with him a simple hand net. He stood patiently in the water up to his waist with the net dangling in the water below while his wife started a fire. As he would catch a fish, he would throw it close to her and she would prepare it in the fire. When he had caught enough food for their meal, he joined her on the banks for their repast. There is an abundance of food to be gotten in the area as the trees all seem to bear edible fruit and in the open fields you can find many types of roots that have nutritive value. Without any knowledge of what these dwelling individuals do I feel most live from the land they dwell on. They farm to live and no more than that. They men seem to be close to their habitat, however I have seen many of them working in the fields growing some nourishing food. I have seen many of the women at work on the roads, or better, on the sides of the roads cutting back the high grass with sticks that have large cutting knifes on the end, working in teams of three and working in three or four groups. They will cut in unison, never hitting one another. They don't wear shoes and are dressed in long dresses, hats, a muffler covering their faces up to their eyes and a hat. They work in every conceivable type of weather and are seen in ditches with water up to their knees cutting the grass. They seldom stop for any reason, but they do carry and use water. I never inquired into the number who suffered snake bites or other life-threatening injuries, but I would think they are not rare!

Another interesting part of the culture here was the modes of transportation. There are many ways to get around, but the most common are cabs. The cab driver is a reckless individual who drives fast in small Toyotas or Datsuns. The cab fleet is called "Popeye Taxi" and the cost is five baht to almost anywhere locally. Sixty baht is the standard fare to the golf course and that includes the return trip when you are finished. Any trip in a Popeye Taxi is not for the faint of heart as they drive very fast, darting in and around trucks, hand carts, other cars and people, honking their horn constantly. They argue about the fare but are very willing to barter. They speak English somewhat, but will act very dumb if you are arguing a point. They are dyed in the wool crooks and will steal anything they see if they can get away with it. They band together and remind me of a swarm of bees when you approach them. If they see someone walking, they will give a little honk and if you raise your hand you are a passenger. Oddly they are hard to find when you really need one when looking for a ride in one of the local towns. They are generally very quiet during a fare anywhere however they seem to understand everything that is said and will acknowledge questions addressed to them. They adamantly oppose student demonstrations and have been known to drive off the students who demonstrate at the base gate. When not driving they are a band of thieves. There are also the popular "Baht busses", which are the small pickup trucks. For a single baht or two you can get a short ride in the areas around the base but watch out who is in the back of this truck as some of the riders in back are part of a team to rob an inebriated passenger and are quick to solicit someone coming away from the local taverns close to the base.

One of the greater problems is the drug traffic as it is said that heroin in Thailand is the purest form of the drug you can find. We have had more than one arrest by Thai police of our enlisted core and once arrested there is an international hold on the person involved, which means they cannot be rotated home. Some end up in the Thai prison system, which is no holiday and others are released to our custody. We can confine them to base or we can send them to the army lock-up in Sattahip. Generally, unless it is a frequent offender, they are told they will work on base until the hold on them is over and then we send them either to rehab in the Philippines or home based on their situation. Some airmen coming up on rotation will try to get caught so they can stay in country for the availability of drugs or because they have married a Thai Poo-Ying and don't want to go home. There also have been cases of married airmen who coming up on their rotation home being found murdered. A contract is put out on them as the family doesn't want their daughter to leave Thailand, plus they reap all the survivor benefits from his death. Those benefits represent a quantum leap in their living status.

NORMAL MILITARY LIFE IN THAILAND

There were many rumors going around that the Thai government was ramping up their displeasure at the presence of US forces in-country. On base not much changed. We were insulated from the pressures outside the gate and I started my checkout in the KC-135 in Thailand. I had my initial check out in the aircraft while at Mather as we had no B-52s for the first few months of my return from Guam during the "Bullet Shot operation. Now I had the best of both worlds, flying both aircraft, at least until, as forecast, the Buffs would leave the country. On the first mission in the KC-135 during this phase one of our B-52s hooked up and I was able to experience what it was like to be on the giving end of the refueling business. The tanker was a bit heavy to work with flying in the traffic pattern, but a good flying bird. The refueling activity and pattern work were interesting and challenging, the rest of the time was a bit boring. During this time I was also given an orientation ride in a Jolly Green over the south coast of Thailand and looked down at the golf course at Sattahip, Camp Samison, an US Army location (where the lockup ((Jail)) for all US forces is at) and the deep water port then skirted over the Cambodian refugee camp (The Vietnamese camps occupants are now gone to the Philippines) then across "Buddha Mountain" and north to Pattya and finally returned to the base. I didn't quite understand the operation of the helicopter, but it was fun and informative as I could pick up the immense area of the confines of this base that needed to be secure. It was only a day later that I had my first B-52D ride I found everything familiar to the "G" model as far as flying the aircraft. I had had "D" rides on Guam after we stopped our raids over the Vietnamese heartland, mostly to stay current, but also I had promised the "D" squadron commander I would go on a flight with him.

This first "D" flight was an exhausting one, mostly due to the conditions in the refueling area. The weather was marginal, in and out of clouds, many turns to avoid cumuliform clouds and the turbulence that goes with them. This was combined with the tanker having an auto-pilot malfunction and no director lights. I did get the required off-load, but it was interrupted with disconnects throughout the hookup. I shot a no-flap landing and three touch and goes, followed by a full stop. All but the refueling went smoothly. It would turn out that I did complete my checkout in the "D" model before the birds all flew the coop but I was then confined to flying the tanker the rest of my time in Thailand.

THE FIRST PARTY

After landing from the "D" ride I had to attend a farewell party for Colonel Austin, the out-going base commander given by Captain Vichit, the Thai commander. It was an interesting party and my first real exposure to Thai food and Thai music. The Thai Navy band played for the occasion and I will say that it was loud and confusing. There was nothing you would recognize. There were many singers and the Thais like to dance! The good Captain Vichit gave up his wife to me so I would have company on the floor for the group dancing. She did not speak English, but I couldn't have heard her anyway due to the heavy brass in the band. I have the feeling it was more to dance with some of the beautiful Thai women who were there unaccompanied. The drinks were "Mekong" (Thai Whisky) or a sweet Thai wine. The food was good, lots of rice and some delicious meat, unidentifiable, but good. Unlike my experience with Thai beer, Thai food was a mystery that I had had sufficient warning about from Billie. She gave me some hints on what I should avoid and others I should pick out at any function where Thai food was the only option. Things to avoid included a small pepper that is served at any Thai function where you pick your food from party dishes. This pepper is very thin and looks harmless, but it can ruin your whole evening as it not only is hot, but the heat lingers in your mouth for hours. It is called a "picayune", which may not be the correct spelling. I would sight these as a choice at every function I went to. The red skin and small size were the warning signals that I was only too happy to pick up on, especially when seeing an unwary party animal chomp into one, only to grimace in the realization his mouth was on fire and he needed to find something to extinguish it. Amazingly, the individual Thai seemed to be immune from its fire. Billie had told me not to eat this very small red pepper. I recognized them on the food trays and despite the urging of others to eat them I declined. As a kind gesture I would warn anyone not aware of this delicacy before they would take their first bite.

There were also this number of young "Poo Yings" (Girls) escorted by Thai Navy Officers, who seemed to also have wives. The abundance of these young beautiful girls seemed strange, but they added to the festivities of the night. An interesting custom! I wandered over to Hal (Colonel Austin) and wished him a fond farewell, knowing he had become the PACAF scapegoat for his actions with the Vietnamese refugees on station. He would be leaving tomorrow on a redeploying tanker. I slipped out and retreated to the Officers Club and had a beer.

Captain Vichit was an enigma of sorts as he was always looking to spend time at dinners and parties being the bon vivant and leading the entertainment. These functions always involved lots of food and women and lots of dancing. There was one serpentine dance, called the butterfly, where you would wind through the chairs and tables waving your arms, trying to keep time with unfamiliar music. I must admit it was very entertaining as you had no choice but to join in. If you were trying to stay un-involved, you would be swept away by a brightly dressed young Thai woman and be in the middle of flinging your arms and feeling enthusiastic about being part of the party. The good Thai commander was a party animal and would look for any opportunity to get one going. He even wanted to visit my quarters and bring food and booze for a dinner he would prepare. I agreed as I didn't want to turn him off and create a poor military relationship problem. I invited a few of the senior staff as I didn't want anyone to feel left out of this interface with the Thai command. The Thai officers outnumbered my invited guests (staff), but I still didn't understand the two women for many of the officers who came. Billie later explained to me that It was a common occurrence for the many functions that the Thai Navy held throughout my tenure, good Thai food and wives mingling with "Poo Ying". This was to make sure that the Americans would have someone to dance with. Interestingly the wives usually sat closest to us! I learned it was best to avoid close contact not only with the harsh red peppers, but also the Thai Navy women, wives and other. This party turned out very well and Vichit to his credit prepared an excellent meal, mostly pork surrounded by delicacies. I was caught up with his ability to be discussing something with me in very good English and turn to someone in the middle of a sentence and speak in a guttural Thai tone to someone at the function. Most interesting was he would be smiling at me and as he spit out his message the smile would turn to a serious look that telegraphed a rebuke of sorts. I would see more of this during my tenure in Thailand.

There were exceptions to the Captain Vichit parties, as some were very formal and had military only, something like our military dining outs. An interesting note on Captain Vichit, he was forty-eight years old and had graduated from the Royal Thai Naval Academy and after being commissioned attended the U.S. Naval Mine Warfare School and the Amphibious Warfare School and later served as the Naval Attache to France and Germany. He had served in the rank of Captain for eight years, had five grown children and spoke fluent French and English.

One of the best affairs happened in early June when all the base dignitaries were invited to Captain Vichit's home as he was hosting the present "National Defense College" class, it was a day of graduations, and involved another Thai meal! It was a very nice affair and I met an interesting group of very interesting Thai military officers. Of significance is the fact that most of the officers were older, in their fifties. There were no young officers in their senior schools which seemed very odd! Captain Vichit didn't disappoint as he was known for his lavish parties and this one even had an exotic dancer, who charmed the crowd with her many sultry moves through the crowd. It was Howard O'Neill's first experience at a Thai party, and it blew his mind as the expressive exotic dancer appeared and she had two flaming tassels and rotated them in opposing directions to the enthusiastic applause of all those older officers in attendance.

A STAFF ADDITION

It was a protocol to meet newly arriving replacement officers. I remembered my arrival as being traumatic as I wondered about what I was going to experience in this remote tour. Also, for all this new country was going to be without family so the feeling of being separated was very much on your mind. The creepy feeling of depression was evident. As the loading platform and steps were wheeled up to the arriving KC-135 I knew there would be a replacement for Phil, my administration captain. Her name was first lieutenant Kathy Michaels. Billie had been told there was a female officer to work with as the new executive replacing Phil when he rotates next month and so I drove her out for the arrival. There were rumors that some key maintenance staff were on-board this arriving aircraft, so I would not be alone when greeting the newest staff officers of the 307th Strategic Wing. I was joined by a contingent of maintenance people who would guide these new arrivals along their way to acclimate them to this, their new assignment and adventure. The first new face to appear as the cargo doors opened was a female officer, appearing fresh and very attractive, a pretty smile and was warmly greeted, if you could see the appreciative glares on those manning the stairs to the door. She was seemingly un-affected by the sudden burst of the humid air of her new home. As she came down the stairs, followed by some fatigue-dressed individuals, on the portable unloading platform. When the crowd pushed to the bottom of the stairs, she was unsure of who she should approach. I stepped forward and stuck out my hand, a smiling Billie on my shoulder. She snapped a salute, which I promptly returned. Her name tag and silver bars on her starched lapels stated she was indeed First Lieutenant Kathy Michaels. Billie surrounded her with a hug, telling her she would take care of her. I grabbed one of her bags and told her I would take her to her quarters in the BOQ (Bachelor Officers Quarters). She smiled and followed Billie and me to the staff vehicle carrying another bag. On the short ride to her quarters she informed us she had volunteered to come to U-Tapao to fill her remote tour requirement. She said she was married to a KC-135 pilot and he would more than likely join her on a deployment soon.

Lieutenant Michaels took to Billie immediately. Billie would act as her mentor for her official duties, but much more than that as they became almost inseparable. Billie also had a friend she could relate to other the usual bunch of men who came into her office. Kathy was a perfect fit and would take much of the workload off Billie. Kathy proved to be as good as she was beautiful. She grasped the position with vigor and intelligence. The efficiency she displayed was noticed by the entire group working in the section. There were also giggles and lots of laughter coming from the outer offices of the command front offices. There would be no scarcity of visitors to the command section as now we had two very attractive women in a place totally dominated with men. Kathy's role as the executive officer for the command group came at the right time as within days, we were faced with an event that would tax our resources and it was imperative that we responded in a professional and responsible fashion. Coordination would be necessary with other commands, the embassy in Bangkok and our own resources up country.

MANAS MANAT (MANASAPUTS)

This mystical man had become an item of interest to me, mostly to his seemingly awareness of all that goes on at U-Tapao and his knowledge of my whereabouts and background. Over the long term of my stay in Thailand and my visits to Bangkok, Manas was always somehow there, whether in person or his driver and car awaiting my arrival. His awareness of the events that were not common knowledge and were protected from being divulged to the outside were something I could never find plausible. One particular day, when he stopped by on one of his many visits to my office, he asked Billie if he could see me for a minute and as usual, I always would ask him to come in. It seemed uncomfortable for him to sit for any long periods, but occasionally I would probe on his life. This day he gave me reason to believe he had some power of perceiving events as he asked me questions about the planned withdrawl of all the Buffs from Thailand. I told him what everyone knew that it was going to happen, but there was no word on when. He smiled, poked at his bun on the back of his head, bowed and gave me a "Wai" and departed. I just had this feeling he knew something. It was very odd, but the knowledge of his life was unfolding, and he was far from being an ordinary person.

Much I had gleaned from information Billie had gathered in her time in country. She had told me there were many stories about Manas. Obviously, his eyesight is very poor, but the story goes that he lost his sight through some sort of an accident and was told he would never see again. It is said that he refused to believe that and "willed" (his words) himself to see again. His coke-bottle-bottom glasses would indicate not too well, but I have never seen him with anyone. He is always alone so he doesn't get any help in going from place to place. It is also a ritual story that at one time during the Japanese occupation that his back was broken and that he would never walk again, but he is always without transportation on the base. It is rumored that his driver stays at the gate and waits for him. His stiff gait would substantiate that story.

One day I asked about his time living in the immediate area and it was like opening the floodgates. He started out by saying he was here in the Sattahip region before there was a base here. After the Japanese invaded Thailand in the Second World War he was involved in the desire of the Japanese to convert the marsh in this area to an airfield. It seems all of what is now the runway and flight line of U-Tapao was a large marsh, surrounded by small jungle hills. Much of that marsh-type environment can be seen, as you drive outside of the base as we are on the edge of the Gulf of Thailand. The scheme for the Japanese invaders was to level those small hills and fill the marsh. Manas was one of the many local natives who was conscripted to work for the Japanese in this attempt. What the Japanese didn't know was that according to Manas, he had been recruited by the OSS (now known as the CIA) to keep them informed of this work and other military matters in the area. He made a statement to me that I will never forget, saying "I worked for the Japanese during the day and I killed them at night". He said at selected nights he would row out into the gulf and meet with American submarines, exchanging items and information on the workings of the area and obtaining weapons for subversive activity, which went on constantly. He said he had transported a significant number of agents into the country from submarines and secreted them to other regions of the country. There was no doubt in the mind of many that Manas had maintained a relationship with those he worked with.

During a future talk he told me he was starting a Buddhist monastery to train new monks. It was to be located close to Bangkok, but not in the city proper. Now, how different was that? His former ties to the OSS/CIA may be how he has so much information. But one thing is apparent he knows a lot of high positioned people in the Thai Government.

On the day before I was to leave UT to go home for Christmas on leave Manas appeared at my door with wrapped gifts, one for Rosemary and one each for my children, with their names neatly inscribed on the designated gift, which turned out to be appropriate for their age and sex. No one on station in the military would have given him those five children's names.

I told him at the time "I can't accept gifts" and he replied, "These are not for you; they are for your family".

Before I was to leave Thailand and the base would close Manas stopped by and asked if I could visit the now established monastery. I told him I was unable and so he asked if I could send some of my officers to visit. I thought it might be a good break for some of the younger officers on my staff. It would be an excuse to see Bangkok and have a pleasant time in the area. So, I sent three of them to visit this august gentleman. Of course, Manas treated them like royalty, meeting them at the airport, driving them around Bangkok, serving them a Thai lunch and showing them around the new establishment. They indicated to me on their return that it was a very nice day and it was well worth the trip.

As a sort of postscript, almost three years after I left Thailand, I received a letter from Manas, that had been mailed from San Francisco. I was then stationed at March AFB in Riverside California. I had been at two duty stations during the interim and he had the correct duty title and the correct home address on the envelope. He explained he was in San Francisco on some form of business and the letter was merely a personal note exchanging pleasantries, asking how my family was. How did he find me? I would consider him the most intriguing and unforgettable man I have ever known.

JOHNY SU

My relationship with Johny Su began with Billie asking me to get involved in his establishment next to the officer's club being saved. Although I really had little to do with its momentary survival, he felt I had, and we became friends. He was indeed a fine individual and I began to learn a lot about him, both from Billie, and from the man himself. He had two places of businesses on the base, the one involved in the dispute and one next to the shopping area on base. He was very unassuming, and in our many conversations it was obvious he was an honest and moral person, who loved his wife Annie and his boys. He also had a thriving business in Bangkok, not just a shop, but a factory for creating rings and things. It was on Fueng Nakorn Road on the edge of downtown. Johnny was a craftsman, but he was also a generous human who was giving of his time and his talent to help others. After first meeting him I felt a warm relationship as he was that type of person, but it was not just a base thing, as he had established many friends in all walks of life in Thailand. He knew people, but he did not use them. He was his own man. He was not Thai, he was Chinese, a Roman Catholic, very popular among those who knew him on base and known for his very fair dealings with those who did business with him. As far as I could ascertain he had had his shop on the base since the arrival of the U.S. Forces. He urged me from the first meeting to visit his shop in Bangkok. He was successful in his business on base and I was in a position of authority, so I had to be very careful on how I dealt with him. There were restrictions I had to live with, and he was most aware of them

As time went on and I assumed the commander's role I had a need to go to Bangkok on business with the Embassy and the JUSMAG (Joint United States Military Advisory Group). I would inform Johny that I would be in town and he would always offer to have someone pick me up at

96

the airport, however I always had an official driver at my disposal. I would tell the driver after being dropped off at the embassy that I didn't need him anymore. I took Johny's invitation to visit his business and after completing my work at the JUSMAG I was picked up by Johny's driver and taken to his shop. I had told Johny before I left. I would be there and he took the time to set up the visit and the transportation to his place, making sure he was there to greet me. The first person I saw upon entering was Johny and beside him a beautiful woman, who proved to be Johny's wife, Annie. She was as charming as she was gorgeous. Also, as I found out very talented.

Unlike many Jewelry establishments, it was not about perusing the counter and looking at displays of rings and other expensive items. Upon entering you were directed to sit down in a comfortable spot and asked to enjoy any number of appetizers, soups and other delicacies. If you were shopping, you could remain in your place and assorted items you had expressed an interest in were brought to you. If you had an interest in some type of jewelry you would see different types and styles of the item. In many cases your interest in some form of jewelry would end up with an original design being created for you, based on your desires and choice of gem.

On Johny's walls were an array of pictures of past U-T Commanders, mine pleasantly included as the present commander. On my first visit, Johnny took me on a tour of the factory. There were rooms set aside for the manufacture of every type of jewelry, artisans painfully selecting and positioning pieces together making a dazzling final product. It was not an assembly line, but individuals working on separate items from orders that had been taken up front in the shop. He pulled me down a hall to one room, called his gold room and inside you saw gold as pieces of ingots being formed into jewelry pieces.

My Dad was an artist, who, in an attempt to make extra money had an avocation and the talent needed to paint signs for various businesses that in his day were very difficult to do as it required the finish to be in real gold. He used a gold leaf, thin strips of gold and after putting on the fresh paint he would attach this thin gold to the sign and with a dry brush, massage it on the lettered lines. It was tedious work, requiring a firm and steady hand, placing the leaf on the wet paint and insuring it had no air bubbles and then edging it to insure it was securely fashioned. My dad excelled at it and was known for his ability to create those signs. I would often watch and hold my breath as he rolled the leaf onto the wet sign. In Johnny's gold room I saw layers of gold thinned down for use for different levels of need on jewelry products being formed in other rooms. It was an amazing place. Looking out of a barred window in the room, you could see little flakes of gold on the bars coming from the activity in the room. It was always a pleasant experience and each time I came to town, with few exceptions, I would visit "Johny's Gems".

Every time I came to Johnny's shop, I would sit and talk to Annie, who was not only beautiful, but also very talented as she would hear a customer's request and would virtually create a necklace or bracelet as the customer talked. I saw her on occasion string a necklace to the satisfaction of a customer and make changes as necessary in it to please the individual while the woman supped on soup. It turns out that Annie was also a source of much of the substantive cache of precious gems that came into the business. Her father was the owner of many of the gem mines on the border of Thailand and Cambodia. In my time in Thailand I would have Johnny and Annie pick out numerous pieces of jewelry and create individual, iconic constructed items for my wife and children. I would watch as Annie would put together a beautiful necklace for Rosemary as she would ask questions about what color of eyes and hair did Rosemary have? She would select pieces and gems to enhance the individual who was getting the gift. I bought a Real Turquoise ring for Rosemary and a Blue Sapphire ring for my daughter, Monique. Annie put time and effort into both of those pieces to make sure they were perfect. Johnny and Annie were a perfect couple, devout Christians, who had among their many friends the Catholic Bishop of Bangkok (also Chinese). This was, of course, in a dominant Buddhist country and Johnny was generous in his relationship with all segments of the country.

Knowing there were restrictions on gifts to the military, he never tried to engage me with a gift, although he did sneak in a gold leafed statue of one of the nine Buddha symbols, "Fukarukagen", spelled exactly that way on the meager piece of paper he taped to the bottom of the nine inch high Buddha, which interestingly enough, was a teak carving covered with gold leaf. He had placed it in my bag when I departed Thailand for my new assignment in March, 1976. I found out later it had to be cleared by the Thai Government to take out of country, which, of course Johnny had taken care of. We enjoyed many fine conversations on world affairs, which he was well versed on. On more than one occasion, Laotian army forces threatened on the northern border to invade in a fashion which could be thought as a form of saber rattling, but It was more than that. It was verified by U-2 Photography and was identified as a sizable force threatening a move into Thailand. I counseled Johny on his safety and that of his family as there were indications that when all United States Forces left the country that an aggressive Vietnamese Communist government and others would make things very difficult for Thailand. Johnny, being Chinese related to me that "invaders "come, and they feel they will conquer Thailand, however when they do come, they are ultimately assimilated and become as one of us". History supports Johnny as Thailand was the only Asian country invaded by Japan that did not show the effects of war when Japan was defeated.

In my year in Thailand I only had one time that I would call a real social visit with Johnny. I was to be in Bangkok on business that would involve me staying overnight. He found out about two days before the visit and called Billie and told her I would be his guest for dinner that evening. Of course, I accepted the dinner invitation. I was staying at the military hotel in the center of town and Johnny would pick me up that evening. After finishing my meetings at the Embassy, I was a bit surprised that Johny's driver met me at the gate exiting the embassy and told me he was there to take me to the hotel. I waved off my waiting military transportation and went with Johnny's driver.

I was already registered at the hotel and went to my room to shower and change into civilian clothes. When I came downstairs, I was surprised to see Johny waiting. We went to his car and drove to a cylindrical shaped restaurant in town, probably six or seven stories high. I should explain at this point that most of those who could afford an automobile usually had a driver as traffic in the city was horrendous. Policeman on corners would direct traffic in many directions at the same time and it was made worse by the large number of bikes, minicabs, baht busses and other modes of travel, all coming together at a cross street or round about, (remember the British influence) many not paying attention to the policeman who was directing them. It was total chaos! I was told there was also a law that held the last person in the car responsible for any accident no matter where you were sitting in the vehicle, so whatever happens you do jump out of the car and stand outside if you are capable of doing so.

Johnny explained that this circular restaurant was arranged in floors based on the meals you were going to eat. The most expensive meals were served on the top floor. Johnny, of course had reservations, and we entered an elevator with an attendant who ran the elevator. No words were exchanged, and the elevator went up to a level I could not identify. It was high, based on the view I had from a window in the foyer when we exited. We were led into a small room where Annie and another three guests awaited. I was introduced to them as his "brudder", which really made me feel comfortable. We were seated on the floor, cushioned by soft pillows with a low table in between the six of us. The other guests were good friends of Johny and Annie, but also people of influence involved in exporting precious gems. They were delightful people and excellent conversationalists, speaking excellent English freely. The meal was served in segments, with a soup, followed by various appetizers and entire process was to lead up to the main course, roasted duck, cooked in mud. I found later that you had to order the duck at least twenty-four hours in advance in order to cook it. Interestingly, with one of the appetizers, which were delivered on a "Lazy Susan" type device, with a selection in each segment I chose an item that after tasting, Johny asked how I liked it. I told him it was delicious and very tender. He smiled as I asked what it was and he replied, "Elephant trunk". It was very good and though I was surprised, I never really thought about it until later. Can you believe elephant trunk? He pointed out another item and identified it as monkey meat, not too tasty! All of this was accompanied by a Chinese "wine", supposedly it was 150 proof alcohol and not to taken in large quantities. At any rate, the duck was everything I had heard it would be and by now I was too full to think about any more food when some sweet cakes arrived. I did take and eat two of them. I'm not sure we were on the top floor, but if anyone was higher, I can't imagine what they could have eaten or could have had a meal any more delightful than we had that night.

We were there for three hours. In departing, I gave a "Sawadee Cup" to the various waiters and a "Sawadee Ca" to our beautiful hostess, who had been present almost through the entire meal. Johnny's driver was waiting as we exited the restaurant and I said goodbye to their exporter guests, who Johnny told me later were some of the wealthiest men in Thailand. I truly enjoyed their company! I can't express how much I thought of Johny and Annie during my time in Thailand. They were truly great people and wonderful role models. They dropped me off at the hotel and I left on the courier from Don Muong the next morning going back to U-T.

I did have one other quiet dinner with Johnny and Annie in Bangkok as I was to leave that night and the aircraft was cancelled due to weather. I found out about it before I left the JUSMAG and Johny's driver was outside, seeing me he said he would drive me to the hotel. He dropped me off and evidently reported to Johnny that I was held over. Johny came by with Annie and we went to a local Chinese restaurant. There would be more occasions when Johny would meet with me, mostly on base and some were gatherings that included Annie, one such was a dinner at Colonel Calhoun's "hootch" where Wayne prepared his usual dinner for the four of us. It was a very loose and informal time where we all laughed and compared notes on family and the happenings in Thailand, which were ominous to say the least. Later I hosted Johnny and Annie, along with Howard, Wayne, and BJ Addison, who was the Director of Resources involving the termination of the contract for Johny's store in the Exchange area. It was a very fishy action as a contract had been signed by previous Individuals, where money had obviously changed hands and now everyone was saying nothing could be done. Howard indicated his hands were tied because the new guy has a legal contract. Johny was disappointed, however he was gracious and comforting to us as we had tried to get the entire process cancelled. It was apparent that the Thai military had something to do with the change. It did turn out to be a pleasant gathering as Johny and Annie talked at length about their three children, a daughter in the University, an older son who had been admitted to Medical School and a fifteen year old son who he was hoping to enroll in Exeter Academy in New England. I passed my limited knowledge of Exeter to them and they were very interested when I described the location and the prestige of the school. They are wonderful parents and good friends. Many of my close friends who had passed through UT knew Johny and his business and I received many requests to procure jewelry from him and send it back home. No one was ever disappointed.

OTHER STRANGE AND INTERESTING MEETINGS IN BANGKOK

I visited Bangkok numerous times while stationed in U-Tapao, always on business, but as was stated on occasion I would combine the trip with pleasure and stayed overnight in the military hotel in the center of town. Never on landing and deplaning was I in need of transportation. On all my official business trips to the capital city, my travel plans were not shared with anyone outside of the command section. However, Billie would tell Johny if I agreed, which I did twice, if I was going to be there overnight. A seat was always left open on the courier which came to UT four days a week for the short flight to Bangkok. It was always saved for official business, no matter who had to go to the MAAG or the Embassy. I was the one who filled that seat, as I was the sole person at UT who was designated as a courier for official business, that had the proper security clearances to carry classified material. Most of the time the seat was left vacant as no one had a need to go there. Yet on every occasion that I used that seat, Manas Manat's driver would be waiting for me at Don Muong. How Manas would find out about my travel was a mystery I never solved. Nobody in the command section was aware of my travel except Kathy Michael and Billie and both were adamant they did not and would not divulge the time, type or the reason for my travel to the JUSMAG, most of my visits were of the sensitive category. Material and topics were given to me by the Chief of Intelligence as he received them through our SSO. He too would not indulge in telling anyone of the trip. I always refused transportation in Manas' car as there was always a staff car waiting for me when I arrived on the courier.

One interesting time when I arrived at Don Muong Airport, I happened to see a former boss of mine as he came off an airplane from an up-country base. He had been the Deputy Commander of Operations at Grissom AFB in Indiana. He was in uniform as was I. Our previous relationship had ended in a contentious manner as he tried to cancel my assignment I had received to Headquarters Strategic Air Command. He was obviously out of uniform due to hair that was coming out of his wheel cap. Seeing him I said hello and we exchanged some pleasantries and present job titles. He was very surprised that I was the present commander of the 307th SW at U-T and mumbled something about his lower level attaché position. As we parted I whispered to him that I thought he should get a haircut. I felt good about that as I stepped into the Air Force Staff car waiting for me to go to the JUSMAG which was located about a half mile away from the Embassy in the designated military area.

On this visit I was to meet one of the most impressive and vital military officers I ever knew. I met for the first time the commander of the JUSMAG, Brigidier General Harry (Heinie) Aderholt. I had heard a lot about this short, muscular, outgoing individual, but I would learn a great deal more in the months ahead. The story was that he was a legend in his time. Most of what I had been told about Heinie was that he had been in the Southeast Asia area for a very long time under different conditions and performing in many assignments. His initial assignment in Southeast Asia was a highly classified program called "The Seven Crowns" and it involved seven different individuals who were inserted into various Asian countries to assess those country's cooperation in the event the United States stretched their involvement in this critical and strategic location. This clandestine operation would have taken place during his assignment with the 1095th Operational Training group, where he was instrumental in developing the Laos airfield complex known as the "Lima Sites" well before the beginning of the Vietnam War. He spent four years at the border of Thailand and Laos. Later these airfields were used throughout Southeast Asia as support sites for special warfare operations and as a CH-3 "Jolly Green" helicopter forward staging bases for rescue and recovery operations in Laos and North Vietnam. You can only imagine the type of work this entailed as dealing with the Laotian government and the many different indigent groups in Laos required great linguistic and diplomatic skills.

That Heinie Aderholt was one of the seven individuals used in this intelligence capacity is further verified as he spent time in the 1007th Air Intelligence Service Group as a special staff warfare officer for two years and then to the 1040th USAF Field Activity Squadron in the same capacity which would have prepared him for the role he played with the 1095th. To know General Aderholt was to like him. He was not a tall individual, maybe five seven or eight, but was a stocky, muscular person, who was impressive to see and engaging to talk with. His language was raw, but not obscene and his constitution is Spartan. He was a no-nonsense person who did not engage in small talk and who emitted professionalism in every situation that I spent with him. Stories about him abounded, most might have had a bit of fiction, but one, in particular was one everyone who knew him verified it was true.

Heine had retired from the military in December 1972 as a colonel from Eglin AFB, a place he had held other previous assignments. Ten months later in October, 1973, he was recalled to take a position as the deputy commander of the United States Military Assistance Command, Thailand and deputy chief, JUSMAG with headquarters in Bangkok. It is well known in military circles that to recall a retired Colonel to active duty is something that does not happen very often and when it does, pressure is being applied from somewhere, or the person has a particular capability or status that no one else has. It turns out that Colonel Aderholt was assigned in Thailand as the chief of the Air Force Advisory Group, Joint U.S. Military Advisory Group in Bangkok from 1970 for a two-year tour. The story is that when the current deputy Commander retired in 1973 from his position and a specific, named individual was selected for that coveted assignment, the Thai government objected to that selection. It appeared they had a say in who would occupy that sensitive position. The popular belief is that they specifically wanted Heine Aderholt. It is a one-star billet, so they would have to first recall Heini and then promote him out of the promotion cycle to Brigadier General. He had obviously made a favorable impression on the Thai government (meaning military) and they wanted Colonel Aderholt to return. Of course, the powers to be said Aderholt is retired and it was a General Officer position (Billet). Harry Aderholt was a colonel. The simple answer was "bring him back and promote him", as that was who they wanted.

Harry Aderholt was recalled and promoted to General in May, 1974. I spent limited time with him, and only once, (maybe twice) socially and that was an occasion when he invited me to a gathering of his staff to watch the heavy weight fight known as "The Thrilla in Manila" between Ali and Frazier, which was to be shown in the bar of the Military Hotel in Bangkok. It was of course a great fight and gave me the opportunity to witness Heinie among his friends and staff. It was obvious that he was well liked, even revered and was very aware of the world around him, engaging everyone in the area with a personable smile or a slap on the back. That fight also gave me an opportunity to meet his wife, a very attractive and personable blonde who would stand out in any crowd.

Going from a scheduled briefing with General Aderholt, and others which followed, where his questions were incisive and to the point, to he being totally relaxed, was a learning experience. I would find in many later meetings this general would demonstrate a thorough knowledge and awareness of the situation at hand. He was possibly the most professional and patriotic officer I ever met. Some of the professional meetings were somewhat tense and troubling, not because of any strain between he and I, but with the conditions that we were confronted with. He would act vigorously in any situation. He carried a loaded, sawed off shotgun, by his side in his vehicle and I can attest to that as I've ridden with him and seen it.

One of his proudest moments was in evacuating Hmong leaders from Laos and Vietnam in late May of 1975. When most eyes were on the aforementioned "Mayaguez" incident, Heinie was busy commandeering three C-130s, found three pilots and scrubbed the aircraft down to eradicate all identification on the aircraft and flew them to Long Tieng. In four days of furious activity they evacuated more than two thousand Hmong including their commanding general and the CIA case officer. All were out of the country in two days. Only that general could have accomplished that deed. His no-threat was too big to overcome attitude permeated his actions.

One of my most interesting trips to Bangkok involved the 3rd Air Division Vice Commander, Major General Robert H. Gaughn. He was coming on an official visit to visit the 307th. It was to be his final visit to Thailand as he was retiring on his return to Guam from his position in the 3rd AD. While in Bangkok he had a tight agenda he wanted to play out. After his arrival, there would be a session with the senior staff, which was really a scenario of what was in store for the U. S. forces in Thailand. We would then go to Bangkok on a visit to the JUSMAG. He would meet General Aderholt someone he hadn't known before. I would fill him in on what I knew. It should be interesting as they are similar in many ways, both well-kept gentlemen, about the same size and known for their bombastic style. After that meeting he wanted to play golf on the professional championship course that had been used for world events. It was the Siam Country Club. He insisted that I accompany him and join him for a day of golf which I was OK with. He had a Colonel with him who would play, and I grabbed one of my golfing friends, Henry Clark to make up the foursome. When at U-T he was going to present me with a medal that I had been awarded from my last tour at Mather AFB. It was a nice ceremony attended by the staff and followed by a cake cutting and that update on our status in country. After that event there would be a tour of the base with Wayne and I and to make it official we would stop by Captain Vichit's office. The flight to Bangkok on the everyday flight would only take about thirty minutes. We would be met by a staff car to take us to the MAAG headquarters for the meeting with General Aderholt. It would be a short courtesy meeting and then to the course. It was a good diversion from the base routines for me and I loved to play golf. I did not take part in the meeting with the two generals, but was told afterwards that General Gaughan was impressed with General Aderholt.

It was a beautiful course and a great clear day. The course was long and had many diversions, such as a five story Japanese Buddha, a Buddhist Temple and a massive Buddha type tree in the middle of the first fairway (which I was told was removed later to entice a pro golf event to play there). The Caddies, although dressed like those at the Admirals course, were very expressive, smiling and saying "dit ma", which I think meant a good or straight shot and then look glumly and shake their heads at you if you went into a bunker or out of bounds. They did not divulge anything about the greens and would not help lining up your putt. I lost three balls, one because the caddy did not tell me there was a water hazard ahead and just shook her head after I hit what I thought was a good shot. General Gaughn was a total sketch, totally relaxed, a blustery fellow, but totally enjoyable. It was a great day and ended up with dinner in Pattya, then a dark drive back to the base as there was no return courier flight. His day of departure would be on my 56th day in country and I got up early to catch his 0500 departure time and see him off. It was a scheduled KC-135 flight day for me, so just threw on my green bag and caught him at the flight line. I was sorry to see him go. He was fun! There is a great twist of irony involved in this as my Air Force history is laced with involvement with this man. As a new second lieutenant assigned to my first squadron, the 715th, in the famous 509th Bomb Wing (It was the wing that dropped the two atomic bombs on Japan) my commander was one Robert H. Gaughn, then a major. He was very proud of the 715th Bomb Squadron safety record which I broke when I taxied over a power cart in a B-47 when coming back from the "refueling pits". This was a task that co-pilots in this six jet engine aircraft were assigned to do. Once the refueling was finished the aircraft had to be taxied back to the ramp and parked in a designated spot. It was late at night and as I was coming into the parking slot a power unit had been parked close to the right side of the aircraft as I turned into position. As I watched the individual waving his parking wand, steering me into the slot, the right wing of the aircraft and the outboard engine clipped that power unit knocking it over. Damage to the aircraft and the power unit was confined to a few minor dents and probably a few noticeable scratches; however, it was a reportable ground incident and as such ended the string of days the 715th had gone without an accident.

After severe counseling from Major Gaughn I was admonished to other duties for a short period. This all happened at Walker AFB in Roswell New Mexico where I played baseball on the base team. On a very hot Sunday afternoon in a game against an opponent who I have long forgotten, I was stretching a hit going for two bases. Sliding into second base a loud snap was heard and pain shot out from my left hamstring as I slid safely into second. I was carted off the diamond and taken to the base hospital where I was diagnosed with a torn hamstring and told I would remain overnight and when I left given crutches to navigate with. This of course was another stain on the 715th safety record, but to make it worse the 509th Bomb Wing, which the 715th was a member was hit with a no-notice wing evaluation, where the wing was graded on all phases of its capability to perform its mission. All crews would have to fly. I had been declared DNIF (duty not to include flying). A substitute co-pilot was found to fly with my crew, which was one selected to fly early in the launch, but lo and behold, the numbers of launching aircraft was one short of the required needed. Major Gaughn talked to the Base Flight Surgeon and told him he needed me to fly with a crew made up of two staff majors as their co-pilot on the second day of the launches. After taking off my hamstring wraps, leaving the crutches at the hospital, procuring an ice bag I mission planned with this made up crew and flew the assigned flight and the results of our flight were very good and added to a high capability rating for the wing.

Despite my heroic actions (at least I thought so) my good squadron commander threatened to end my baseball days with the Walker AFB team. The overall results of the squadron changed his mind, plus the urging of the very persuasive Aircraft Commander I flew with, Major Jennings O. Larson, one of the finest pilots I ever had the honor of flying with. I was allowed to remain on the team although I didn't play for a good period of time due to my hamstring injury. Things were going well after that, until on a crisp winter day I was going to the hospital for a routine visit, the nature of which was merely to get a required shot, which I among many others had our names posted on the squadron bulletin board and were directed to accomplish by a very near cutoff day. As I turned on the road facing the hospital, traveling at a very low rate of speed and approaching a cross street, a motor scooter shot through the stop sign and collided with me. Although not seriously injured the Master Sergeant driving the scooter suffered a large gash on his thumb as his hand had hit the throttle lever on his handlebars. Others who saw the collision helped me get him to the emergency room, where I met with the Air Police and filled out an accident report. The meeting with Major Gaughn followed that afternoon and I was told by my very red-faced Commander that I was accident prone and he was transferring me to the 393rd Bomb Squadron, where I found some relief from dealing with him but remained for only a short period of time. Major Gaughn was subsequently transferred and other members of the 715th urged the new commander, Lt. Colonel Dick Arnold, that I be reassigned back to the 715th. I was placed on a very good crew and I became a favorite of the new commander of the squadron. The following year was uneventful and in fact I was considered as a very good pilot and crew member.

It's not the end of the story as I left the Air Force in December,1957 to finish my teaching credential but found going back to school dull and unfulfilling. The following November I received a call from March AFB from a good friend of mine Lieutenant Colonel Ken Lidie, he and his crew plus Colonel Arnold were there for a Bombing Competition. He asked if I could come out for a visit that night. I had little to do so accepted and took the hour drive from my home To March AFB in Riverside, found Ken and my former roommate, Chuck Pfeiffer and felt a sense of belonging that evening with old friends. During this eventful night I was asked by Colonel Arnold if I wanted to be recalled. I jumped at the chance to return and said certainly. It was only a matter of ten days, just before Thanksgiving, 1958 when I received official notification of my recall and was given a date to report to my old wing, but first I would have to get a flight physical. I was told to go to March AFB, the closest location from my home to complete the physical. Upon arriving I went right to the hospital, completed the physical and was walking across the street to my car, with exciting thoughts of reporting to my old squadron, seeing all of my old friends which had now moved from Roswell NM to Pease AFB, Portsmouth New Hampshire. As I waited for a car to pass by I was a bit surprised as it screeched to a halt, the window rolled down and a lieutenant colonel poked his head out the window and blustered out "Dugard, what are you doing here". It was my old squadron commander, now stationed at March as a Lieutenant Colonel, waiting for an answer. I meekly told him I had been part of a limited recall program and was rejoining the 509th in New Hampshire. He paused for a second, looked intently at me and said, "that's far enough, good luck" and departed.

I never saw him again until my stop in Guam on my way to U-Tapao for our very short meeting in which he greeted me warmly and with a pause and a knowing wink. Now we meet again with some extended meetings and a day of golf. I had been told before I left the base to go to Bangkok that it was a sort of retirement trip for him as this was a gift before he departed the Air Force. It proved to be a very enjoyable time. It was a difficult course, but the wide fairways and the verdant surroundings were not at all like the jungle course at Sadaheep. The only similarity was the heat and humidity and of course the yellow clad caddies. General Gaughn was a good golfer and enjoyed his time with me on the course. He didn't take the game too seriously which I was happy for as I didn't want to experience an angry Robert H. Gaughn at this late stage of my career. He was really a nice man and obviously had had a successful career. An ironic postscript of sorts, while on the golf course General Gaughn confided with me that he sat on my promotion board to Colonel and approved and graded my promotion.

A Medal for Colonel Dugard, pinned by Major General Robert H. Gaughn

THE B-52 WITHDRAWAL
FROM SOUTHEAST ASIA

There had been many warnings and threats toward the United States Government toward the B-52 and the F-111 presence in Thailand. There had been internal protests of our continued presence and our present status in Thailand. In addition, the Thai government supposedly controlled by a civilian democratic government but dominated by the military was reacting to threats by the North Vietnamese. These were viewed as serious threats for an invasion of Thailand by their now victorious army. We had received messages to the effect we could expect a with-drawl of the B-52s and the F-111s very soon. The FB-111s are not part of the 307th but our tankers are needed for them to complete the long journey home. We were very active in the number of sorties being flown by both our aircraft and we had built up our KC-135 force in order to support the F-111 drag to the CONUS so the time had come for the Tankers to get active. There were also only so many holes the B-52s could carve in the skies over Thailand as there really was no mission for the Buff any longer.

Finally, the order came to send the remainder of the B-52 force home. For the returning crews and staff, it was a joyful occasion. This would have a large impact on the total force as there would be no use for the operational and maintenance support segment of our command staff for a B-52 operation. There were a couple of exceptions who would have to stay longer in some capacity as they had not spent the required one hundred and eighty days for an unaccompanied tour. One of those who would be leaving was my golf partners Major Karl Kaufman, the chief of flight management. I would miss the left-handed swings of Karl. He was as strong as an ox and could hit the ball a mile and scored well but lacked the finesse of Pat Richmond who was a very good and precise golfer who had a very low handicap. Both had little trouble in their rounds with me and on a very difficult jungle course. Pat was a KC-135 Instructor Pilot (IP), so would remain to torment me on the course. Sending the last of the B-52s home would be historic to say the least. The first of these monster aircraft came to Thailand in the late 1960s and proved to be a fearsome weapon. There were times when there were more than one-hundred and fifty Buffs in U-Tapao., We were now down to sixteen.

Official orders for the B-52s to leave were received with dates of departure, but it was our responsibility to set in motion who would be going and on what days. The departure times were set to start this rotation home, with three to four aircraft departing each day for three days. The first of the black beauties would leave on Friday, June 6 and others would continue the process through Sunday June 8. The fact that the wing commander was not on station meant that I would be in command of the redeployment of these majestic aircraft. I felt privileged to be a participant in this event even though I was not a long- time B-52 pilot. I had still flown it long enough to appreciate its great capacity for delivering iron on an enemy. I had logged over three hundred hours of combat time during my "Bullet Shot" and "Linebacker II" B-52 flights. My greater experience and background had been in the six J-47 engine B-47, logging over 3000 hours and then into the supersonic B-58, the fastest and most significant aircraft in my form five (The Air Force official individual flight log), outlining flight time and experience. I loved the B-58, having logged over 700 hours of flight time and left it for a headquarters assignment after over twelve years on a combat crew.

I was very fortunate when arriving at the headquarters as flying time there would be in the T-39, a two engine, six seat aircraft that I had flown during my time at the Instrument Pilot Instructors School (IPIS). I immediately checked out and was installed as an instructor, so was able to get many flying hours and interesting trips around the country, transporting many of the senior staff, including my bosses in and out of Washington DC for Pentagon trips and to other interesting places. One of my more interesting flights occurred late in my time at Offutt. I was told to be at base operations to plan a flight to the Orange County Airport (Now John Wayne Airport) in California. All I was told was I would be taking I would be taking a high-ranking dignitary to that location. I planned the flight along with an assigned co-pilot and was told my aircraft was parked in front of base operations, something that seldom happened on normal ferry flights, so I assumed I would be transporting a General officer to that location as normally a bus would take a crew to a parking spot to pick up the aircraft for flight. After finishing my mission planning the co-pilot and I walked out to the aircraft for the customary pre-flight of the aircraft and wait for our passenger(s). Our designated departure time passed and as it was a hot day after completing the interior checklist up to "start-engines, we stood outside the aircraft for our passenger(s). It seemed a very long time, now well after our programmed departure time, but finally a stream of vehicles appeared entering the flight line. The lead vehicle was flying its identity flag, four stars which identified it as the vehicle of the CINCSAC, the SAC commander. I didn't look beyond that car, but as people disgorged from the three-vehicle line I could see most of the general officers on the command staff were in the group, but most interestingly there was a civilian who I recognized immediately. It was Senator Barry Goldwater. He was joined by three other civilians, who I assumed were members of his staff.

The CINC himself introduced me to the Senator. After some amenities we boarded the aircraft, the senator his staff of people with him and they took their seats in the rear section of the T-39. While entering the aircraft and before starting engines I remembered that Senator Goldwater was a pilot and a retired Brigadier General, so I sat in the co-pilot's seat for takeoff and departure. After leveling off I told the other pilot to go back and ask if the general/senator would like to fly the aircraft and within moments he appeared in the cockpit indicating he was eager to fly. He strapped in and took the controls.

We had exchanged some pleasantries and I told him of our route of flight and that we would have to make a refueling stop at Nellis AFB in Las Vegas, before going to his destination. We exchanged some information about my flying experience and he his time in the Air Force, then as the flight progressed he told me some of his personal history, telling me that his father had been the Indian agent in Arizona and he had great memories of his youth in this area we were now flying over. He asked if we could go lower and check some of his boyhood locations, so I called center and canceled our flight plan, going visual flight rules and descended to a scenic tour level as he pointed out areas he was familiar with all the way to the vicinity of our desired refueling base at Nellis AFB. He knew of the many native Indian tribal locations and his familiarity of their locations and status made for a very enlightening history lesson. I called Approach Control and told them we had a code two on the aircraft, which signified I had a very high-ranking passenger on board. (This was something that should have been in my flight plan, but due to not knowing the identification of the passenger and his staff, this was the first indication of the status of my passenger). A code one is the president! They put us on a very long downwind, taking us over Hoover Dam, pretty much ignoring the priority designation call I had made. I then reiterated the code to approach control. Someone must have finally recognized priority designation and immediately gave us vectors to final approach. I asked the senator if he wanted to make the landing and he jumped at the chance. He flew a nice final culminating in a smooth touchdown.

Pulling off the runway we were met by a "Follow-Me" vehicle which took us to a parking spot in front of base operations. After parking I was surprised that we were not met by the base commander or some other appropriate ranking individual. I told the ground crew all we needed was fuel and we would be on our way and turned to go into base ops to renew my Instrument Flight Plan (IFR). The Senator said he would go with me. As we entered and went to the weather station to get an upgrade on the weather enroute, and at our destination, people started to realize who this civilian was who was accompanying me. I finished my business and we walked out toward the aircraft and out of the corner of my eye I saw an official vehicle, with lights a blazing coming at a high rate of speed down the ramp, followed by a line of other vehicles. I turned to the Senator and said something to the effect that his arrival had now been noticed. He smiled and we continued walking to the aircraft. We were met by the ground crew saying refueling was completed. This was interrupted by the sound of a car braking to a halt and a very ruffled Colonel, leading a group, running to meet us. We hesitated as the colonel approached and arriving, he was apologizing for not being there when we arrived, and the senator was graciously saying it was okay as the refueling stop was not in the original flight plan, which was not true, but left the embarrassed base commander a good excuse. We quickly mounted the stairs, leaving the colonel, sweating profusely, watching dejectedly as we entered the aircraft.

The Senator went directly to a seat in the back, telling me he had been into the destination airport before and advised that I needed to make that landing as it was a difficult approach over obstacles and he was not prepared to attempt it. ("That airport", later became "John Wayne Airport", a bustling and busy Orange County destination with high tension wires hanging high above the end of the runway that have since been removed). Upon landing we were directed to the far side of the airport, where military aircraft were serviced. After deplaning, the senator and his staff, thanked me for the flight, said warm farewells, entered a waiting vehicle and departed. There were many other interesting flights with many interesting individuals while stationed at Offutt AFB, but that was the top one.

When my headquarters assignment was over, I was told I would be going to Southeast Asia on a tour. I had been angling for an OV-10 assignment to SEA with my friends at the Military Personnel Center (MPC) in San Antonio. I was in the stream for that, but I had not officially been given the assignment, until one day while sitting in my office I was told the sitting CINC (Commander in Chief) wanted to talk to me about some personnel matters. The commander of 15th Air Force, Lieutenant General P.K. Carlton, was filling that position while the commander of SAC was off station. I had had many previous meetings with General Carlton and had briefed his wing commanders at his request at March AFB last year. The meeting began as a discussion about certain officers he had been asked to intercede for in promotion matters. I had pulled the records of these officers and was prepared to answer his questions about the merits of each. When finished, I started to leave, and he said he was not through talking to me. General Carlton said he was aware that my time at the headquarters was almost completed and he wanted me to be one of his squadron commanders. He asked me if I wanted a KC-135 or the B-52 squadron. I had been flying bomber type aircraft since I was a second lieutenant, some seventeen years ago. To go to the "Buff" was not my favorite dream as I thought of it as a huge, cumbersome truck in the sky, but there was no choice in this matter as the B-58 was phased out of the inventory shortly after I left Grissom. I had once made fun of my friends who were assigned to that beast. I realized suddenly there was no exit to avoid this assignment. I wasn't asked if I wanted the assignment, only what aircraft. I replied that I was a bomber guy and would like a B-52 squadron. I was told I would get some maintenance training as an Organizational Maintenance Squadron (OMS) Commander with the 55th Air Refueling Wing on station, following which, I would go to one of the 15th AF bases as a squadron commander. I slowly felt this assignment had been worked out before our conversation with our own personnel people in the headquarters. A phone call to the Military Personnel Center after I returned to my office acknowledged that my proposed assignment to OV-10s was scrapped and the B-52 was to be my next role in the Air Force, location not known.

I was shortly thereafter was assigned to the OMS squadron. It was a matter of just parking my car daily at another location on the base. It was to be a six-month indoctrination in the maintenance world., an assignment I really enjoyed as it brought me very close to the maintenance personnel that made the mission flourish and thrive. It was a great entrance into future assignments. After I spent those short six months as the Organizational Maintenance Squadron (OMS) CC I was sent to Castle AFB in California for training in the Buff

After flying the T-39 for almost four years the B-52 was an imposing aircraft. My initial experience was that it was a huge, eight-engine aircraft, however I found it easy to refuel and very different on takeoff as when you hit S-2, takeoff speed, minimum pressure on the control column and it lifts into the air. I compared it to be in an elevator that goes forward. On landing there was no "round out", just a flat approach where you could see the runway throughout the landing process, but after those years at the headquarters flying the twin engine, hot little aircraft T-39 out of base flight, a bird that I really enjoyed, this was work. It was six weeks of separation from the family, but one dedicated to understanding and flying this 525,000-pound flying machine. Completing the checkout requirements, I was transferred to Mather AFB in California, only to find my squadron deployed to Guam as a part of the "G" force deployment for the "Bulletshot" show of force in Vietnam.

Flying this aircraft on missions to Vietnam from Guam and return gave me a new perspective of the aircraft. It was highly maneuverable and responsive and as I indicated was a piece of cake when refueling in flight. I actually found out that the refueling lights on the tanker made sense as they were put on the tanker for the "Buff", whose refueling receptacle was behind the pilot position, not on the nose like the 47 and 58. You could not see the refueling lights in the 47 or 58 as your cockpit position was too far aft.

It was always a matter of flying formation and using the "boom" to assess your azimuth and distance from the tanker. There were a series of colored bars and a green circle in the middle. Fly the middle circle and you were in the "Green". Using the now significant lights was another cross-check to hold your position. So, my new feeling about this great, strong bird changed over the six months I spent flying out of Guam. It was enhanced in the following three years flying from various stateside locations. It would never replace the B-58 as my favorite aircraft, but it was a real pleasure to fly and it proved over-and-over again it could withstand a great deal of damage! On a returning aircraft from one of our Linebacker II missions, one of my squadron pilots flew his damaged aircraft back to Guam from Hanoi and we counted one hundred and forty-eight holes in his aircraft upon landing. The best part, he never felt anything, and he didn't realize he had taken a hit!

This was now the end of United States combat force involvement in Southeast Asia. The B-52s were the source of great fear in the hearts and minds of the North Vietnam and their Viet Cong allies. I've talked to many former Army and Marine veterans of Vietnam who told me stories of the sound of the huge bomber and seeing contrails in the sky, knowing that soon after there would be a rain of bombs on a selected target. Going into target areas where there had been a series of B-52 sorties, total devastation would be apparent. In one instance during the battle for Hue, the Marines had asked for the B-52s to drop their stores on their own battle line. With the ignition of the bombs release the marines fell back as the horde of NVA came across the river into the area where the marines had been as the bombs struck, ending the battle for that key city.

As someone who participated in those raids, I can attest to the atmosphere among the crews who flew the "Buff" as we knew our missions had an effect. On one such raid my flight of three B-52 Gs were vectored to a target from a ground control facility in the southern part of Vietnam.

From our flight altitude of 31,000-feet I could discern no visible target. In fact, all I could see appeared to be rice paddies. We were told to release our bomb load by ground control as there was no radar return to bomb from, which after release I turned into a gentle thirty-degree bank and watched as the first bomb hit into the ground below. It was like hitting a big mud puddle and then a small explosion, followed by two or three others and then as the rest of the string hit the world erupted as the target must have been a weapons storage area of the VC. They had used the expansive rice paddies as a hiding place for their weapons and ammunition thinking it would be safe. Little did they know of our intelligence capabilities! As the other two aircraft released their bombs and they struck the same area, the cascading roils of eruption was a magnificent display of fireworks, although somewhat muddy. The ensuing clouds that were emitted rose in splendor to the same height as our departing bombers.

My personal memories of the raids were many especially during "Linebacker II", the eleven-day Christmas raids of 1972. They are dwarfed by the many years that the B-52 was the dominate force in the Vietnam War. Now it was over and this small force of now sixteen was all that was left, and they were about to leave. The legacy has been established. A B-52 was a legend in Southeast Asia that won't fade because of their departure.

The sixteen B-52s remaining in Thailand were all "D" models and they came from bases throughout the United States. They were the last of the force that hit a zenith in number during the Linebacker II raids of over 240 aircraft stationed here at U-Tapao and on Guam. This count included a comparative number of the "G" model stationed in Guam who were brought over during the "Bullet Shot" program to intensify the number of sorties against the North Vietnam government and their puppet Viet Cong forces. The "G" model flew only out of Guam where my involvement as a squadron commander took place. The "G"s were not the war horse that the "D" was as they could only carry an internal store of twenty-seven bombs, whereas the "D" had the same internal capacity, and due to a set of "hard points" could carry an additional load of hundred pounder bombs under each wing. Both were formidable weapon systems. The Guam based aircraft mission length was over twelve hours, whereas the U-Tapao mission was around four.

As the preparation for this final departure was initiated, I wanted it to be memorable. The three days would be something to remember as the black B-52"D" hulks, the BUFFS (Big Ugly Fat Fellows, for want of another word) most definitely needed to be remembered for their role in Vietnam!

REFLECTION

My memories of the "Linebacker" raids would persist during these days as the launch on the first day, December 18, 1972, of those missions from Guam was imbedded in my mind. I along with three other "G" squadron commanders would fly lead aircraft in the raids over Hanoi in the significant missions against the North Vietnamese, in an aggressive attempt to end the conflict in Vietnam. It was determined that the four commanders would be split into no more than two to have some commanders on the ground coordinating pre-flight activities and two in the air as "Airborne Commanders". Due to my limited time in the aircraft compared to the other three commanders (they were long time Buff pilots and I had spent five years flying the supersonic B-58 after eight years in the B-47) I was selected to fly Day Two. The activities I would be doing were to select crews to fly Day One as well as designating who would be wave leaders. In meetings with the crews early in the evening before the first missions would launch, we selected those who would fly "Day One" and put them into crew rest. This included selecting standby crews and position spares, who could fly and bag-drag aircraft crews, who would not fly. In addition, we were tasked to coordinate with our personal equipment (PE) people and the in-flight kitchen to insure they were prepared for this surge in activity. (The in-flight kitchen would more than likely need to be ready for feeding the six-man crew on those aircraft as they would be flying a fourteen-hour mission from Guam to North Vietnam and return). There would be over a hundred and twenty aircraft flying on December 18. This would be a combination of the "Ds" and "Gs".

The "D" force had two additional squadron commanders who also were split into a single airborne commander/leader for Day One. Each Guam "G" squadron was made up of three ordinary squadrons from bases in the CONUS (Continental United States) my squadron had fifty-five crews. In

Personal Equipment, current date inspected chutes, survival vests, handguns and other survival pieces would be needed for this force which would launch mid-afternoon the following day. Of course, our activity to prepare started on December 17 and continued through the night to include transportation to the briefing theater and then to individual aircraft. Crews on busses had to be coordinated by aircraft location on the ramp. Each bus was pretty much limited to two crews due to the PE and flight equipment of each crewmember. The base theater was used as the pre-takeoff briefing forum as there were too many crews and spares for the usual location, bomber operations, as approximately eight hundred crew members were in attendance along with staff all the way up to the Eighth Air Force Commander, General Johnson, my former wing commander in B-58s, and of course me.

The briefing was historical as it would be the first use of the B-52 against Hanoi and Haiphong, targets that the fighter guys had had the exclusive use of for all the years we had been in Vietnam. These designated targets, when announced, brought silence to the crews. Though combat veterans, many had flown SEA tours in other combat aircraft, they were stunned at the targets they would be confronted with. The silence continued when they were informed that they would be going into the most highly defended area in the world, with multiple SAM (surface to air missiles) SA-2 and SA-3 sites surrounding the targets. The briefing ended in a prayer for the safety of the crews and departures were made after the command section left the theater. It was a very bright sunny day and the crews went to their assigned busses and I went to my truck as I had work to do preparing for the next day's launch. I would be the Airborne Commander, leading a twenty-one ship cell to a yet unknown target.

Sitting in my squadron office, on Guam, which was just a bedroom on the second floor of what we called the concretes, that was cleared out so that two of the four squadron commanders each had a desk. The doors were left open to allow air to pass through, as the heat would not allow the air conditioner to keep up with the humid environment. I knew that I would have to leave to witness the launch and so I puttered around doing odd things until I heard the first power units start up and knew engine start times would follow shortly.

I left my office and went to the railing outside the door and could see the white puffs of smoke from the APUs. Takeoffs would start in less than thirty minutes. The interval between aircraft in cell (cells were usually twenty-one aircraft) would be fifteen to thirty seconds, with a pause of maybe a minute until the next twenty-one would depart. All aircraft would be airborne in less than an hour. This was an event I wouldn't miss! The launch of over a hundred and twenty aircraft would be an incredible show of power. I finished what I was doing and ran downstairs to my truck, picked up my compatriot "G" squadron commander, Lieutenant Colonel Herb Jordan, who would also be flying tomorrow, and raced down to the flight line, pulling off the hardtop to a vacant dirt area on the takeoff end and on a slight incline with an excellent view of the end of the runway and parked on the dirt next to a phalanx of pickup trucks and bread trucks of the working crew chiefs and support personnel who were not working at this moment. We were facing the takeoff end maybe a hundred feet from the hammerhead as the first of the "D" models and flight approached the end of the runway waiting for takeoff to commence. As we heard the power come up and the roll began, a raucous sound of horns from every vehicle started, along with the waving of flags, towels and cheers. It was the most amazing display of patriotism I had ever seen or heard. It was absolutely stirring. It brought tears to my eyes!

As each Buff brought up power the noise level accelerated, both from the aircraft and the crowded area around me. The water injection firing brought about a cascade of black smoke that was covering the area, but not before the first of the "G" models began their dance down the runway. The very first "G" aircraft was commanded by Lt. Colonel Don Rissi, a good friend and former B-58 pilot in the same squadron with me, who was supposed to depart for home today, but was held over due to the need for crews. I told him last night that although he was supposed to leave tomorrow as he had completed his 180-day tour, they were holding him over and he would have as I told him "one more flight" before leaving. Those words have haunted me ever since, as does the picture in my mind of his aircraft, taking the runway, spilling water as he turned onto the runway and fired it on his takeoff roll. He was probably the most experienced Buff pilot in hours and mission lead time, as well as having a combat tour in F-4s. He was a logical choice to fly that position on Day-One. He never came back! His aircraft was the first to go down on that historical day and he and his co-pilot did not survive the SAM missile hit that brought the aircraft to its uncontrollable state, reportedly slamming into downtown Hanoi. The rest of the six-man crew survived and spent time in the Hanoi Hilton.

THE FINAL SORTIE FOR
THE BUFFS IN SEA

Colonel Dugard and the last Buff with farewell garlands on the nose

Today would be a bit calmer and a great deal less noisy than the launches of Linebacker. It would be Day One of the departure of the last B-52s in Southeast Asia. (SEA). Tout Fini!

I was excited to take part in the final departure of the B-52s from Southeast Asia (SEA). It was also a moment to pause and remember the political fiasco I had experienced in my time associated with the Vietnam War. I was privy to the results of our Linebacker raids in 1972 as we daily would examine the BDA (bomb damage assessment) from the previous night. It was obvious that each day's raids had exacted heavy setbacks for the North Vietnamese. As each day passed it was apparent through photos taken by the SR-71s flying each night that it was becoming more difficult for this enemy to continue the fight.

By the ninth day, the bombers were facing little if any SAM action against them and our intelligence photos indicated that their resupply system was entirely shut down. Haiphong Harbor was blocked and mined. No ship could get in or out. The rail system was completely shut down from the continuous raids with rail stock destroyed or on its side along the approaches to and from supply neighbors and/or allies like China and Russia. There was no chance of an enemy fighter aircraft getting off from their destroyed runways.

Day Eleven saw no opposition to our aircraft flying unopposed while dropping their bomb loads on the already destroyed targets. From any experienced perspective the war was over! The programmed raids, which I was to take part in for Day Twelve were cancelled before engine start. It was announced that Henry Kissenger would return to Paris and meet with the North Vietnamese and conduct "talks"; surely it would result in a total end to this war?

It did bring about the return of our POWs, but that was basically it. We halted all our efforts in the North at a time when minimum raids would have insured no further hostile activity. We had total freedom to fly over North Vietnam to make sure supply lines stayed closed and their war-making capability would be forever ended. A single cell of B-52s flying constantly over selected targets would have rendered Hanoi's military chiefs unable to mount a return to war making status.

However, political and media pressure cut off our capability to wage this conflict. Flight restrictions were made, limiting our ability to attack enemy resources, also where we could fly giving the enemy areas to build up their weakened ability to continue the war. Our own congress cut the funding necessary to keep North Vietnam from continuing this war. Continued sorties over the north were forbidden! Straying into Cambodia was forbidden! The mined harbor of Haiphong was cleared, shipping in and out of the harbor was allowed to come and go as they pleased. Their supply lines were repaired. Our war making capability was undermined by the docile dudes and demons of congress, most of whom had no idea what war was or how to fight it. Von Clauswitz said in his treatise on war, "You must destroy the will of the people to fight". It worked in reverse in the early 1970s as congress and the media certainly did a number on the American public as our American citizens had no will to continue this war. (The media did such a great job on the military that Vietnam veterans were spurned and castigated after the end of the conflict). The result was covered on my first days in Thailand, the day Saigon was lost, and the South Vietnamese became refugees or prisoners in their own country. Saigon became Ho Chi Men city. It was a shameful era in American history!

SIXTEEN TO GO

It is Friday, June 6th, 1975 the initial day of the departure of the last B-52s to leave Southeast Asia had arrived. I had been bombarded with news inquiries about the departure and the event was getting national attention. It was obvious to me that this was a significant historical event. Once again, the wing commander, Colonel Calhoun, was not on station as he had gone home on leave so as the vice wing commander, I was in charge. It was day 44 in my time in Thailand and as I prepared to brief the first departing crew at 0430 hours, I was very emotional as I started my comments to the departing crews on their role in this happening. This would signal the departure of the last B-52s in Southeast Asia, something that started over ten years ago. I gave the second group of crews essentially the same emotional briefing at 0600 hours. The news media was to be allowed on station at 0630 hours and I left the crew briefing to run the ramp and found a beehive of activity. Two tanker aircraft would support the departing Buffs with refueling on their route to Guam.

True to their schedule, the launch of the U-2 took place as I prepared to meet the press. The weather had been kind to us as it was a clear and windless morning. The heat index was on the rise, but now within my tolerance level. The press was being transported to the ramp from the front gate by government busses and as they disgorged the number of cameras, sound booms, microphones lights and other gear was staggering. All the major news agencies were represented as well as Bangkok news media to include ABC, CBS NBC, the International News Service (INS) and Reuters and with them came individuals representing the U.S. Embassy and JUSMAG. There was also a Japanese news service, one representing Australia and a couple of free-lance reporters. They seemed English, at least they spoke the language. Even the ADVON commander, General Baxter, flew in from U-Dorn and was present. There was a designated area set aside for interviews which would take place before and after the launches. An Air Force film team was present to preserve the moment and seemed to know what they were doing in contrast to the group of motley civilian press, however there were exceptions. The press period was to last about a half an hour and the questions ranged from very good to a bit on the far-side. I was careful in my answers as I was not about to embarrass my service or my country. Some questions concerned the relationship and on-going negotiations between Thailand and the United States. I gave pat answers and deferred most to Embassy personnel. Others about my experience and of those I flew with on various missions. Reuters and INS seemed most inquisitive about my experience in the Linebacker II raids which I kept low-keyed but did answer their questions. The information people from the Embassy later told me my answers were well chosen and appropriate.

The Thai Government hung flower garlands on the nose of the departing Buffs as a "Sawadee" tradition. The crews loaded up and we were ready for the first of the launches. The Buff had flown thousands of missions over Vietnam, both north and south and this air armada had disgorged millions of tons of bombs on selected targets and now only sixteen of the force remained and they would soon be gone. It was indeed an historic event! First day departures would be in two three-ship cells, the first taking off at 0900 local and the second followed one hour later at 1000 hours. Takeoffs would be at one-minute interval and each three-ship cell would have a manned spare aircraft with a crew ready to depart on the seven- hour flight to Anderson AFB in Guam, in the event of an abort by any of the designated departure aircraft. Each three-ship would be accompanied by two Tankers which would takeoff prior to the Buff launch.

It was a typical I was now going to witness my second historical departure and would do so with the vivid memory of that December 18th launch from an island in the Pacific. Three lovely black buffs would leave in the first three ship cell for Anderson AFB Guam. They would make up "Ruby Cell". Captains Nelson in tail number 5069, Swanson in tail number 5079 and Bippert in tail number 5673 were the three aircraft commanders and Major Bob Rodriquez would go as the airborne commander (ABC) in the lead aircraft. He had been one of the first individuals I met when coming to U-Tapao AB. He was an experienced B-52 Instructor Pilot (IP) and the designated Operations Officer of the Temporary Duty Crews (TDY) and a person I would miss as he was a true professional. Maj. Barngrover would be in tail number 6696 and would prepare the spare and be ready to depart if any of the three primary aircraft came up lame. Departure time was affirmed at 0900 local with one-minute separation for numbers two and three.

The second three-ship cell would follow one hour later, with Captains Miller in tail number 5086, Stanicar in tail number 6585 and Shelfler in tail number 5073 as the aircraft commanders (ACs). Captain Johnson would be the AC of the manned spare aircraft in tail number 6663. Engine start time for all aircraft would be forty minutes prior to the departure time. At engine start time, all aircraft in Ruby Cell and both Tankers indicated a "Go" status. The KC-135s took the runway and launched one minute apart as the B-52s waited on the hammerhead and at precisely 0900 aircraft 5069 initiated his roll, taking the active, fired his water and the "beginning of the end" was taking place. Aircraft 5079 and 5673 followed one minute apart on a still, windless, humid, on the way to 92-degree, summer day, filling the runway environment with thick, black smoke from the water injection takeoff.

All cameras were blazing as the flawless departure of three sleek black birds left the ground. The launch drew praise from all, but there was an empty feeling of remorse from those assembled to watch the departing aircraft as the engine exhaust emitted a trail of recognition of the airborne Buffs. Major Barngrover would wait for another day for a scheduled departure as he cut his engines in his designated parking slot. The pause between cells was short as maintenance trucks went back to the revetments where the next three aircraft and spare were getting ready to start engines.

I drove with Colonel Dennis O'Brien, the deputy commander for operations (DCO), back to the parking area as we exchanged memories of time spent flying the B-52 during the many operations we had been involved in. We both agreed it was an event that we would remember as significant in our memories of the Vietnam War. As we approached the sandbagged revetments, we could see that the three primary birds and the spare were locked up and ready for engine start time. Power units were drowning out our conversation as we took in the whine of the engines being started by the soon to be departing aircraft. All seemed well, until we heard a call from Captain Miller in aircraft 5086. He was having a malfunction of his number one hydraulic pack, which was a major malfunction. Unless maintenance could solve the problem, the manned spare Captain Johnson would go as number three in the cell and Captain Stanicar would be the lead. Other than 5086, all other aircraft were in the "Green". At taxi time, 5086 had shut down engines and we officially decided to go with Captain Johnson and the spare aircraft 6663.

After a long pause I raced back to catch the exit from the revetments for the aircraft leaving at 1000 hours. I noticed that the flower garlands were in place and all seemed ready to go, however most of the news media and Embassy personnel had departed, with a few cameras left to get more departure photos.

After the launch of the two supporting tankers the three in condition to launch aircraft, taxied to the pre-takeoff position, followed by a group of maintenance trucks and my vehicle. Again, as takeoff time approached, engines were brought up to the stop and Captain Stanicar, as lead aircraft, took the active, fired his water and was followed at one-minute intervals by the other two aircraft. The runway was hardly visible from the ensuing black smoke. The absence of any wind only allowed the black cloud to settle, masking any sight of the departing aircraft from our present position impossible, so we drove down the ramp to the departing end to see the three aircraft joining up over the Gulf of Thailand.

We thought the day's effort was over, until we got a call from Captain Sheffler in aircraft 5073 informing us that he had zero oil pressure on number five engine and was shutting it down. I told the command post to have him terminate his flight to Anderson and return to base (RTB), (U-Tapao) and land as soon as fuel burn-off permitted him to land at his max gross weight. We now had two aircraft that would have to be rescheduled for their exit to Guam. Captain Sheffler successfully landed two hours after his launch time. Later that day, maintenance informed me that both of the aircraft that aborted have been repaired and could be ready to leave on Day Two, June 7th. After talking to the crews it was decided that Captain Miller's aircraft, 5086, would launch as the number two aircraft in the first departing cell and Captain Sheffler would depart in 5073 in the second launch on Saturday at 1002 local, allowing the crew to get the required crew rest before departure.

Day two would follow a pattern similar to the launches on the first day, with the mentioned changes, except there would be no news media to bother me. I did invite Father Don, our base Chaplain to join me for the launch and he was delighted to be able to witness the event. Major Schnabel with the designated airborne commander, Major Myers on board, one of our B-52 planners in aircraft 6690 would lead, with Captain Miller as two and Captain Barngrover in aircraft 6696 as three and the addition, Captain Cartwright in 5090 as number four. Captain Wathen would be in the manned spare, aircraft 6687. Two tankers would again launch to support the departing aircraft and start their takeoff five minutes prior to the first B-52. The good padre sat in on the pre-takeoff briefings, saying later he was very impressed with the professional manner with which it was done. His curiosity was raised when the crews got together to discuss join-up procedures and the tanker rendezvous. They patiently answered all his questions. He was like a little boy in a toy store.

Day 2 dawned much like day 1 with no wind and high humidity. Engine start time for all four aircraft was right on schedule. Captain Schnabel led the four deploying hulks out from the revetment area. Four black beasts, doing the familiar taxi conga, not loaded for war, but with men who were happy to be going home. Imagine those over half a ton birds as they scuttled down the taxiway to their launch. "Send the beasts east" had been a familiar cry during my days on Guam when we hoped for some relief from the tedium of missions to Vietnam and recurring six-month tours flying those missions. These birds would be going east to home. The taxi was reminiscent of many I had seen before, however it seemed more symbolic as they wended their way to the end of the runway in full view of "Buddha Mountain". They were followed by the phalanx of support vehicles and were watched by many who had seen these launches before, most of whom realized the meaning of this group departure. The many B-52 maintenance troops who would soon have no role in Thailand were especially aware that this meant they would soon depart for home. As the black tails sped down the runway, systematically firing water as the power came to full throttle, there was a thrill of pride that seemed to emanate from the sound. It would be repeated in the 1000 local launch, but for some reason this departure had something that was indefinable. I couldn't pick it up, until I heard the tower sound out "Sawadee Buffs" on the radio. It was a term that had been on the front page of the flight schedule for this week and had been picked up in the Bangkok press headlines, actually using the term "Buff" when referring to the aircraft. On the inside of that flight schedule was a tribute to the role of Strategic Air Command and its crews. It read:

"A chapter, a glorious one, in the history of SAC ends with this final issue of a flying schedule which sees our "Beloved Buff" returning home----homeward bound, indeed. Never-the-less, let it be said in the chronology of military history that; we came, we saw and we performed the task which had to be done. And so, the dedication of so many of us who were involved in the Southeast Asian conflict can now be catalogued as an event within an era which saw our resolve rise to every task, every challenge and disregarding the dangers meet its goal.

To those of you flying home to your loved ones---fly safely. Those of us remaining, understand that our mission is paramount to secure the peace. To our enemies, whoever they may be, let us serve notice that the mailed fist of SAC shall and will prevail. With virtue we depart. Letting things be what they are, mount on clouds, ride on the sun and moon and wander at ease beyond the seas for SAC is there. Well Done."

As the last Buff rose above the stagnant black smoke disguising the runway you could taste the emotion of the day. I don't know why this launch brought about that feeling, but it was there and the memories flooded my consciousness---the visible SAMs on my first mission over Hanoi, the desperate breakaway from the target, after the release of our twenty seven 750 pound bombs, the relief I felt departing the lethal target area, the words I spoke to Steve Rissi the night before Day 1 of "Linebacker II, "one more mission Steve" and the clearing out of Randy Craddock's crew room, fingering his radar navigator, Major Poole's pipe after his crew was shot down. All later reported as KIA (killed in action).

This follow-on departure would be a standard three ship cell with the manned sub. Leading this fourth departure was Captain Weller in aircraft 5063, followed by Captain Davis in aircraft 5077 and following would be Captain Sheffler in 5073, the airborne abort from yesterday, whose loss of oil pressure on engine number five forced shutdown of that engine and his return to U-Tapao. The manned spare would be Captain Martin in aircraft 6697. Engine start and taxi was normal, no apparent problems with the aircraft and it might be appropriate to cite at this point that causes for abort would only be those which had an effect on flight safety, so some aircraft malfunctions that did not compromise safety were acceptable for flight, among these would be radar problems necessary for bombing and navigation as in-cell aircraft had the capability to be assisted in those matters to a destination by the gunner, using his "Gun-Laying" radar (this procedure was called "bonus deal) and other aircraft in the cell as well as in visual sightings by the pilots. The taxi to the end of now smoke cleared runway was much the same and with a short pause on the hammerhead the lead aircraft started his takeoff roll, followed closely by the other two aircraft. A light breeze had stirred the water-firing smoke to dissipate so it would be possible to see the three aircraft for their climbing join-up. Captain Martin did not leave the revetment area and shut his engines down as the last aircraft left the runway on its climb out. Takeoff commenced promptly at 1000 hours. There had been no change in the weather, except the temperature had risen a couple of degrees and the humidity was now out of sight and despite the air-conditioning in the car, the open windows had already induced sweat coming out of my hat. That gentle wind had come upon the scene which now gave a slight cross wind of sorts and allowed forward visibility to be much improved as it cleared the smoke from the aircraft to waft to the west in the direction of Buddha Mountain. Visual following of the three departures was now possible allowing you to see the lead aircraft starting a gentle turn to the left and the other two trailers to join up as they climbed to the south. On one of these three aircraft, one of my constant golf partners, Major Karl Kaufman had departed. Pat Richmond and I would have to find more willing golfers for our visits to the Admiral's course!

There now remained only four B-52s in Southeast Asia and they would leave tomorrow. I returned to the command section, only to find Manas Manat sitting and chatting with Billie. He stood as I entered and asked if he could spend a moment with me and I said sure. There was no clear message except that he was inquiring about the health of my family. In the process, it was clear he had more than a casual knowledge of each of my children and of Rosemary. It was not offensive, but it was puzzling! The meeting was short and as he wandered out to the outer office, I followed and asked Billie where he got the information. She pleaded ignorance. I was very perplexed about this man, but there would be more that would add to my confusion as my tour grew in length.

It was Saturday and I shooed Captain Michaels and Billie out of the office, told them to go home and decided I would look up the new interim base commander, Bob Janka, and see if he would like a tennis match. After calling his office, it was apparent he was hoping for someone to take him to task and said he would meet me on the court in fifteen minutes. He must have already been dressed and I told him to make it thirty as I had to go back to my quarters to change. Arriving at the empty court I found "LBJ" stretching and swinging his racket. He had on a crinkled floppy hat and was wearing a "real" tennis outfit, red and white stripes on his collared shirt. I was wearing my normal gym shorts but did have a nice white floppy hat. We played three sets, despite the heat and humidity. He had told me previously he frequently played tennis and he was a good opponent. I had indicated my desire to play handball, however he said he only played the one sport, that being tennis, but could do paddleball if I wanted. That was not my sport, but I had played and could take it up to accommodate him.

I had found a wide cadre of handball players, most of them not very good, but a couple were very familiar with the game and made for a good match. I had a history of playing handball throughout my Air Force career. I picked it up with the three wall courts at Laredo AFB during pilot training and it continued at every base I was stationed. It reached a high point while at Bunker Hill AFB, playing against my two greatest adversaries and two best friends, Jack Lee and Ed Collier. We played while on alert and off alert. We played all the time. It became the nature of our being when not flying. The competitive nature of the three of us was always good for friendly needling and great games and matches. All it took was a phone call or a casual challenge. The courts at Bunker Hill were first class and had a gallery for viewing. When there was a match going on involving the three of us, either a cutthroat or one-on one there was always a huge viewing group watching, not only to see the game itself, but to hear the barbs and comments among the participants. Playing handball at U-Tapao was very different and truly an adventure. They were excellent courts, totally enclosed and because of that, very hot and sweat promoting.

After a single game you had to take a break to get some fresh air and if you can believe it to cool down in the above ninety- degree weather outside the court. The temperature in the court had to rise twenty degrees as you played. There was no air-conditioning, nor any way for the heat to dissipate except to open the door to the court that even I, at five foot six, had to bend down to exit. A match of three games needed to be completed only with breaks and large doses of water to prevent complete dehydration. And of course, after the match a trip to the Officer's Club or to my refrigerator for a beer or two was in order.

After the tennis match, I was told by my opponent that he was being replaced on a permanent basis in a couple of weeks and would return up-country to his OV-10 outfit, so we better get in some more games quickly. I said that was a doable thing and returned to my trailer to find my newly washed and dried clothes neatly folded on my bed. Lum thien sensing my need also set out a fresh towel for my shower. Forsaking an immediate shower, I opened a can of beer and ventured back outside to catch some sun and watch the grass grow. I was not that tired but felt the need to just sit and reflect. Tomorrow would be the last day for the redeployment and would see the departure of the rest of the B-52 crews and their staff, some of the senior permanent staff, Al Merril and John Thigpen, my intelligence guru and the DCM (deputy commander for maintenance) who I had become good friends with these last two months. I had attended a "Sawadee" party for them last night and it turned out to be a night of happiness, but also of sorrow. You never know in this business if you will ever see your friends again as we travel in different circles. I was very sad to see them go but knew their time had come and they were looking forward to going home to their families and the move to a new permanent duty station. The day was not done though as I would join Jim McGrath, the 3rd AD Director of Operations, here on a visit from Guam (shopping tour) for a dinner after Mass and return early to get some shuteye before the 0400 briefing on the last day, a Sunday, of the B-52 in Southeast Asia.

THE FINAL DAY FOR THE BUFF

The first B-52s arrived at U-Tapao in April, 1967 and flew the first combat missions the next day. Now on my Day 46 since I left home, June 8, 1975, the last B-52s would depart this historic base. The bedside phone rang at 0300, no time to do anything but get to the first briefing. I wanted to be early to the pre-takeoff briefing as I wanted to remind these last four crews and the additional staff members riding this last wave home of what they were closing. It was the last chapter of B-52 involvement in the Vietnam era. Most, if not all of them, had taken part in "Arc Light, Bulletshot, Linebacker I or II" or any other name applied to the effort. Now it would be Sawadee, the final farewell and I want them to get the impact of this flight. Walking out of my "hootch", (it was really just a trailer on a blocked foundation), into the dark morning I was caught up with the still surroundings. It was probably around 75 degrees, no wind at all and the quiet surroundings seemed to envelop me. I paused long enough to grab a banana off my tree, opened the gate and then my car door. Stepping into the car I turned on my communication system and called the command post. I asked for a maintenance update on the four departing aircraft and was told they were all in the green. Satisfied I traveled the five-minute time it took to get to "Bomber Operations" and found Dennis waiting outside along with some of the departing staff members going home. The 0400 hour first briefing started normally, but there was an air of anxiety among the crews The two Tanker crews were lamenting with the B-52 crews about the fact that after taking care of those aircraft going home, they would have to return to UT to continue the role they play. It is a fact that the withdrawl of al the F-111 squadrons from SEA will begin next Saturday and ten to twelve of our KC-135s will be tasked to support their departure. It was also obvious that these B-52 crews didn't need any pep talk about the importance of their flight out of Thailand. I told them I didn't want to keep them long and imparted to them my feelings about this last flight. Bomber Operations was a sea of excitement as the briefing ended and they were obviously excited to be leaving for their journey home. The bus loading outside in the dark morning was reminiscent of other times and a more somber atmosphere.

Inwardly, I was very proud that I was the guy in charge, thanks to Wayne leaving station. Some of these last crews had been in my squadron on Guam and two of them from my squadron at Mather, my last duty station, and I felt the bond between us. I wished them a safe flight home and then asked the aircraft commanders to hold up a minute. I told all four of the ACs (Aircraft Commanders) that after departure to circle around and that I expected a fly over the runway at a safe level above it, fifty feet would do. I grabbed Major Bob Kogel, a long time Instructor Pilot (IP), and told him that after he was airborne I wanted him to take his aircraft

5104 on a 180 after takeoff, parallel to the runway, establish a long final, accelerate and make a low, high speed pass over the runway. "Keep it low, but safe" I told him. He nodded smugly and with a smile, departed the room while talking to the other three pilots. I had told Denis O'Brien what I was going to do, and the word had gotten out that there would be a low pass on departure.

Now the B-52 "D" model is not a "clean" aircraft as it has an array of Electronic Countermeasure probes, extending from the lower underside of the fuselage that must be taken into consideration when flying close to the ground. It would be much like having the gear partially extended, something I never considered, but Denis reminded me as we watched start engines at 0820. For a moment I thought I should remind Major Kogel, but thought he was an IP and would know enough to consider those extended paddle-like probes. Again, it was a perfect flying day, despite the almost always threat of rain. It was hot and humid as usual and a nice soft crosswind for takeoff, which would insure the water burn-off would not impede the viewing of the departing aircraft, nor of the low pass, that would take place after all four aircraft had departed. I left the crews at the now loaded busses to ride the ramp and was amazed to see that the activity level surpassed anything I had seen since Guam Linebacker launches. It was unbelievable as the entire 125-man bomber branch Organizational Maintenance Squadron (OMS), plus almost every specialist from the Avionics Maintenance Squadron (AMS) and the Field Maintenance Squadron (FMS) were on the line. I counted forty-two trucks surrounding the four lonely black tails in the gray dawn giving the appearance of a spooky line of empty revetments. The crew chiefs were a classic example of Nervous Nellies, walking round and round their aircraft, anxiously awaiting their crews. Again, the garlands were on the nose of each buff and something different was the written on the tall black tail of each aircraft. They worked all night and still took the time to write departing messages on their aircraft. I've never seen so many cameras!

The crews arrived on their busses, walking to their aircraft, resplendent in scarves, jungle hats with appropriate sayings embroidered on them and began to take care of business. There were a lot of handshakes and many tears and finally "load up". As the launch time got nearer, some of the trucks departed the area to go to the beach to watch and take pictures from there. The rain held off and the ceiling would be scattered, but good visibility for the launch and the flyovers.

Engine start was normal and the taxi of the "Lumbering Elephants" took place. It was beautiful as the four left the UT revetments for the last time. All four ships moved to the hammerhead and prepared for takeoff. A minor problem arose with Ball 15, the number three aircraft. He informed control he had a low Hydraulic Pack. The hatch was opened, and maintenance went aboard. After a short period of time maintenance departed the aircraft, the hatch was closed, and all was in the green. It seemed like an hour before everyone was ready to roll, but it was my internal jitters taking over. You could almost hear the cameras buzz and click.

Major Lacklen's aircraft 6596 took the runway on time followed by Major Walther in aircraft 6687 and then by Captain Martin in aircraft 6697 and finally Major Koegl in 5104. The garlands were flying off the blunt nose of each aircraft, the chalk marks on the tails telling a love story and four gorgeous birds leaving the ground. As Major Koegl lifted off I caught all the aircraft turning in trail back toward the base. They never got more than a couple of hundred feet off the turf; I lost sight of them on their extended downwind as they fell behind objects and buildings on the base. I sighted the smoke from the engines of the entrail aircraft as they turned back toward the runway a good distance out and then stopped their turn as they lined up on the runway.

There were no obstructions on the approach end of the runway, so they were very visible as they approached. The first two came in tucked together in a loose formation at about two hundred feet, blazing over the runway. Two five-hundred-thousand-pound aircraft passed by us, looking like they could dance in the sky, lilting ever so graceful as they fled toward the Bay. Wild cheers could be heard from the large assembly of 307th maintenance and operations troops, even with the engines accelerating. Number three followed a bit higher but still an impressive show for the Big Ugly Fat Fella. I got on the horn to Kegel in Ball 16 and said, "bring it down, but do it right and give them a show". He was a pilot who had over three-thousand hours in the aircraft and he was someone I could trust. He had extended his downwind to separate from the first three aircraft. He was slowly inching it down, getting lower and lower as he hit the approach end of the runway. I was located about a thousand feet down the runway, standing outside my vehicle with OB. As he crossed the threshold of the runway, he was approximately ten feet above the runway. I caught a glimpse of the extending probes as he passed my position and could see a minimal space above the surface as he passed. The applause, honking horns and wild cheering was deafening. I had my microphone in hand and was about to say something, but all that would come out was a proud "Good Show", as he climbed to a hundred feet and started waggling his wings in a final "Sawadee" over the gulf. I'm sure those on the beach were ducking for cover. It was a stirring demonstration of airmanship! I said again, "Good Show", which he acknowledged with a "thank you" and a verbal "Sawadee" to anyone monitoring the tower frequency. I watched with my 20-20 vision until I couldn't see any trace of the last flight of Buffs from U-Tapao and finally stepped back into my car, listening on the tower channel to see if there were any last words from them, knowing they had already switched to departure control by now. O'B and I were still on a pink cloud and talking about the pass over the runway by Major Kogel. Of course, the aircraft, in our memory, as-long-as we talked, got closer and closer to the deck. A series of blown-up pictures later showed he had more than sufficient clearance above ground as he passed our position, all eight engines probably at 100 per cent and an accelerating airspeed.

All the bomber branch vehicles picked up the remaining people now ready to leave and were wending their way back to their now empty revetments. It was hard to believe in reading the extended history of the base that at one time, as many as seventy-four Ds had been there, a total of 67,038 sorties were flown from UT, dropping over two-million tons of bombs and 340 tons of that total had been used during "Linebacker II". Seven didn't return and two others were lost to hostile fire, one prior to Linebacker II and one after, in January 1973.

Charlie Tower was being vacated for the last time by "Bomber Charlie", LT. Colonel John Yaryan. Scars of previous sapper attacks were apparent in one of the revetments. History had been well served and I was honored to be a part of it as the commander of the last launch. It was a trick of fate that the Vice Commander of 3rd Air Division at the time and the one I reported our successful launch to was BG Robert H. Gaughn, my first squadron commander in the Air Force.

139

Day 46 was far from over! A beer party was being held in the J-9 revetment with speeches and kudos given to one and all. One of the crew chiefs, Staff Sergeant Bailey was given the water bucket treatment as his was the only aircraft that resulted in a delay in all the launches. Denis and I paid our respects to their great accomplishment, drank a beer and went to the next gathering in the AMS hanger. Of course, their specialties were no longer needed as there are no fire control Bomb-Nav or ECM systems in the KC-135. They had a rip-roaring party that saw everyone of any authority was summarily thrown into the beer cooler, which is a twelve-foot long engine case, three and a-half-feet deep, filled with beer and of course---ice. I was no exception and I was the big event, so they did it with great flourish. I tried to keep my shoes dry, however realized I had to step out of the deep case in order to exit. It was refreshing and again, having supplied them with some entertainment, OB and I left to dry off and find other pursuits. I remembered I had a tennis date with Bob Janka at 1300 hours and it was now well past noon. It did occur to me that the Director of Maintenance, had not gone to the AMS bash and left the flight line before the dunking of O'Brian and Dugard and missed out on that treat, so called him and Bob Janka and told them there was trouble and they should respond immediately to the AMS hanger. They did and as they arrived individually and opened the door it was "Whoosh" and into the icy engine case. At least they were in civilian clothes. Never did get in the tennis match that day. Needless to say, I am awaiting their revenge, which I'm sure will come at some future date.

After their dunking Colonel O'Brien and I went by the base post office, which of course was closed for business on Sunday, but access to our mail-boxes was easily attained, so we wandered over to see if anything had fallen into them. I hadn't stopped by yesterday, so hopefully I would be rewarded for my optimism. I could see through the pane and saw I had a letter, so opened the box to find a letter from Rosemary. I still couldn't get used to the address, 2416 Stonehaven, Sacramento. I had spent so little time there before departing and leaving for this assignment that I was still looking for the address I had living on base. At any rate, she said the front yard now had grass and the bushes I had planted in the back yard had survived and were now growing, then came the blockbuster as she wrote that my friend from Mather, Howard O'Neill, the Mather Base

Commander, had a new assignment and guess what? He was going to be the new base commander at U-Tapao. Strange things happen and this was the top of the pile. Mather was a Training Command Base and SAC was the tenet, so I knew Howard on a professional basis. He had been the base commander and as such worked for the training wing and although we were never close, we had become friendly through our wives as they were fast friends. We had some disagreements on some base functions, but never on an adversarial basis. Also, she related that Howard was moving his family right down the street from our new home. That was a good break as it would give Rosemary someone to talk to close by. I would tell Father Saulnier about Howard as he too was stationed at Mather as the former base chaplain and would certainly remember the cheerful colonel.

THE PADRE AND THE ELEPHANTS

One day in early June, Billie told me a local Catholic Priest wanted to talk to me. I told her to send him in and he shortly stood before me, dressed very casually in a hardly, priestly, Hawaiian shirt, a necessary move from the "Roman Collar" in the heat and humidity of Thailand. His name was Father Sweeney, a ruddy Irishman who looked very familiar, but I sloughed it off as I have seen a great many Irishmen and many priests who looked like him. He was an American who had lived in Thailand for many years, originally coming as a missionary and stayed to start an orphanage not too far from Pattya. It seems that he has used the base as a point of support for the orphanage for many years, counting on the generosity of the men and women stationed here. But his method of raising these funds was out of the ordinary as he would once a year bring a circus to the base and needed permission to do it again this year. He said that July 4th had been a standard date for the event and would like to do so then. He was very convincing, but I didn't need to be convinced as it sounded like a great way to pass the day. He indicated they had used an area on the base that was open so they could bring on the elephants, and I emphasize the plural as that was the main attraction, plus a few minor characters, such as an Ape and an aged tiger. He indicated our own "Mike" the gorilla was also used, but basically the attraction was complemented by the use of the military as "Carnival" men.

It sounded like fun and I told him we would not break such a long-time tradition and invited him to bring his group to the base for the July 4th celebration. I told him I would have no problem finding volunteers to help make it a great day. He stated that he would also bring many of the orphans with him. He said most of them were fathered by base personnel who left when their assignment had expired, never knowing that they had fathered a child. The children were then abandoned by the mother, most who were teenagers when they got pregnant, and had no way to support the baby. It seemed based on his story we owed him and those children a day of fun and adventure.

Many of the local merchants had supported this happening in the past and knew about the priest and his work in Thailand. Billie indicated that others on the base would support the setup for the arrival of the Padre and his elephants. She had made many friends on and off the base so was the perfect catalyst to get the ball rolling making a number of calls and set things in motion. Our maintenance section took on the responsibility to set up the many venues for entertainment. Many of the crates that were used for shipping material into the base now became wood for the structures that would become stands for native wares and food. One such setup was for a dunking type of contest. With an individual sitting on a pedestal over a large pool of water a direct hit on a target would send that individual into the drink. I was one of a large number of volunteers, who would be on that pedestal and suffer the fate of a direct hit. It became a major event as when you are on a remote tour away from family these types of diversions are a God send. Despite the long hours supporting the mission there is little to do in our free time and so enlisted and officer alike became involved in the creation of the carnival at hand. There were stands already made that the good father sent in along with an elephant and a handler to move material from point to point. The elephant was a wonder to watch as he would pick up a long plank and the handler would direct it to a spot where he would drop it into a usable spot. The maintenance squadrons supplied most of the construction gang and really enjoyed doing it. It was a place where activity was constant as when individuals had some free time they would go to this area and work on something that needed to be done. It rose seemingly overnight into a very credible and finished event location. It now awaited the big day.

POST BUFF DEPARTURE ACTIONS

Life would go on, but the departing freedom birds was taking away many of the close friends I had here and now I had to pick up the pieces and press on. I am kept busy with Medal recommendations for those involved in the Mayaguez incident and Officer Effectiveness Reports (OER) on those departing, some with barely their six months in country. I'm a bit envious but realize it is the nature of the beast. Our monthly "Sawadee" party was last night and we all wore party suits, made in Thailand of course. Mine is blue and it has butterflies on the shoulders for rank and is replete with patches, foremost is my "Buff River Rats" and B-58 patches. It was the biggest event by far since my coming to UT, and also it came with the introduction of a new arrival. Father Saulnier introduced Lieutenant Colonel Hill, the new Catholic priest. Father Don has been the sole chaplain for a good while and could use a break. Strange that we are getting an added chaplain and are losing a large contingent of airmen including our tanker skilled specialists, with no programmed replacements.

Other spigots of news find Wayne returning on Wednesday, day 49, the same day that Colonel McGrath, our Maintenance Commander leaves. We will be down to three 0-6s (Colonels), once Wayne lands. I expect we will have other personnel moves soon. Wayne did come in on a tanker on Wednesday and true to form, once he was on the ground back in UT, took command sort of and divulged that he will leave as soon as his six months are up which is early August.

Message traffic is picking up on the external threats to the base. In addition, the Thai government is getting restless over the possibility of our leaving as they will be without any external security. The menacing gestures from neighboring countries, especially Laos and Vietnam and the Communist incursions from Malaysia have everyone in Bangkok a bit nervous. JUSMAAG and General Aderholt have sent a series of highly classified messages indicating the need for us to beef up base security and to brief our airmen to be vigilant when leaving the base for entertainment. The political structure is a mess, as the civilian leaders are like a weathervane, one minute they want us here and then they want us gone. It is apparent we will be totally gone in the next few months and they worry about the consequences of our leaving and the void it could create. On the other hand, they are aware of the saber rattling of their aggressive neighbors and their threats. Specifically, we are to be prepared for protestors from students and the labor unions as they are dominant factors in the internal problems facing Thailand, both being communist inspired. They disrupt everything, appealing to the emotionalism of the people, and stir them to the point of chaos (not the farmers or the people in the country as most of them could care less). The civilian government Has long depended on the United States and its presence to thwart potential problems. Now they are in a quandary as they stymie the logical chain of events and due to civilian leadership inaction, have now stirred the military, which is very pro-American. The military leaders have told the civilian leaders to get things under control or they will take over. A coup could happen at any time!

The United States plan for the removal of forces will go as planned and could even accelerate due to the instability of the government. We are a Strategic Wing without bombers, but we have a mighty force of tankers. A build-up of the force has been in process and we now have twenty-seven in place now to support the F-111 wing exit this next Saturday.

To add to the distrust that permeated the air there were a series of local incidents going on that had the local and some government sources wary of the presence of the remaining US military. I was asked for an interview by a reporter from a Bangkok newspaper about our remaining Tanker aircraft. I had met him the day of the B-52 exit. Our contingent of tankers had always been fifteen but due to the need to support the with drawl of the F-111s and later, other fighter groups at U-Dorn, Korat and Nakom Phenom as I indicated we had been building that total, adding twelve tankers. It was a touchy subject and I had been told by the U.S. Embassy officials not to discuss numbers. However, during the interview and confronted with a direct question about that number I told the reporter that we had brought in the new double-tailed tanker aircraft. Reports had reached this reporter and others that we had more than the fifteen we were supposed to have on station. They could count the tails sticking up from the surrounding roads and were recording a number beyond our supposed total of fifteen. I was a bit surprised, but that really seemed to satisfy him, and he departed after a lengthy time in my office discussing any and all topics about the base. The next day there was an article on the front page of his paper, with a picture, showing the tails of the parked tankers, obviously taken from a distance and the headline talked about the new double-tailed tanker on the base. Incredibly, I did not receive one phone call from any source, including the JUSMAG or the Embassy. Even Wayne thought I pulled a fast one, even though his ego was a bit damaged as he was not asked to participate in the interview. Maybe the powers to be were as astounded that someone would believe that story as I was.

Wayne indicated later that I appeared on national television in my role as the person in charge in the departure of the B-52s. He now feels left out and regrets his long absence, missing events of a national nature and I can feel a sense of resentment on his part, as I have carved out a niche with the operational personnel on base. He stayed in the background from his return until his departure, spending most of his time in the office and letting Denis and I take care all the operational activity.

Saturday, Day 53, was the day of the departure of the first group of F-111s from U-Dorn. The first briefing was to be at 0200 hours, followed by one at 0400 hours. It was a miserable morning, raining, hard at times with a strong wind down the runway. There would be two cells of tankers and they would escort the first group of F-111s to Guam and then return to UT tomorrow. These early briefings for the ten tanker crews involved in supporting this event would be an indicator of things to come. It was going to be a busy time for the next few weeks as the end of the Buff era was just the tip of the iceberg in this exit of our forces from Southeast Asia. The early launches were made on time despite the weather and the first refueling rendezvous with the swing-wing F-111 flights were accomplished without a problem according to a report from the lead tanker aircraft.

No sooner than they left the ground we received an OPREP (operation report) tasking us with support for a flight of F-4s going to Clark AFB in the Philippines tomorrow, Day 54. I called Tanker operations and told them to set up a launch of four tankers for this drag. Two of the tankers would then take the F-4s to Kunsan, Korea. I decided that would be a good day to take a flight and complete my checkout in the tanker, but flying on one of the two returning to UT. I put in another call to the tanker scheduler and found that Major Jerry Reese, the Instructor Pilot (IP) I had been flying with, was on the schedule for tomorrow and asked them to put me on board. They were happy to do so.

The 0400 briefing for the second launch for the F-111s went off without a hitch and the weather had not improved enough to launch on time. It was still very marginal but the tankers in flawless fashion taxied to the end of the runway and waited. It would turn out that the last cell was delayed until 0820 as the ceiling dropped to less than 100 feet. They managed to get off when the ceiling lifted long enough for them to get off the ground. They disappeared into the low clouds almost at the same time as the gear went in the well. If they had been delayed any longer the mission would have had to be cancelled as the F-111s had launched and were already waiting for their first "top-off". A return to base (RTB) for those aircraft had already been discussed by both of our operation staff. Hopefully things would get better. Recovery tomorrow would be difficult if the weather does not improve. We were short on diversion bases, so I may have to spend the night at Clark AFB in the Philippines.

Sunday, Day 58, Flying different aircraft would seem to many who have not experienced controlling an aircraft in flight to be a problem, but it is much the same. You must adapt to the characteristics of the aircraft. The tanker was a bit more responsive in flight than the B-52 and takeoff and landings were much the same with rotation being the difference. The checkout was different due to being on the front end of "passing gas". Instead of gaining gross weight, you lose it. I was able to complete my checkout on this add-on "drag" and it also give me an opportunity to be at the controls when the flight of three F-4s were individually on the boom getting their programmed offload. After the disconnect on the last fighter we turned around and returned to UT. I had to complete pattern activity and perform a landing, plus a missed approach and then a full stop landing. All the work was accomplished during some heavy rain and a slight cross wind on final. I will admit I did not have a dry flight suit when finished. Once back on the ground Wayne picked me up at the aircraft and while driving off the ramp greeted me with yet another support frag, with a drag now scheduled for tomorrow, supporting F-4s and A-7s, some going and some coming in. The tanker pilots will not complain about getting flying time. Zowie--- Rain, rain and more rain, was forecast for the next few days!

The following day's drag was to be just one of a series of movements that our tanker crews would be involved in during the upcoming weeks. Interesting was the fact that many of the movements were to units in Korea and Australia, which made for some weird planning. The first week of preparation for the next series of launches, more F-111s and F-4s, was difficult as the tankers had both "boom" and drogue refueling to accomplish. What was most significant was we were very short of mission planning qualified personnel and our tanker maintenance troops were very thin. Destinations were as close as the Philippines and as far away as back to Guam. In most cases the tankers would recover at the location they were taking the fighters to and return the next day. The overlap in missions had a debilitating effect on the crew-rest requirements for individual crews. We were not limited by aircraft, but we were stretching crews to the limit. We managed by working the initial refueling by the launching aircraft and having them return to UT. The second refueling was performed by a returning tanker. This would work for destinations like Clark in the Philippines or to Kadena in Okinawa, but not to Guam or other longer "drag' destinations. To make matters worse the monsoon season was upon us and weather conditions were not helping.

I also learned that the OV-10s might disgorge from the country as someone realized close air support is the last thing needed now. The OVs however would not need tanker support. The next series of retreats (which really is the name of this exercise) will take place next Sunday. We are seriously short of qualified planners, due to the disgorging of personnel at an alarming rate. Wayne has his departure date of August 10, which may be a good thing as he has become very distant from the staff, passing down tasks for others to do. He also informed me he is going TDY to Kadena AB for some reason, so I better get in a golf game with OB and Pat Richmond soon. I have had some difficulty with a pinched nerve (at least that was the diagnosis) in my neck which hampers tennis but doesn't seem to bother my golf swing. Strange! Sunday, Day 60, turned out to be the worst of days;

rained all night, very soggy pre-takeoff briefings and I believe I sense a fatigue factor setting in for the planning staff as well as the crews.

The weather report for the first refueling area was not good, but doable, as we all have managed in the worst kinds of weather to pull it off. The crews would use their radar to complete the rendezvous if needed and then find the fighters and latch on. But, as fate would have it the tanker lead aircraft in the first cell screwed up the rendezvous. Two of the fighters aborted and had to jettison their empty fuel tanks; both declared an emergency and landed here at UT almost out of gas. The second cell was even worse. They lost forty-six minutes in the rendezvous and almost lost total control of the situation before ultimately diverting to Clark in the Philippines without getting clearance and almost out of fuel. Some really, bad decisions were made, both from operations on the ground and from pilots in the air. Thankfully, all ended without the loss of aircraft or personnel. I had a long talk with OB about the decisions that were made, and we resolved the problems before we met with Wayne, who is leaving for Kadena today. He could become a bit irrational these days but was not in a mood to discuss the problem and felt all's well that ends well. We are woefully short of qualified officers who are knowledgeable in Tanker-Fighter operations and are working our three to four good men to the nub. No complaining though; just visible fatigue. The HHQ people were attempting to withdraw more of our qualified people along with some of our tanker crews, until I called the 3rd Air Division and pointed out our needs and the fact that there are continuing frags for the withdrawal of units up country going on. We need the tankers, crew and staff to remain at least stable until the drawdown ends. Finally, they were convinced of our needs and reluctantly let us keep our aircraft and crews, without divulging it to any higher level. The Embassy had already announced the with-drawl of twelve tankers and are very "mum and glum" over the sustained status. I haven't received any requests for interviews so hopefully we can go on with our business without any other distractions.

Day 65 and 66 were days of changes as Little Bobby Janka left for his flying job as the commander of OV-10 wing (He can lead them home!). I will miss LBJ as he was easy to talk to and provided me with some semblance of an avenue to the PACAF world. Howard O'Neill arrived the next day and officially took command of the CSG and seems ready to roll.

He has inherited a bucket of worms as thefts are on the rise on base and incidents are increasing off base. Captain Lee Steininger, the wing executive officer and a master parachutist was leaving our command section and I would miss him in the court, a good competitor in handball, as well as in the office. He was a great athlete. He would be replaced by the newly promoted Captain Michael who seems well qualified to take up the task, a very busy one. We also lost our wing personnel officer, Captain Charlie Zulpher, who would not be replaced. On one of the tankers coming back from Guam Lieutenant Colonel Jose Stuntz arrived. He will bolster our maintenance as the Assistant Deputy Commander for Maintenance.

There was a brief lull in activity, giving us time to catch up on some needed crew rest time and to clear up some of the delayed discrepancies on the aircraft. With that stability is something we are not used to and won't see much of anytime soon. Word has come down for heavy activity as preparation begins for another launch to support what we perceive as the biggest "drag" we've had. There will be three massive cells and it will require all our tankers to support the mission. We had a all crew briefing the day before all our activity was to begin. I talked about the need for "Air Discipline" and reminded the crews of the previous problems two weeks ago and the communication errors that were made. I also reminded them that it was better to abort a mission if marginal conditions existed than to push the limits to the extent that we have a bent aircraft.

Day 75 would be an early start with a 0300 hours crew briefing. The forecast weather was perfect, and you just knew it was going to be a successful one. The rain had abated as we had about three inches the last two days. The sun came up in a cloudless sky and the engine start for each cell was without incident. All three cells launched on time in textbook fashion. They subsequently delivered the fighters who joined a cell of tankers out of Kadena over the Philippines for the remainder of the flight to Guam. Our tankers landed at Clark for refueling and are programmed to return to UT later tonight for missions tomorrow. We will turn the aircraft around and see if we find fresh crews in the air for those missions.

Our maintenance personnel are working by rote, the operation planners are groggy from the constant frag orders coming down from above and our crews are quickly wearing down and the requests were definitely pushing our crew-rest requirements. Where are all the fighters coming from? I had no idea of the extent of the numbers of aircraft stationed in Thailand during the war in Vietnam. Surely there has to be an end to this! The final surge for at least the present, came the next day. After recovering our tanker fleet last night, crews who had met their crew-rest requirements were put back in the air to support a group of fighters out of Korat being sent to Korea. It was forecast to be the last major drag for at least a week or two. It was sort of an interesting period of time after that last major drag, as the withdrawl of the fighters halted to the extent that they were no longer a major part of our flying time. Most of our active support was for in-country fighters still flying training missions. We were very active and my time in the tanker was growing as I was able to get in the air at least once a week, flying short sorties hone my feel for flying the KC-135.

DAY 72 THE FOURTH OF JULY

The day started with a bang! I had heard what I thought was the daily, 0615 launch of the U bird, but moments later I was called and told by the command post that the U-2 had aborted his takeoff and ran off the end of the runway. As the president of the base accident board (a position the vice wing commander traditionally fills) I proceeded to the scene. He had come to a halt about five feet short of the runway lead-in lights stanchions on the end of the runway. There was not too much apparent damage, but it would be a logistical problem to get it back to the U-2 area. After some discussion, an OMS Chief told me it would be done before noon. Knowing he meant what he said, I left it in his hands. Fortunately, it was a stand-down day and there would be no interference of our flying operation. At noon I found out the U-2 was in the hanger and undergoing repairs. A mechanical problem had been cited as the cause of abort. It would be a short accident board! Other important things were on the docket for today as the long-awaited arrival of our circus participants were ushered through the front gate, eleven elephants. Kept outside of the gate were a large number of "students" demanding we leave the country.

It turned out we had a grand Fourth of July Celebration, despite the U-2 dump and the fact we were in the midst of student demonstrations, surrounding the base and occurring at the base gate. At 0800 hours, the carnival began with the parade of elephants onto the base, eleven in all. It was the beginning of different performances by them and their stunts continued the entire day. They were more than entertaining and wowed the assemblage and performed to raucous applause by the crowd of people, both US and Thai military and some selected friends who Billie had hit up for donations. To quote Father Saulnier about the elephants, "They do whatever they do better than anyone else can". Elephant rides were plentiful along with free food, Thai food was in evidence, as were many of the Thai military indulging themselves, including a certain Captain Vichit, but there was also a hot dog stand which served buffalo burgers and French-fries in addition to hot dogs, thanks to our food service squadron.

There were many game booths and all in all an old fashion state fair atmosphere right here on the gulf of Thailand. The center piece was the dunking spot! Of course, it was a hot and humid day, but it did not deter the crowd who took great pleasure in unseating the command section and others from the perch into the pool of water below. There was a too-large target that when hit by a thrown ball, that released the mechanism and the sitter would be dunked. Four balls for a quarter. I noted that the staff took steady aim at the target when I sat on the perch, dropping me into the cool water below. Billie was especially deadly, and she would shriek each time she hit the target and continued while I was falling. I was successful in dropping Wayne into the pond a couple of times before I took my dunking turn. The water was very refreshing, cooling me off, but after a time, others took my place, even the temporary duty TDY tanker commander took a turn. We couldn't convince Vichit to take a turn.

There were the usual races pitting one squadron against another, obstacle courses, a punt- pass-and kick contest and a race from the beach to the entrance of the event in which I ran. It did turn out to be a contest with everyone involved having a good time. There were tug of wars between squadrons with the winning squadron getting a case of San Miguel beer. The ending tug of war involved fifty husky men on one end of the rope and a single elephant on the other. Needless to say the elephant won, despite two tries. It was never close as once the handler told the Elephant to back up the fifty on the other end had no chance. We even had a group of base guys jumping out of an airplane and repeating it again.

There were a number of orphans who came to the celebration and during the heat of the day they were escorted by some of the airmen to the gym where they could occupy themselves inside or rest on some of the cots that had been placed in there by the gym staff. They were all in a uniform shirt, so they were easily identifiable; some volunteered to work the stands, dispensing food and trinkets. There were places where you could donate to the orphanage and it was obvious that it was a giving atmosphere. It all ended well after sundown with fireworks fired from the beach. This was followed by a dinner for the staff and Father Sweeney, sponsored by the 0-6s. OB was absent as his mother had died and he had returned home for a brief emergency leave. Last seen at sundown was the sight of the eleven elephants, even more impressive as they left then when they arrived, trunk-to-tail wending, their way down the road. It was a happy and fun day; everyone was weary, but happy and the orphanage had succeeded in not only picking up needed funds to sustain their mission, but they provided us a respite from our work and a wonderful reminder of our national heritage.

THE THAI PEOPLE, THE WOMAN AND DAUGHTER FROM THE GIFT SHOP.

Lam Tien, Johnny Su and his wife Annie, were the only people I really had gotten to know that were natives of the country, but I soon became more aware of others as I grew accustomed to the base and its surroundings. I had picked up a few words in Thai from Lamtien and the cab drivers who took our golf players to the course, but most of those I interfaced with spoke English to me. I don't mention Manas Manat at this juncture as I still categorize him as a mystery man. I had identified Captain Vichit, the Navy Commander as a person who I felt would take advantage of anything he could and of course Billie had set me on this path. Now after almost three months in-country and having acted often as the 307th wing commander due to Colonel Calhoun's continued absences, I was being invited to social affairs with the Thai military and other base operatives. Billie cautioned me about some of those I would meet as her experience in this area had armed her with a large dossier on common players I would see. The Thai military had many functions that demonstrated their penchant for partying, and all had three common ingredient--- food and dancing and women. The food was excellent if you avoided the choices that were harmful to your health. The dancing was very different, but fun. After a while nothing seemed to be embarrassing, even floating in circles, waving your arms or to bend at the waist as you addressed your male counterpart, as men seemed to be the principal ingredients in some of the dances. Billie told me I would need a party suit for some of the affairs I would attend. There was a tailor on base who created a two-piece blue flight suit with epaulets of colorful butterflies. This was very appropriate as the favorite dance at these events was that butterfly dance where grown men would dance in meandering paths waving their arms in what was called "the butterfly dance". These events were generally Thai Navy events for some country or military remembrance.

I made many excursions outside of the base on informative matters, checking the nature of the many small hamlets close to the base. I was always accompanied by someone who knew the territory and could speak the language. I became accustomed to the fact that if you wore any kind of uniform in Thailand, it was common that you had a long-barreled gun strapped to your waist. Most of the men were not tall, so the effect of this long-barreled gun seemed to be one of a "macho" nature as the gun seemed to go to the kneecap of the person wearing it. Many of those in uniform had no affiliation to a military or police outfit. Of course, my journeys outside of the base were never made with a weapon of any kind. If I ventured out with an Air Police escort, they would be carrying a gun. Going to the golf course was always a test of the day and the time and the circumstances, but I never had a problem. I always felt a little ill-at-ease on these trips and it was for good reason as it really was a country of opportunity, meaning that if you looked as if you could provide some form of livelihood, such as a camera, watch or if you looked like you had money, you were fair game. Someone would seize the opportunity!

There were instances where airmen would leave the base and never return, found dead in some alley and with his valuables gone. This would become very prevalent later in my time in-country. We also had a problem where the enlisted personnel would marry a local Thai girl and upon coming to the end of his tour, would meet an untimely end. The system was well known where if you marry a GI and he dies, you get all his death benefits, which in Thailand would give you a very comfortable life. Many of these marriages were for that reason only from the bride's family perspective, so coming to the end of a tour, the family of the bride would contract to have the husband murdered to gain these benefits. The local justice system was such that the individual hired was never identified or found and the family would now have a steady income through the widow.

There were many instances of robbery, resulting in the death of the victim, and justice, when meted, was swift. In one case close to me personally, it happened to a friend of mine, Captain Walt Ray, who I had been stationed with and played tennis and squash with. He was stationed up-country and I had seen him here just a couple of weeks before when he came down on some sort of business. He was very athletic and a good natured, professional officer. In his quarters at an up-country base late one night, he was awakened by someone in his room going through his pants pockets looking for his wallet. My awakened friend grappled with him and during the melee was stabbed to death. The thief escaped, taking Walt's wallet and watch, only to be found the next day in possession of the wallet he took. Before sunset that day the thief was hung in a public spot. Another similar incident happened before I arrived when a Lieutenant Colonel stationed at U-Tapao had gone down to Samsung to shop, bought expensive items at the local jewelry shop and upon leaving he was accosted by a thief who took the jewelry the colonel had just bought and when the colonel resisted, he was shot to death. The thief was quickly caught a short distance away with the jewels in his possession. Justice again was swift and at daybreak the next day he was executed, for all to witness, close to the spot he killed the colonel, executed by his own handgun. Yet, most of those I ran into outside the base were gracious and helpful despite language differences.

All of those conducting business on base spoke excellent English and were very friendly to all. One such woman ran a novelty-type store close to the 307th headquarters building. She was honest and her prices for her inventory were very fair when compared to those on similar stores in Bangkok. She also lived in "Pattya Beach", a resort area close to Bangkok. She offered Dennis and I, plus three other command post off-duty officers, a day at the beach near her home, which sounded like something we could do, so we took her up on the offer. Five of us traveled to her home, which was barely a block off the main strand of the beach. After arriving and changing into appropriate wear she led us to the beach, where we were met by a glass bottom boat with three smiling guys, wearing headbands and colorful shirts and shorts. We boarded this fairly, long boat and were taken to a small island. As we left the boat, we were set up with chairs and towels by two or three attendants, who then started to prepare a lunch for us over a fire, cooking delicious strips of fresh fish and some sea urchins. After a three-hour or so time on this seemingly, uninhabited island, as there were no other people in sight, we were taken back to the main beach area.

There was one small problem on the island as when we decided to go into the water, I stepped on a sea urchin, which promptly shot something into my foot. The pain was very harsh, until one of the attendants, succeeded in pulling the "spear" out of my foot. We were met once again by our benefactor, who provided us with some cold drinks for our trip back to the base. It was a very special gift from this kind woman. I frequented her establishment often to get a soft drink as it was close to the command center. I would often stop to talk with her and on one occasion her teen-aged daughter was there. When I was introduced to her I put my hand on her head, only to be greeted with distraught looks from both her and her mother. In the Buddhist religion the head is the most sacred part of the body. You can step on their toes, but don't touch their head. I apologized immediately and it was over, but it was a lesson learned.

Pattya was a favorite spot for the natives who could afford it as it was a sleepy area devoid of tourists, although anyone could see it was the beginning of being discovered by the tourist traffic. It had a good start and the restaurants situated there were of high caliber. The beach area was a long strand of sand, only interrupted by areas owned by charitable groups and as it turns out, one segment of beach was owned by the wife of Bill Gilmore, a B-58 pilot friend from Grissom AFB. They had married in Thailand and were now permanently living there. It was a very desirable location and was right next to the USO beach. I traveled there often as it was a (a scary) cab ride from the base, and it was amazing how it changed in the short period of my time in country. The beach areas which had been owned by the USO and my friend's wife sold their property while I was still in Thailand, and she then opened a restaurant off the beach. I visited it once and was impressed at the décor and the familiarity it had to pleasant American places to eat and have a cocktail. It appeared entrepreneurs were moving into the prime locations not designated as public beaches.

It was interesting to note that travel by vehicle out of the base was on two lane roads, where it was common to see elephants in trail going to and from areas where they were used for many tasks including the movement of recently cut trees. Although there were paved roads most of the roads in the U-T area were unpaved, dirt roads off the main two-lane roads, such as the one going to Pattya

The Thai navy personnel, other than Captain Vichit and a couple of the other Thai officers assigned to the base, were non-communicative and if they spoke English, they never attempted to engage in any language other than their native tongue in my presence. The Thai golf course was run by the Thai Navy and most of those working there did speak passable English. I did pick up some Thai words for good and bad shots from the caddies that I would hire each time I played as well as those who would get the attention of the players of an impending thing to avoid or warnings, such as what could be lurking in the surrounding jungle or what not to eat hanging from a bush or tree.

I did learn to never walk under an overhanging bush or tree as the tiny snake known as a Krait (sometimes spelled as Crate or referred to as a Habu in Okinawa) would often hang in trees waiting for some unsuspecting food source passing through, dropping from their perch and grabbing hold, knawing their poison into the victim. Krates did not have fangs and therefore had to grab a soft spot on your skin in order to penetrate and kill the victim. Once bitten by a Krate, there was no known recovery. They are relatively small, eighteen inches to two feet in length, ringed in changing green hue stripes around their bodies. They blend in with foliage and are very hard to see. I only saw two of that deadly, snake while in Thailand. The first was as a result of a frantic call from one of our security guards in the SSO. He was the mid-guard in the closed inward path to the secure area and was in a small opening before you would reach the door to the building. It had a desk and a wider section to allow one to pass through when cleared by the guard. A krate had entered through a small opening on the ground and was spotted by the guard who upon seeing it, climbed on the desk, calling for help. Another security guard entered and killed the snake with the butt of his rifle. Carrying it out for all of us to view who had heard the call. The second occasion happened during a softball game which we were having one very hot summer afternoon. We had standing softball league games every Sunday and often would get up such games on stand-down days between the operational permanent party and the temporary (TDY) crews. Sometimes it was maintenance versus ops, but on this day in one of the games, we were between innings when a newly arrived pilot who had been watching the game strolled to the dugout, (actually benches in the sun) and asked if he could play and we said "sure, go into right field the next inning". He grabbed a loose glove and trotted out and took his position and during the ensuing at bats was seen stamping his foot around as he moved from one spot to another. It should be noted he was wearing shorts and had running shoes on. When he came back at the end of the inning, we asked him what he was stomping on out there. He replied that it was a small snake, green in color. Without hesitation we ran out, bats in hand, found the little critter and summarily killed it. We told the new member of our squadron who now seemed bewildered by our actions about the "small snake" he had seen. He was very impressed when told of the type of reptile it was and a bit unnerved by the experience.

THE KC-135

Despite the fact that I had flown the KC-135 Tanker at Mather, I was informed that I had never received the formal checkout, which includes a number of checkout flights and the formal simulator program, and a 60-4 "Standboard" flight check necessary to fly without Instructor supervision. I had been doing things in a reverse fashion at UT as I had now completed the required number of instructional flights in the KC-135, but in order to be totally qualified to take it on a mission without an IP, I would have to complete six simulator sessions plus another check ride and to do that I would have to go TDY to Kadena AFB on Okinawa. On day 91, I departed UT for Kadena and was met upon arrival by the 376 Air Refueling Wing Commander Ray Horvath, at 0300 hours. I was led off to the BOQ (Bachelor Officers Quarters) and awoke the next day well after the sun had come up. My formal sessions would not begin until tomorrow. I had some time to gather myself, so visited an old B-47 friend, Tom Benagh, a former instructor pilot in the B-47, now the base commander here. He was older (I last flew the B-47 in 1965) and was a very busy man, so I didn't want to interfere with his busy day and left to visit the Base Exchange. I would like to tell you, it was hot and humid on Okinawa, but beautiful. When entering the air conditioned Exchange, it was like I had gone through a metamorphosis of sorts as I was stunned at the array of goods and gifts offered here. When seeing the stock of items here It became obvious why they called UT a remote tour! I slowly recovered from the shock, vowing to buy a birthday gift for Rosemary before I left and called my old B-58 friend, Larry Duval, who had been so active in the rescuing of refugees from Vietnam. He was also a teammate of mine on the best softball team I ever played on. He was the first baseman on the team at Grissom Air Force Base, where every member of the team flew in the B-58. It was made up of athletes like I had never seen before and Larry was the left-handed slugger, batting fourth in a lineup of real "studs". I had a wonderful time with him and another old friend, Jim Webb from B-47s, going back even further to my days as a co-pilot at Walker AFB in Roswell New Mexico.

The next day reality took over and I started my simulator rides. Each session was for three hours plus critiques and I did two rides with different co-pilots on the first day. More social time with good friends and Ray Horvath and his wife took me out to a Japanese restaurant for dinner that night. Gene Templeton, the 376th CV (Vice Commander), an old friend from SAC Headquarters and I discussed the foibles of being second in command, however his relationship with Ray seemed very compatible. The following two days the routine was the same and I finally took my simulator check ride and passed. I was now a qualified KC-135 pilot, plus I was still qualified and current in the B-52D. Of course there were none around! I felt like superman1

I left Kadena AB at 0330 hours on Saturday morning on a returning tanker which was flying back to it's home base. After landing in Guam I would meet a deploying KC-135 in which I would return to UT. It was to be a short delay before launching for UT. We landed in the middle of a typical Guam rainstorm and once again sought a dry place to stay. Guam had changed as now everything on the base had a normal feeling to it. The refugees were gone and for all intents it was a peace-time environment. The concretes, where I had spent six months during "Bulletshot" and "Linebacker" days, was now what it was programmed to be, Airmen barracks. The Gym, once opened twenty-four hours a day, was closed at 0800 hours, didn't open till nine and the BOQ, once overflowing with senior officers, was essentially empty. The war was most definitely over for those assigned on this tropical Island. It turned out I would now have a day to kill as the deploying tanker has a twenty-four-hour delay due to a mechanical problem. This now very wet warrior (I had been walking on familiar roads) checked into the BOQ and I contacted Jean Pierre Beaudoin (Bo), my first navigator in B-47s, truly an old friend. We spent many a week on Nuclear Alert in places like Spain and England, not to forget the "mole hole" (Alert Facility, called due to no window environment, where all the crew quarters were underground) at Pease AFB in New Hampshire. He spoke with a decided French accent as his family was from Quebec in

Canada, however he was born in Berlin, New Hampshire. I spent some quality time with him and his family and recounted old times. Bo's wife Muriel had spent many a reflex tour helping Rosemary get through being without a husband. I left Bo's quarters on base, stopped at the Officer's club and had a meal. The memories flooded out as I remembered the many nights I had been the "sheriff", trying to quell the crews from doing damage to the Christmas time decorations out of frustration on missing another time at home. I finally got out of Guam the next day and landed at UT at 1830 hours Sunday night. I was met by a very affable Colonel Calhoun, seemingly very happy to see me back. His mellowing nature continued to his departure on August 10th.

KC-135 taxiing on wet ramp

On Mission

DOCTOR PEPI BARRERO

I had had a number of people who I played tennis with since the departure of Bobby Janka upon his return up-country, but most of them were the B-52 personnel, both the permanent staff and the temporary B-52 crew dogs, all now departed. Most of the games since were with KT (Kathy as she liked to be called), Lieutenant Colonel Jose Stuntz, now appointed as the new LG (Chief of Maintenance) and some others in the staff. KT and I also played paddleball, a game she was very good at and one I didn't enjoy very much. She was a very tough athlete and would pick me apart in our games, always ending with both of us covered in sweat. The new flight surgeon arrived on one of the deploying tankers and with his arrival I found a new source to play Tennis with. Pepi was a great athlete and very formidable opponent on the hot courts. When we first met, I immediately liked him, and after our initial conversations his declaration that he was a tennis player set in motion a new challenge. We set a time on the next Sunday to play a few sets to get to know each other. It would prove to be a great friendship both socially and on the court.

Shortly after his arrival I invited Pepi to a crew briefing on one of the redeployment drags, in support of the withdrawl of the up-country fighters from SEA. I introduced him to the crews as their new flight surgeon. Pepi regaled them with his declaration that he would welcome the "business" and his desire to learn more about their mission here as the last vestige of the US forces in Southeast Asia. In one of my initial conversations with the new doctor I told him I would manage a flight or two each week as I did enjoy flying the aircraft. He indicated he would like to join me one some of those missions. Doctor Barrero was a very serious and handsome guy; he was also a very engaging social person. I had very little to do with him professionally as my doctor until the result of a later incident he would express concern about my neck and I would tell him I felt no pain. Of course, it was a lie, but he nodded in his doctor glance and tell me to take it easy. There were many times that Pepi and I would compare notes on life. As a bachelor he had a free-wheeling side to him, but when pressed, you could see he was a man of many interests. I found him to be easy to talk to and during our conversations, he indicated he really enjoyed being in the Air Force but told me he eventually wanted to be a "micro surgeon" working on hands and fingers. He had the demeanor to do that. I asked him how many of those specialists there were in the United States and he said maybe five or six in the U.S. Our conversations would always turn to sports and his tennis game.

I mentioned to Pat Richmond, who was a tanker Instructor Pilot (IP) that we should make the new flight surgeon earn his flight pay on a flight with the two of us. Pepi was more than willing and would prove to be an apt listener on all aspects of flight. Later we found that Pepi enjoyed his flights in the KC-135 and I enjoyed having him along for the ride. He was very impressed with the in-flight refueling of the fighters from the up-country bases and spent time in the boom operator well watching from there. He was a great asset to the close-knit wing. He became a favorite with all the staff members, especially Kathy and Billie. He didn't really understand the Air Force celebration scene at first, but later became accustomed to it and participated in our many high points. I became fast friends with him and a fierce competitor of his on the courts. We played at about the same level on the tennis court and we had really tough matches, however his work on the handball court, which he agreed to play on occasion, was less competitive, but they were still good contests. Athletic he was and you could sense the fire in his belly every time we took to the court, emerging from each set on the tennis court, sweating and laughing at how we would anticipate each other's shots, grabbing our water bottle, swigging a quick drink and going back for another set.

In one of our conversations I found out he was a U-Control (Wires were attached to various flight surfaces to control the moves of the aircraft while you stood in the center of flight) model airplane builder. It was an interesting hobby and one that required many hours building and then flying these model aircraft. He evidently had one model he was particularly pleased with that he flew frequently in an open space near the softball field.

I told him to let me know when he would fly it again as I would like to see it. He set up a time when both of us could take the time to do this and we met one nice Sunday morning and he spent fifteen to twenty minutes telling me how to control the model in the air. It seemed simple enough as it was matter of using the wrist action for climbs and dives and a steady hand for level flight in circles around a large circumference.

The model itself was an intricate display of workmanship and you knew Pepi had spent many hours in its construction. He fired it up after ensuring his flight path would have no obstructions in its flight and took off in flight. He started in level flight and then went into a pattern of climbs and dives and then into loops, missing the ground in a comfortable fashion. After ten or fifteen minutes, he brought it down for a smooth landing. He asked me if I would like to try it and of course I said "sure". He went over the controls again and standing with me he told me to start the takeoff after he refueled it and started the engine again. Once going, he let go of the model and I launched it into the air. I whirled it around in circles and slowly worked into a few climbs and dives. On one of the climbs I realized it was a bit steep so instead of leveling it out I made it steeper and was in a loop that was very wide and now the model was going down. I heard Pepi yell at me to pull it out, the model crashed into the ground, shearing the wings and embedding itself into the turf. There was silence for a minute as if the world had come to an end and both of us looked at the model in disbelief, then at each other. I was in shock as was he and the exchange between us was one of apology and forgiveness. He was not angry, but I could see the disappointment in his face. All the hours he had put into that model were displayed in that look. It was devastating to say the least, then suddenly he began to laugh and commented on my ability to fly large aircraft and unable to manage something as small as his model. Needless to say my competence as a U-Control pilot took a hit, and was eventually known to all as Pepi made sure the story got out to my staff. It grew in importance as time passed. It was an event I would not live down for the remainder of the tour.

LAST DAYS AS THE WING
VICE COMMANDER

I had a series of neck problems and had been going to physical therapy for a couple of months. In the early days of August as we were preparing the Sawadee party for Wayne which was to be on the 8th, I took some time to play a game of tennis with Pepi. We warmed up with a few volleys and finally we said we were ready to play. I threw up the first ball to serve and as my arm got above my shoulder, the racket fell out of my hands. I picked up the racket and tried again with the same outcome. Doctor Barrerro came to my side of the net and asked what was wrong, and I told him I had no feeling in my arm as I raised it. He took it through a couple of cycles and told me to see him back in the hospital in an hour. We left and I returned to my quarters with a neck now so painful I could not look left or right. My right arm was OK but tingled if I moved it around too much. As directed, I went to the hospital and was met there by not only Pepi, but the orthopedic specialist, Doctor Alltoff. They went through a series of motion maneuvers, some other tests and a couple of X-Rays. I was still experiencing pain in my neck and back and a tingling in my right arm. I was told to take a couple of pain pills and to rest and they confined me to quarters. In the meantime, the orthopedic said he would consult with the Ortho-Neuro-Surgeon at Clark Air Force Base in the Philippines.

I was very involved in the night for Wayne, which was to be at my place in my large enclosed yard, so I bypassed my trailer and instead returned to the office. Billie handed me an official message informing me that the CINCSAC (Commander in Chief Strategic Air Command) General Russell Daugherty was going to visit on the 20th of August, with an entourage of generals to include, General Ryan, The SAC DCS Operations, a person I knew and greatly admired, and General Rew, in his new role as the 3rd AD commander plus others. Pepi had called and told Billie of my condition, so she was surprised that I had come. She told me to go back to my quarters, but I refused and swore her to secrecy and stayed to get things ready for the party. Wayne had left that morning on a fast trip to Guam for the change of command at 3rd AD, involving General Rew and General Minter, so I felt obliged to be close to the business of the day. Pepi called me on the brick and admonished me for being in the office (somebody squealed) and asked that I return to the hospital to see Doctor Alltoff. I said I would. Upon arrival, they sat me down and gave me some doctor looks, they said after studying the X-Rays and with the consult with the Neuro surgeon in the Philippines that I had a pinched nerve in my neck in the T-5 and T-6 vertebrae. After some conversation, they said I needed to go to see that Neuro-Surgeon at Clark as he was a specialist and alluded that because of what they found, I probably would need surgery to alleviate the pain and the problem in my right arm and shoulder. Further tests would be taken at Clark, along with more X-Rays to determine the extent of the problem. It was not something that could be delayed as it needed immediate attention. They said prolonging the problem could have serious consequences. The impact and the timing couldn't be worse as the Sawadee party for Wayne, his departure and the change of command on the 12th, plus now the visit by the CINC, very much complicates getting this done in a timely fashion. The hospital administration called and indicated they were setting up an appointment for me on the 13th of August, the day after the change of command. It sounded doable as if surgery, which was on an outpatient basis, was to be done I could be back in time for the visit by General Dougherty. A tanker was going to Clark on that day and I convinced Pepi not to take me off flying status so I could fly in the seat to Clark. It would be interesting as we are still very much involved in the support of forces up-country and our attention to that is the highest priority. I would have to be involved in the planning and execution of this important effort.

Wayne returned on the 8th from Guam, the day of his Sawadee, and was totally involved in preparation to leave, packing and such. It was obvious he was not interested in any of the pending activities and just pushed the pending business my way as there could be no delay for him now. The fact that he had not been here for many of the significant events had pushed him from the working staff, so this would not be a problem for them in getting the necessary work accomplished.

The night of the Sawadee party arrived and it was a tremendous affair despite heavy rain on this outdoor party held in my fence-confined yard. There were over sixty invited dignitaries including Captain Vichit and Admiral Samut. Howard, the new base commander and Roger Cooper, the 99th Squadron Commander' were also among those attending. We had picked up steaks from Guam and decided to do French75 punch instead of having a bar. No one seemed to care about the rain as there were many funny presentations and speeches given that did not elicit departures for cover. Vichit and Samut crowded into the small overhang at my front door and thought we were all crazy, but soon joined in the revelry of the moment and were as soaked as the rest of us. The next day I learned from Admiral Samut's office that he had a marvelous time and wished to thank me for the invitation. He had indicated as much when he and Howard were seen laughing at the French 75 bowl late in the evening and the rain was at a fierce level. It was hard to believe that I had been in country four months and have experienced so much. I feel comfortable with the Thai environment and the people surrounding me. Tonight's event cemented my feelings of being a contributor to our mission and feel I have a very good relationship with the Thai military and the powers to be in Bangkok. It was a great "wet" send-off for Wayne, but his departure will have little effect on the remaining staff and the mission.

I have been reduced to sleeping sitting up with pillows behind my back due to the pain in my neck but have been able to get some much-needed rest, in that fashion. Tanker operations picked up as we were supporting aircraft who were staying in-country for the time being. I think much of the slow-down in departures is a bit of response to the saber rattling of the Laotians and North Vietnamese who have upped their threats to the Thai government. We are in the middle of nervous feelings on the part of the Thai leaders, the military wants our protection and wants us here, but on the civilian side they were saying things would subside if we left.

FRIDAY, AUGUST 12TH, 1975, THE 112TH DAY

New and Departing Commanders of the 307th SW

The C of C Dinner Photo with Manas Manat at the table

It had been an interesting time since I arrived as Colonel Calhoun had been absent for much of the time. He has been gone for some of the peak moments during my first months here. He has passed the magic 181 days to complete his remote tour requirement which he really has been pointed to for the last three months. He had said goodbye to me at least twice, thinking he was gone, however the personnel people said he had to be in country to complete the tour, so spent early August on Guam returning for three days and the change of command and taking part in the official passing of the flag. The day started with an interview with AFTN (Air Force Television Network) lasting twenty minutes. The ceremony itself was well attended with Thai dignitaries, the base commander and his staff and the entire 307th Wing staff, (plus Manas Manat, who appeared out of the blue, expecting a seat at the official reading of orders) other than the command post controllers on duty. It was a simple ceremony with the reading of orders, after which Wayne left to catch the waiting T-39 for his flight to Bangkok where he was to pick up a commercial flight home. All the rest of us retreated to a luncheon at the club. Nice bunch of people and Captain Vichit seems to have become accustomed to my presence and spends time joking about my neck problems, indicating it has cut down on my running. He even joked about Colonel Calhoun, wondering if he was gone for good this time and I assured him that after the final days of his appearance he was totally and officially gone!

On August 12th, I received orders that I was now officially the 307th Strategic Wing Commander. It was a role I had performed periodically for these last three months, but now the designation gave me pause to reflect on what had happened over that period. A lot has happened over that period, hopefully the next few and remaining months will be as exciting and successful. The permanent party and many of the temporary duty crews seemed pleased at my new designation. Billie informed everyone at the luncheon there would be an impromptu, but well-organized party at the club that evening. It seemed like one sustained celebration as little work was done for the remainder of that day, despite the need to plan for a full flight schedule for the week ahead.

Evening arrived and it might have been two separate events, but the only noticeable change was in the attire of the group. They were not dressed for the business we are involved in but instead all arrived wearing shorts and bright colored shirts, packing the place, and exchanging barbs. Also, coming up with a very funny skit that lampooned the cervical collar that I had been wearing for the last few days and had a small helium balloon that they attached to my collar to hold up my neck. They gave me a series of free (faux) tickets to some of the local hangouts, such as Madam Tees Massage parlor in Newland and other "nice" establishments. It was hilarious. A book of possible incidents was given to me "to ease me into the routine of remote living" and saying, "the charming Thais will appreciate your efforts to learn about their way of life". They also presented me with a desk plate as the commander and gave me a beautiful brass bell with my name inscribed as the Commander of the 307th SW. We stayed till late in the night, singing songs and having a great time. It was a fitting and hilarious start to the remainder of my stay in Thailand.

The next day I was told my departure to Clark was delayed for some reason and had been moved to Friday the 22nd of August. They would run tests on the weekend and if necessary, do the surgery early the next week. I would catch a "Young Tiger" deploying aircraft on the 26th to return to UT. It sounded fine and would turn out to be a work of fate as the day after I was to depart, we experienced the loss of an aircraft. My therapy and other concerns had to take a holiday. "Fate is the Hunter"

THE U-2 INCIDENT

On August 15, The 99th Strategic Wing launched an early aircraft, a redeploying U-2 back to its home base. Uncut 72, piloted by Captain Jon T. Little, 99th Strategic Reconnaissance Squadron, accompanied by its KC-135 escort, Uncut 75 departed from U-Tapao with a final destination of Beale AFB, in California. Less than two hours after departure, the 307th Command Post received an emergency call at 0350 local time from Uncut 75 that the accompanying U-2, Uncut 72 was down, last known position as 7N, 101:47E. Our command post alerted the Search and Rescue Command Center, call sign Joker at U-Dorn AB. It was the ringing of the secure phone in my quarters that induced me to jump out of my bed at 0400 hours. "Aircraft down" got my attention. No matter how many times that phone rings I am instantly wide awake, and the message had me scrambling to get dressed. I pulled on an ever-present flight suit, grabbed my hat and departed for the command post.

I received the notification a mere ten minutes after they got the call from Uncut 75. After they gave me the information, I told them to call the 99th Squadron Commander, Colonel Roger Cooper and then notify 3rd Air Division. The 3rd AD Air Rescue was ruled out for any kind of assistance due to the distance involved. I arrived at the Command Post minutes later. The scene was one of frenzied activity, but all was seemingly in control. After a short update of what was known at the time, I initiated a call to General Rew, who had been informed by the 3rd AD command post on Guam of the incident. I was interrupted by the duty controller indicating he had the Joker Commander on the secure line. General Rew told me that I was to take control of the operation and to keep him notified on any information concerning the state of the search. Activity had already started at U-Dorn, thanks to our command post quick actions, and in telephone

173

conversations, Lieutenant Colonel Charles Trapp, the Joker Air Rescue Commander and I agreed that U-Dorn would commence the search and rescue attempt at first light. We scrambled a duty crew and launched an alert tanker to the area to assist with the search and to maintain voice contact on UHF.

Communication with Uncut 75 was very sporadic as they were in a wide circling pattern and having descended to a lower altitude, radio transmissions were difficult. After three furtive hours, we got a call from Uncut 75 who notified the 307th Command Post that a five-minute beeper had been heard, indicating a chute had opened at the automatic fourteen-thousand foot level, however no chute was sighted and no voice contact was heard. They also were able to bring us up to speed on what had unfolded prior to the pilot leaving the U-Bird. Uncut 72 which was at base plus twenty-thousand feet altitude (base is fifty thousand feet) had complained of autopilot problems just prior to declaring he somehow had become inverted, felt the aircraft was out of control and was leaving the aircraft.

Uncut 75 immediately firmed their location and started an orbit of the area descending from thirty-thousand feet to 10,000 feet and estimated a nine-hour orbit capability prior to a needed return to U-Tapao for fuel. I detected a voice I knew during this radio transmission and asked the controller if Lieutenant Colonel Sinclair was on board the aircraft and the response was affirmative. I knew at that time that we had a knowledgeable individual aboard that aircraft that would give us information necessary for this endeavor. Subsequently, Colonel Roger Cooper, the 99th SRS Commander, arrived at the Command Post and was updated on the present situation. He suggested that a deploying U-2 could arrive at the scene shortly and assume a high orbit in order to maintain UHF radio contact with all involved in the search and rescue and allow Uncut 75 to go remain at a lower altitude. We could release the alert tanker, which was en-route to the targeted position when the U-2 was in position. Up to this time, there had been no voice contact with Captain Little or any other information that would assist in the search.

One hour and ten minutes after initial notification of the loss of Uncut 72, Joker Search and Rescue stated that two C-130s, King 21 and King 22 from Korat AB were preparing for the mission. King 21 would launch immediately and go to the crash area. He should arrive there at sunup.

King 22, a tanker capable aircraft, will accompany two HH-53 helicopters, Jolly 50 and Jolly 63, from Nakom Phenom AB. A coordinated OPREP -3 (Operational Report category 3) was submitted by the 307 Command Post to all commands. The chopper ETA (Estimated Time of Arrival) to UT was an hour and forty-five minutes or 2355 Zulu and after a loading of water rescue material and refueling stop, it would take another two hours to the search area. We were informed we would need to upload several articles on the incoming HH-53 including hospital personnel and other rescue items such as survival flares necessary for the search. In the meantime, Uncut 75 informed us he had established a low orbit, assisted by Uncut 46, the deploying U-2, now in place in a high orbit over the search area. We could now sustain UHF capabilities with all search aircraft. He gave us his coordinates as 7:22 N and 101:34E. In the meantime, King 21 was off the ground at 2209Z and Jolly 60 took off from Korat at 2226Z. At 2300Z, Uncut 75 was given clearance to descend from 10,000 feet to five thousand feet. Weather in the area was reported as 2000 scattered, good visibility and water surface, light swells two to four feet.

At first light there was no sighting of Captain Little or his bright yellow, one-man dingy. The scattered clouds were interfering with any attempt at a clear sighting. Repeated calls to Uncut 75 on any voice contact with the downed pilot were answered in the negative. The tanker updated his needed departure from the orbit area as 0400Z and we relayed that to Rapcon and Bangkok Center. At 0040 Z, Jolly 63 arrived at UT and five minutes later we were told Jolly 60 diverted to Korat for a minor maintenance problem, but that they expected a quick turnaround. They would upload all the MK 25 flares and half of the other life support equipment and would await the arrival of Jolly 60. 17th Air Division at U-Dorn had dispatched Scatback Alpha, a SAR (search and rescue) command section to UT to assist and it arrived minutes after Jolly 63 with a flight surgeon on board. I told a disappointed Pepi, who had volunteered to go to the scene with the rescue helicopter, he could stay here and assist if needed. The plan, pending Captain Little's condition, was to bring him here as we were the closest hospital to the scene. Uncut 46 gave us an ETA to UT as 0200Z.

At 0130Z, now over four hours since the first report Uncut 75 notified the CP he had voice contact with the downed pilot, however there was no visual sighting. The tanker gave us a present location, later updated to 7:38N, 101:34E. Jolly 60 had departed Korat and King 22 followed within ten minutes. At this time, I asked Uncut 46, the U-2, now close to the search area, to remain on scene, fuel permitting, as it was essential that UHF communication be sustained until we could rescue the pilot. King 21 reported he was now on scene and had a beacon lock-on and was in voice communication with the pilot and was tracking to his location.

Thirty minutes later at 0220Z, King 21 had a visual on Captain Little. He was in a fishing boat and appeared to be okay. Jolly 63 launched from UT to rendezvous with King 22; now en-route, Jolly 60, would refuel in the air from our alert tanker who was subsequently launched to meet with Jolly 60. At this point I directed Uncut 46 and Uncut 75 to return to base (RTB). Thirty-five minutes after the first sighting, King 21 had sight of Captain Little on a beach being tended to by the fishing boat crew. He was in voice contact and his location was given as 06:52N 101:03E. I called General Rew and gave him the update on the search, and I also asked if I could form an initial board of inquiry to preserve facts pertinent to the incident and to interview SAR crews from Uncut 75 and Uncut 46. Permission was granted. I asked Joker to allow King 21 to remain on scene and recover at the Malaysian Airport HAT-YAI which was on the other side of the peninsula from the beach where the pilot was located. A Thai helicopter was now airborne and could pick up the pilot and deliver him to HAT-YAI. King 21 would then pick up Captain Little and return him to UT.

I convened a board of inquiry at 0400Z, with Colonel Cooper as the presiding officer. (All recorded voice transactions and other data from the time of first transmission and the final pickup information were secured for use). Joker advised King 21 to remain on scene and recover at HAT-YAI for the pilot pickup. The Thai Chopper reported a mechanical and had to RTB. I turned back to the closest chopper to the pickup spot and Jolly 63 was designated to pick up the pilot. At 0550Z, I made an official request to the PACAF command post, with 3rd AD approval for permission to use the local C-130 and crew, which was on TDY basis at UT from Clark AFB in the Philippines, to go to the crash area and conduct a search for wreckage. The duty airlifter gave us immediate approval to go ahead. Local MAC authorities had the crew ready and prepared to launch.

At 0600Z Joker advised that Jolly 63 picked up the pilot from the beach area and gave us a 30-minute time in route to HAT-YAI. In the meantime, King 22 and Jolly 60 were directed back to UT, followed by Jolly 63. King 21, now on station at HAT-YAI, awaiting the arrival of Captain Little, reported he was having difficulty getting fuel from the military at HAT YAI. We initiated necessary, calls to MAAG in Bangkok for assistance and finally Jolly 63 was given the fuel. He later called, back in the air, and said he had Captain Little on board and was proceeding directly to UT. He gave an ETA of 0920Z. Upon arriving, Captain Little was met by Doctor Barrero, the now pleased SAC flight surgeon, and was taken to the base hospital to be examined. I hustled to get there, and I was relieved to see him propped up in a bed and outside of two black eyes and some sore spots, and a little waterlogged he said he felt in fine shape. 3rd AD, 17AD and Joker were notified. I talked to General Rew and gave him the up-to-date progress of the search and the final outcome. He was pleased that we now had the pilot on station and that he appears well. I told him I would let him know of any other developments in the search for wreckage.

THE AFTERMATH

At 0750Z, the C-130, Klong 91 piloted by Captain Everitt Rowe, launched to start a wreckage search. Jolly 60 and Jolly 63, now both on station, were met by our life support section to recover the equipment placed on board at the beginning of the operation. King 22 recovered at UT and Joker was notified that all three aircraft were now at UT. The crews would be detained long enough to compile debriefing information. The debriefing of all these crews would entail a brief intelligence inquiry followed by individual statements to the board of inquiry. Each crew member, in turn would be asked significant questions about their participation in the search. As the board of inquiry was all inclusive, I was asked some minor questions on my involvement in the overall activity. The SAC and MAC command post personnel involved in the coordinated effort were also involved in the board questioning, all giving statements concerning their involvement. The duty controllers who initiated the action were personally congratulated by General Rew by telephone. After the on-station command post controllers, the first to be interviewed were Lt. Colonel Sinclair and Captain Kopplin, who were aboard Uncut 75, who gave their statements and were released to quarters. They were followed by the King and Jolly crews, who when were finished with questions and gave their statements were cleared to return to their bases of origin, Korat AB and Nakom Phenom AB up-country in Thailand.

Upon arriving at the search area at 1030Z, the C-130 pilot, Captain Rowe reported that no wreckage was sighted, but would run search patterns in the vicinity of the crash coordinates. I told the command post people thanks for a spectacular job and sent kudos to all the participating crews and commands. It had been a long arduous night and it was a successful one. A pilot was saved and even though a valuable aircraft was lost, the combined efforts of all commands and all the participants had kept this from becoming a personal tragedy. I told the command post controller to keep me informed of the search progress and left the building to a nice sunny humid day. Yes, I was getting acclimated to the heat. I hesitated in going back to the hospital as Pepi had indicated the examination of Captain Little would take some time and that he felt that after the exam Captain Little should be in isolation for a decent period of time and at least overnight. I stopped by the Base Exchange and met some of the tanker crews roaming around. They had heard of the search but were unaware that the pilot was recovered. They were very impressed we found and recovered the pilot and upon thinking about it, so was I. Most of the credit for finding him so quickly goes to Uncut 75 as they had the position of his bailout and started an immediate orbit of the area, despite the dead-of-night conditions. That fix was the key to the area of search and the notification of the event that started the immediate work by the command post to notify agencies that initiated the search activities. Captain Jim Rowell and crew E-122 did splendid work and it should be recognized. Also, the advantage of having on board Lt. Colonel Sinclair, and also Captain Bill Kopplin, both experienced U-2 pilots was a huge advantage in the search. Jerry, of course being the Operations Officer and a long-time pilot of the U-2, had extensive knowledge of the aircraft. His work on the radio was essential in providing on-scene advice throughout the long operation and contributed to the coordinated operation of the various commands.

I grabbed a bite to eat at the bowling alley and headed back to the trailer and hoped to get a nap before hitting the five o'clock mass. It was Saturday and the evening mass was a habit I had gotten into since my arrival here. It was an attempt to, not only do my weekly duty, but also to enter the air-conditioned chapel after a hot day on the courts, which was also a weekly habit. Then on Sunday, the golf bunch could try for an early golf time at the Admiral's course. Arriving at my home away from home, the gate was open and as I entered, Manas Manat was sitting at my outside table, munching on one of the bananas off my tree. He flipped me a sincere Sawadee and a Wai and asked, "how was the pilot"? Where was this guy's source I thought to myself, he knows everything that goes on and appears when things seem to take place on this station. Not knowing what else to say I said, "he's fine". Manas dropped the subject and said he dropped in to congratulate me on taking command of the 307th. I thanked him and at the same time thought maybe he had talked to Billie after last Tuesday's announcement of the new designation. Again, he inquired about my family, mentioning Rosemary by name. It was all pleasantries and he departed with the gait I was becoming used to, slow steps, but firmly forward in his pinned back grey bun and his long flowing Thai dress. I needed a nap!

I was about to enter my abode, when my brick sang a song to me (we affectionately called our hand-held radio a brick because of the size they used to be). The command post told me that the C-130, Klong 91, sighted an oil slick and debris at 07:01N/101:43E & 07:04N/101:51E. They said they saw a cylinder and a black hatch approximately three-feet by four-feet. I was their first call and I didn't have to tell them to let the other participants know as I could almost hear the background calls going out. 3rd AD notified our controller that they had heard the report on HF radio. I routed my call to General Rew and informed him before his people could notify him. He was again glad to be informed, but he was not a person to show great emotion about anything. I recalled when he was my wing commander on Guam, we were at our standard morning standup briefing going over the day's sorties and crews and in the middle of the meeting he nonchalantly said to all of the participants that the new colonel selection list was out and that I had been promoted to colonel, then a salutatory congratulations and immediately went back to the business at hand.

Finally, I made it to my bed, took off my shoes and dropped into dreamland. I awoke with a start, thinking I had a bad dream, but then realized I had not and that the loss of a U-2 did happen today. I must have slept for two hours. Looking at my watch, I still had plenty of time to go to mass. The chapel was around the corner, but I could walk there in short time, going by the tennis courts and the back of the gym, but as always, I would need a car if something more were to happen. It was about a ten-minute walk and a five-minute ride, but again it was hot outside and the humidity was hovering at about the same temperature, so all things considered I would drive. (Incidentally, the heat and humidity in Thailand seemed to build during the day, with the hottest portion late in the day, mornings were very pleasant, temperatures at about 72-74 degrees and build from there. Once the sun went down the temperature would fall, but the humidity lingered until early morning.) Now I knew the car was the right choice and took the five-minute trip to the chapel.

I was a bit early, but the coolness of the air-conditioned chapel made praying easy. I selected a seat in a pew about a half-way up the aisle on the left side of the small base chapel. I settled into the mass at hand and while sitting and listening to one of the readings before the Gospel, the side door of the chapel, which was about ten pews in front of me. When the door to the chapel opened, it made a grating, informing sound, but it was not offensive. It wasn't the sound of the door opening it was what came through it. In walked Jerry Sinclair, The 99th Operations Officer, followed by four other U-2 Pilots all in their orange flight suits, hats in hand, searching the chapel, looking for someone or something. Jerry suddenly spied me and took long strides to my pew which was not occupied to my left and motioned that he needed to see me. A bit startled by the interruption, I hesitated for a second and he emphasized his request for me to come to the end of the pew. Now Jerry is a very spiritual person and a devote Christian, but not Catholic so I guess I was a bit hesitant, but then thinking something terrible had happened I grabbed my hat and walked to the end of the pew. In a subdued voice Jerry said, "I need you to come to the officers club and give permission to open the bar". At first, I thought, what is he asking? Then I remembered that the club had regular evening operating times for the bar and only the 307th commander could open it outside of those hours. How Jerry knew where to find me was a mystery until I remembered the command post was aware of my location. I had told them where I was going when they notified me of the C-130 search findings. I smiled as I knew the other participants at the mass must have wondered what was going on and as I looked forward I realized the lector had stopped reading the second epistle and Father Saulnier was staring at our group from his seat by the altar. I motioned for Jerry to get going and now the four orange suits turned and were exiting the way they came in, followed by me.

Outside, my car was in its usual parking slot reserved for the 307CC and Jerry said they had not called the command post, but instead had been looking for my car. They started at my residence and drove to familiar locations, the chapel being their third spot when they finally spotted the car. They had spirited Captain Little out from the hospital and taken him to the Officers Club, where he and others in the squadron were waiting to celebrate his recovery. When they initially arrived as a large group and wanted to open the bar the club officer told them they would have to wait until 1800 hours (6PM). The only way it would open early would be if the 307th commander gave his OK, thus the search. Hearing this I took the quick path to the club, followed by the 99th contingent in the squadron commander's vehicle. We entered to loud huzzahs from a very loud and boisterous crowd of orange flights suits and some hospital personnel, among which was Doctor Barrerro, the friendly SAC flight surgeon, who obviously was in on the conspiracy to get Captain Little to the celebration. Jon T. Little was there and the center of attention as I motioned to the club officer to open the bar. A beer was thrust into my hand and the party was on! Howard appeared and joined in and another raucous party was starting. I left after three hours and It was still raging. I learned later that it had even grown beyond what I had experienced until Captain Little was told he had to return to the hospital by a sober SAC flight surgeon. Slowly it died out, but the club officer told me the next day it never got out of hand despite the crowd. When the bar shut down for the night at 0100 hours, it was quiet. It had been an amazing twenty-four hours.

The next day dawned to a series of OPREPS from Headquarters USAF, down through SAC, 8th Air Force and the 3rd Air Division channels that recovery of the crashed U-2 would take place with appropriate equipment being airlifted to the sight of the wreckage and was already in-route for that effort. Further information was never shared with the 307th as to the results of that effort. A Fifteenth Air Force Accident Investigation Team arrived on day 119 and found that we had done most of their job. We had already compiled all the logs and detail that was not in the initial reports and had interview tapes to coordinate the initial report and all this was given to them. They indicated they would like to just interview the pilot and substantiate his story. It was a short stay for them. We learned later through the JUSMAAG that the U-2 was recovered, at least all the important parts and highly secretive intelligence systems, such as cameras.

LIFE AND THE PLACE WE LIVE IN

Amidst all the turmoil that was going on, I received a congressional inquiry concerning the Airman who was shot downtown six weeks ago while shopping. Unfortunately, he had his American wife and two children with him, which is very much discouraged. Of course, they were living off the economy as there is no accompanied housing on the base, as this is a remote tour. A remote tour is designated as a one-year tour without dependents. It is for good reason as these are areas considered unsafe in some fashion, but mostly there is no accommodation for dependents to live here. No housing on the base, usually due to the nature of the mission and living off-base here can be hazardous. Thailand is considered a war zone and the living areas around this and many bases like this is close to squalor. After the incident happened his squadron commander had spent an entire day moving the wife and children on base into some visiting quarters, small, but functional, which was against all regulations, but felt it was for her safety. Her husband was air evacuated to Clark for his hospital stay and recovery. Subsequently, I had set up transportation for her and her children to join him at Clark AFB, which was not totally in the regulations, but we skirted them to accommodate her. She was otherwise taken care of in great fashion. In the congressional complaint it said we didn't supply her with security, that she was unwanted over here and that she was harassed and further, her father and mother were not notified and lastly, all the men over here lead immoral lives and have Thai women and live in a degraded state of morality. (There are some who marry over here, which is discouraged for many reasons and have to live off-base and it is typical off base housing in a foreign country) She also complained that she had to pay her own way to come here. In my response I noted that she came over here against regulations and it is called "an unaccompanied tour". I also stated that there was no level of harassment once they are here, but they can't stay on base as there is no housing (once on the base she stayed in visiting NCO quarters which are very small apartments meant for short stays). She claimed the squadron commander was intoxicated when he arrived at the hospital. (It was five AM and the hospital staff and superintendent said he was perfectly sober and expressed great concern for the airman and his wife) I had a "seven-day" suspense to get it out, but was so irritated I had the report answered in three hours. I received no further mail from the congressman!

THE VISIT, DAY 120

The SAC Commander's Visit", L-R Colonel Dugard,
General Rew, General Daugherty, Colonel O'Neill

The Generals were scheduled to arrive at 1650 hours local. General Daugherty with wife, and Generals Ryan, Murphy, Brallier, Rew and a large entourage (sixteen) of staff members would be landing in the SAC command plane. To complicate matters I was told before they arrived, I had to go to the Thai community relations meeting and there was no way out, fortunately it would be over after another Thai luncheon. Going off base to these functions I use a motor pool car with a driver and a staff (Air Policeman) member to take me. Admiral Samut had become very friendly with me and his entourage gave me the courtesy Wais and I noticed the position of their hands indicated they treated me like a superior, except for Captain Vichit, who gave me an equal position. It included a few of the Province Governors and was not a bad meeting. The location had a lot to do with it as it was held on the beach at Sami San in the Thai Air Force Officers Club. The Thai interpreter was funny and kept them laughing with my remarks. I'm not sure he said what I said, but Samut and Vichit, who both speak English didn't indicate a change from what I said, nor did they laugh. I guess they just thought the remarks were comical. I've never been known as a comedian.

I got back to the base with two hours to spare before the arrival of the CINC aircraft and found everything was ready to convince them that we knew what we were doing. I greeted the group and having met General Daugherty before, I was still impressed with his candor and knowledge of the local scene and operation and he called me Al. Mrs. Daugherty was a stunner, looks a lot like Lauren Bacall, looks and voice, so gracious. I loaded the CINC and Mrs. Daugherty in my car along with General Rew and took them for a ride to view the remaining aircraft that left Vietnam on the 30th of April. I took a bit of time to tell them the story of the C-45 with the two CIA agents who disappeared after giving me the keys to the aircraft, then took a swing towards the bay and showed them the Cambodian refugee camp and other points of interest. I hoped that this trip would give the general's aide time enough to get all the bags and other things into the general's quarters. I purposely took the long way back, but when arriving at the designated VIP (Very Important Person) quarters (Wayne's place) found everything outside. It seemed the door was locked from the inside of what had been Colonel Calhoun's trailer.

I jumped up to unlock the door with the key I had been given by the housing office and it only opened the outer door. I apologized and was trying to think who should I call? As advertised, General Rew became very nervous while General Daugherty and his wife nonchalantly walked around the area and remarked on the flowers in the region. Of course, I had to look like I knew what to do so with brick in hand and beginning to get an answer from the command post I spied now Captain Kathy Michael walking toward me with the General's aide. Cancelling the call, I asked her what happened to the lock on the door. It seemed that the aide had locked it and had the key to the inner door. He explained he had helped getting the luggage of the other generals to their respective trailers and was a bit embarrassed that he hadn't put the CINC's luggage into their quarters. I would be sure to check other venues before taking anyone to them.

That evening we had an outdoor dinner in Howard's driveway which bordered on the lawn of the CINC's quarters, catered by the O'Club with cocktails before and Shish-kabob, rice (why not) and fresh string beans. There was a plethora of fruit and a fruit salad made up of watermelon, pineapple, bananas and cantaloupe. It was a grand evening and fortunately it didn't rain. It was a very pleasant gathering, and everyone seemed very much at ease and enjoying themselves. (Why not they get to leave tomorrow after shopping and go back to civilization).

The CINC and his wife excused themselves and left the party early. We took the rest of the Generals to the Top Three Club so they could hear the only western band in Thailand. All were in civilian clothes, but it didn't fool the assembled crowd of non-commissioned sergeants, as many served under this high-powered group, and were on their best behavior. After an hour of good western music, we went to my trailer and discussed manning and administration problems with Generals Rew, Murphy and Ryan. We broke up with some promises of help at 1100 hours. It was to be an early wake-up call the next morning as General Daugherty and General Rew were to have breakfast at the NCO (Non-Commissioned Officers) Club.

The next morning after the on-time launch of the U-2 gave me a good time hack I picked up General Rew at 0650 and General Daugherty at 0655 and arrived at the event for breakfast with fifty of my senior NCOs, mostly master sergeants and above. The CINC gave an impressive talk on just about every imaginable topic and answered questions from the audience for over an hour. He is such an impressive man!

We left to catch a helicopter to take us to the Embassy in Bangkok. There was a minor hiccup as it was not parked in front of base ops as it was programmed to be there but found it close by as helicopters are hard to hide. We first took a tour of the area, much like one I had taken when I first arrived, but a bit more extensive as we followed the coastline up to Pattya Beach and then into Bangkok. It was a short courtesy meeting with the Ambassador and his senior staff and kind words were shared by all.

The return trip was a lot quicker and as we landed the CINC remarked that it was "A nice, productive trip". General Daugherty then met with the tanker and the U-bird crews, again a fine talk and when told Captain Little was in attendance, he went on about the great successful recovery effort coordinated by the 307th BW. General Rew was very happy with the comments as he slyly winked at me. We then had an internal meeting with the General and his entire accompanying staff where I elaborated on some of our problems and seemed to get the right answers from the CINC. We did rile some of the personnel worker bees from headquarters, but the General seemed pleased, at least I think so! We retreated to my office and met with General Aderholt and a member of his staff. The base commander was asked to attend the meeting with his senior staff. Heinie talked about the political climate in Thailand, local area problems and other matters for forty-five minutes, giving me pause to reflect on our present situation. It was truly fascinating and made me wonder why more of this sensitive information had not been given to us at U-Tapao before. It was an eye-opener and explained some of the situations we have encountered in the past. Following the meeting General Daugherty talked to me about items peculiar to the 307th and Dennis and I voiced our concerns about some of our urgent problems. He suggested we approach our host military with caution and keep them at "arms" length (his words). He asked General Rew to take care of a couple of items that could be solved at the 3rd AD level. The entire group was then whisked to the flight line where the summer rains discovered our presence and unloaded just as the door closed on the departing aircraft. I dove into my vehicle, escaping the downpour, and felt a sense of relief that the visit was over and had gone well. As the rain was pounding on the roof of my car, I watched the CINCs KC-135 taxi to the hammerhead, take the runway and depart the station through sheets of rain and a now bellowing wind.

CLARK AB, THE PHILIPPINES

The day after the CINC departed, I was to fly to Clark AFB in the Philippines to see the neuro- surgeon about my neck. I had been told he was the very best in the business and I was at a point where I was looking forward to getting the tests over with. General Daugherty and General Rew had expressed concerns about my health (neck), both telling me I needed some rest time. I agreed of course telling them I was going to take some leave time after the SAC Commanders conference in September. They agreed that was a good idea. I asked if there were any plans to send in a Vice Commander to the 307th during our meetings and the personnel gurus said no, that Dennis O'Brian would be cleared to carry the brick in my absence as time did not permit a new colonel being assigned for that billet. It was disclosed that I would be the last of the string of commanders of the 307th Strategic Wing. Time does not permit a new arrival to get time required to complete a remote tour. At any rate, I would fly the tanker there as the left seat pilot and the IP would go in the right seat. Of course, I should not be flying, but as I mentioned I had convinced Dr. Barrero that I could fly. He made some reference to my crashing of his U-Control, but, with a suppressed smile, let it go. The initial delay in going to see this great doctor had given me time to sort of deviate from my doctor's orders. I had started to feel less pain and was able to eat something without pain. I still slept sitting up but thought I should at least walk. Slowly in that two-week delay I had gained total control of my arms below the shoulders and my pain had subsided a lot. In the last couple of days I had tired of sitting up in my bed in order to sleep and I was bored with the absence of running or any other activity, so took to the street one early morning and started out in a slow jog, thinking I would stop the instant I had any pain. I jogged for seven or eight minutes when I felt it would be best to stop, so walked briskly for a few more minutes. I had done that for the last few days and lengthened the time I ran each day and it did seem that there was improvement. Of course, the neck brace and the physical therapy I did not miss helped. So, with a set of X-rays from every angle of my neck, I crawled into the left seat, started engines and we proceeded to launch for a meeting with a flight of F-4s, who were on a training flight, refuel them and wend our way over the Gulf of Siam and then to the beautiful Pacific Ocean to Clark AFB. It was a cloudless flight and a successful rendezvous with the flight of three fighters. The refueling went without a hitch and when complete, we had a short flight left into the Philippine capital.

I had noticed on my first trip to Clark AFB how the white buildings of the base were. They acted like a beacon on this very clear day and they stood out amidst the contrasting areas of congestion around them. Approach control had turned us over to the tower for a visual approach to the runway. It was a smooth landing, pretty good for a bad neck on an aging colonel. Once in base operations I was met by a driver who would take me to the base hospital for my scheduled appointment. I said goodbye to the crew of the tanker and thanked them for the ride and said I would see them back at U-T when I returned on a Military Airlift Command aircraft scheduled to come through here on Friday. They said they were going to the officer', the ever s club for something to eat and then stop at the exchange to stock up on some gifts while their aircraft was being refueled.

Billie, the ever efficient secretary, had given me all the information I needed to find the Orthopedic Specialist in the huge complex that made up the hospital area, so I arrived at the main entrance and went promptly to the second floor and found the right office. I was a good thirty minutes early for the scheduled time with Doctor Danielson, so gave my name at the front desk, sat down and waited. A nurse appeared about fifteen minutes later and asked me to follow her and ushered me into a typical second room where she went through the cursory checks. An X-Ray technician took me to an appropriate room, where he said the doctor wanted a current view of my neck, so took a couple of pictures. I was met by the nurse who took me to an office type room and said the doctor would be right in. He appeared, tall, very neat in his white coat and talked with a Texas twang and asked for my X-Rays. I handed them to him and one by one he put them on a display screen and compared them to the most recent ones just taken and at the same time asked how my pain level was. I told him it had subsided somewhat as he asked me to move my head in various directions, then moved my right arm into a corkscrew position and then testing the strength and feeling in my hand and fingers, all the time wanting to know my pain level, 1-10. He showed me the recent X-Rays pointing out the source of my problem and then showed me those taken at UT. He narrowed the look to the spot three weeks ago and showed me a comparison of the two. He then sat me down and wanted to know what I had done since the first days of the loss of feeling and tingling in my arm above the shoulder and I confessed the morning jog-walk regime I had started in the last few days. He indicated the most recent X-Rays showed some significant improvement.

He took out his pen and drew a diagram on a view of the throat area on a piece of paper and indicated the type of surgery that would be performed. The repair or corrective measures he would take would involve going through the front of the neck, exposing the spine and fusing the affected discs. He indicated that going to the spine from the back would involve cutting muscles that would take months to heal, from the front was it was just in and out.

After going through all his drawing and over-view of the surgical procedure he said, "the movement you have in your neck right now and the freedom of your right arm is what you would have after surgery. You have as much freedom of movement now as you would ever have after I would operate, so whatever you are doing continue it. "I could operate, and I am the best at this surgery, but I would say you are doing well in your recovery and I would not recommend surgery".

He also said if there was any regression he would not hesitate to operate. He also indicated again that he was the very best in the field in or out of the Air Force, and no one could do more or do it better. He did tell me that he encouraged me to run as long as I did not experience discomfort and that the jogging regimen, I had been doing was OK, but to not overdo it. He gave me printed instructions outlining ways for gaining strength in my arm, hand and fingers. It included arm exercises and small scale weight-lifting, such as wrist curls. I didn't need to hear anything else and thanked him for his time and asked him where a base phone was that I could get ahold of the tower. I found the phone in the hallway outside his office and asked the base operator to connect me to the tower. Once I got an answer, I asked them if the tanker going to U-Tapao had departed yet. The answer was, "They are on the hammerhead ready for takeoff.

I told them to hold the aircraft for me as I would be there in ten minutes. I called base taxi and asked to be picked up at the hospital entrance, ran downstairs, caught the taxi which took me to base operations where I got in a "Follow-Me" vehicle that took me to the awaiting aircraft, whose entrance ladder was down. I crawled into the aircraft, got in the jump seat behind the two pilots and thanked them for waiting. They said they were glad to do it.

After takeoff I explained to them the interchange between the doctor and me. I didn't tell them that as a result of the visit, the doctor had put some limits on me and placed me on DNIF status which took me off flying status and backdating it to the start of my problems. I didn't get into the seat for the return and would talk to my friendly flight surgeon when I returned so we could fix the paperwork. I couldn't believe how this turned out and was pleased with the outcome. Fate, once again worked in my favor as if I had gone there on the original date there would have been only one set of X-Rays to consider, or at least the comparison between the one taken when I arrived would not have shown any improvement in the condition of my neck. It was a very happy and smooth dead-head flight back. Upon arrival surprise, followed by everyone being genuinely happy to see me back and glad I didn't have to have surgery, so was I!

"THE COMMANDER'S CONFERENCE"! A BREAK!

I would be afforded a good break in September as there would be a wing commander's conference at SAC Headquarters in Omaha Nebraska. I would fly from UT, stop at Kadena AFB and pick up Ray Horvath, then to Guam where we would change aircraft, flying with General Rew through Hickam and then directly to Omaha. This trip would involve Rosemary, as here were certain items I didn't take to Thailand that I would need at this conference. My Mess Dress was essential attire for the conference. It would be delivered to me there by Curtis Smith, the Wing Commander from my old duty station at Mather AFB. Rosemary would deliver it to him at Mather and he would kindly carry it with him.

I would arrive in Omaha on Monday, the eighth of September, and after the conference fly to Sacramento a week later and after a ten-day leave, catch a tanker to March AFB where a deploying "Young Tiger" will carry me back to UT, through Hickam and Guam. The Commander's conference went off without a hitch, seeing old friends and making new ones. It was a busy three days and a commercial flight to Sacramento for a ten day leave which as all leaves are it was too short and once again, I left my family for the final months of my tour. I caught the deploying KC-135 out of March after lucking into a T-39 flight going to March out of Travis AFB. The aircraft landed and refueled at Hickam and then departed for Guam. I was still off status so watched from the jump seat for the entire flight. I was met in Guam by a life-long friend, Pat Halloran, the new 3rd AD vice commander and a new general selectee. He informed me that General Rew was planning an inspection tour to UT and would bring a large contingent of his staff with him. (another shopping trip for most) I would have mere days after I made a required visit back to see Doctor

Danielson at Clark to prepare for that visit, but hopefully things will smooth out in time for his visit. The stay in Guam was overnight and I left early the next day for UT with mixed feelings about my future days in Thailand as Pat had said there were some significant changes in the tone now being fostered by the Thai government. It is strange how an almost three-week absence can seem to change everything. Would this hasten my departure from the country? I was not past the safe 180 days needed for tour credit. A flight from Guam over the stormy south Pacific to UT did not bode well for the coming days and months ahead. It was a tough flight, dodging building thunderstorms the entire way. The landing was made during a blast of rain and a good cross wind. The pilot did a great job.

Upon arriving back at U-Tapao after the all-too-short break on a dismal, rainy Sunday, the 164th day of my counting time in Thailand for remote tour credit I was met by the entire operational staff. After exchanging pleasantries on the ramp, OB and I retreated to the command section where he briefed me on the present status and more salient happenings on the base.

It has become obvious that the base here at UT is slowly shutting down as replacements are very hard to come by and resupply of items has virtually stopped. My trips to JUSMAAG and the Embassy usually end up with some comment about moving non-essential items out of the country on redeploying aircraft. Many of the base facilities have been shut down. The officers club has been shut down due to kitchen problems, however access to the bar opens at the end of normal duty days. Other eating facilities such as Foodland, an on-base place to eat have been shuttered. The BX was no longer getting new goods to add to their inventory, so shopping was very skimpy, however the Thai operated shops were open and doing well. Many of the other on-base facilities, such as the gym, were restricting the hours of operation to a bare minimum.

To make matters worse, thievery on base has been stepped up and there have been instances of terror tactics inside the gate. PACAF has implemented a high security status on base due to the instability of the political environment and the lax on-base security. I became immediately aware of the increased security as armed guards with dogs had been placed around the trailer area where I lived. As I went out for my morning run the next morning I was greeted by a jeep with gun-toting security police who were to accompany me on my neck limiting run/walk. If nothing else, my pace quickened for the route I usually ran. I was later told to change my route as it was too much of a pattern, so I did.

Billie informed me that the hospital called and said Doctor Danielson had informed them that he would like to see me to assess my progress and for me to arrange a return to Clark AFB to see him. With all of the activity with redeployment, I was able to work my required return visit to Clark around two fighter support sorties, one going from UT and one returning. I was going to have to hand the brick to OB for another two days and so two days after arriving back from the CONUS, I would venture to see the good neurosurgeon, Doctor Danielson. An uneventful flight, a three-hour mission, completed as advertised and upon landing, I once again told the crew, who would be my transportation back that I would see them tomorrow at an early "first stations" for the return flight.

I was hopeful that I would see my return to flying status as a just reward from by my good, scalpel threatening, doctor. Upon arriving at his office, he started out by testing the strength in my right arm and shoulder. He was very pleased at the increase in strength in both areas, but also says my wrist and my grip left something to be desired. He final approved my return to flight status, taking me off DNIF status, but he said I was still at increased risk and though coming along just fine, the possibility of a recurrence is high! He said to not play handball or any other such exercise just yet but do indeed keep running as he feels that was the source that helped my recovery. He also had his nurse give me a typhoid shot as mine was out of date. He wished me well and said he hoped there would be no reason to see him again. I was very fortunate to have such a competent doctor.

I spent the night visiting some 509th Bomb Wing friends of B-47 days, had dinner at the very busy officer's club and departed the next morning. Back on flying status I was afforded the left seat for the return trip so was feeling I was back where I belonged. On departure into a just arriving sun, the Philippine islands stood out as I had seen them so many times, but this time I ventured on a sort of historical jaunt. Leveling off at a low visual altitude, I took my young co-pilot over Bataan and Corregidor. He was born at least five years after WWII, but being an Academy graduate I felt he at least knew the history and impact of these two areas. I had the boom operator and navigator looking over our shoulders as we navigated the area. I was like a little kid, gawking and pointing out check points to all of them. It was very impressive as the red rising sun and the very blue Pacific made it very special. I discovered that the shot I received yesterday was like a load of rocks in my left arm, now I had two bad arms!

Climbing back to altitude, it would be a routine rendezvous and fighter refueling then off to UT. At least I thought so, as after the successful refueling something happened on the way to the field. We arrived during very turbulent weather as we were notified that the base was closed due to severe thunderstorms and brutal cross winds. We set up a holding pattern off the coast, watching the cumulonimbus clouds building into hammerheads and had to wait over an hour before we received approval to make our approach and come in for a landing. The southward-bound monsoon had arrived! Once on the ground, I realized that the wonderful Third Air Division team and General Rew would be here tomorrow.

General Rew and fifty-two staff members hit the ground at 1000 hours local time, not on a social visit, but on an inspection tour, obviously to do a little shopping too. I offered General Rew a staff car and he turned it down as he didn't want to drive, so I would be his guide for him the entire length of the visit. This would include his personal desire to see Admiral Samut in Saddahip. I would have to use a motor pool driver to accommodate that trip as I don't drive off base. The short trip to see Samut is through the very seamy side of the local area. Road is narrow and small GI hangouts are obvious with their gaudy exteriors. We were greeted very formally by the Admiral. The conversation was one I had heard before as it involved his desire to cooperate every way possible to safeguard the base and its personnel. The pleasantries over we departed for the base and traversed along the same road we came on. Fortunately, there would be a trip to Bangkok to address the situation in our immediate area to break up the visit. We would arrive in time to get to our aircraft for a flight to Bangkok. Actually, it would be a good break as General Aderholt informed me he wanted to treat General Rew to some touring in the city and a golf game at the course downtown that had been selected for the World Cup Golf Match in December. A MAC-Thai U-21 aircraft picked us up for the thirty-five-minute flight to the Thailand capital; It proved to be a pleasant ride despite the rain.

The U-21 was the courier aircraft that I had used for my flights into Bangkok on business. It was an eight-passenger, reciprocal engine aircraft, very comfortable, however it can be tossed around a bit in turbulence. Today, the General, his aide and I were the only passengers. It usually is full. After landing, we were met by an Air Force vehicle and taken to our downtown hotel where we dropped off our bags and then went directly to General Aderholt's office at MACTHAI. The General informed us that the Ambassador would return from Washington tonight and meet with us tomorrow morning instead of today.

The briefings were very informative and after staff discussions, Heinie downplayed the political problem, saying he had seen it much worse in the past. One item discussed concerned me as General Rew had heard through our intelligence sources there were substantial reports that a contract was out on my life. It was a result of some curfew restrictions I had imposed on my personnel due to increased activity against the airmen on base. The story had a yellow Volkswagen whose driver had been paid to do away with me. It was news to me, but both generals were aware of these reports. Now I knew who had put my morning Air Police Jeep escort on my morning run. It was to ensure I was safe as I went from pillar to post. I had already changed my morning routes, as most knew where I generally ran. General Rew expressed concern for my safety, but also for the enlisted personnel at UT who were so unaware of the dangers in the local areas surrounding the base. General Aderholt tried to play my situation down, saying he had verified contracts out on him but ran the streets of Bangkok on his daily run. Rew was not convinced! Aderholt did say that if the situation around the base didn't improve, he would personally get involved.

Golf was in the agenda the rest of the day. That early afternoon in the sweltering heat and humidity (it had rained but had stopped just prior to teeing off) we played at this beautiful course close to the center of Bangkok. It was like playing on the great courses at home which were used for all the golf championships. Both General Rew and Aderholt were very good golfers and it was really a fun time despite the required golf attire, long pants and collared shirt. At times it seemed like I was swimming in my clothes! Their scores were in the low eighties, mine a bit higher. General Aderholt said anytime I wanted to come he would send a car to meet the courier aircraft and meet me at the course to play. In the drive back to the hotel General Rew brought up the threat to my life and the yellow VW again. I was sitting in the front seat with the driver, a staff sergeant and the two generals were in the back. We were waiting at an intersection in Bangkok for an indication to move forward when General Aderholt raised his voice to the driver, who hit a spot near the dashboard, causing it to open, displaying numerous weapons, to include a forty-five and and thirty-eight handguns. I saw other weapons and clips of ammo as the sergeant closed the dash to its normal position. The general told my general they would look out for me. He opened the door, got out and told the driver he would see him later and started running down the crowded street. (according to General Rew, Aderholt told him he wanted to get to the embassy and the traffic was keeping him from something important). It was mostly silent the rest of the way to the hotel.

At the end of the day It was indeed refreshing to get back to the air-conditioned hotel and take a shower, followed by an American beer in the lounge. General Rew didn't drink so I had two beers. In the declining daylight Johnny Su's driver picked us up and took us to Johny's shop, where the General unloaded Mach-Mach Baht for some spectacular jewelry. Johny was the perfect host and spent time over noodle soup, displaying different jewelry items to the General. Johny's driver took a very satisfied general and I to a local Chinese restaurant where we ate a delicious meal. Upon departing the ever present Johny's driver was waiting and took us back to the hotel. It was a short night as early the next morning we went to the American Embassy to meet with Ambassador Masters, the new head of the Embassy and his military advisors. There was more information on the current political situation in Thailand and the impact of the US military presence was discussed and more specifically our place in the geo-political situation that we were currently involved in. It was again a revealing discussion and gave me some insight and some disturbing thoughts about the civilian situation. Again, I was left with the advice to not trust the Thai military.

Thanking the Ambassador for his time and the information he shared with us, we left and were sped back to Don Muang airport by a military driver, caught our U-21 and returned to UT. It was a whirlwind tour. It was felt that things had gone well with the inspection team while we were away according to the "whispering" in the halls. The "out-briefing" from the team followed a short time later before their late departure. It was very complimentary and General Rew was extremely impressed and couldn't tell me enough how much he enjoyed the visit. After they had left, almost like a dream I felt it had been a trying, but beneficial visit as I was with the general constantly the entire time and it did sometimes get nerve wracking! My feeling though now was my remaining time in Thailand would be eventful. The information I had gained had placed be in a position of knowing things would continue to be interesting and hazardous. I would be sure to look out for the "yellow" VW.

THE PIG ROAST

After the departure of the inspection team I thought we needed a break. There were no large drag requirements scheduled for the next three days. We needed something to celebrate our success and to demonstrate to the group the appreciation for the effort and hard work they have shown during a very complex period-of-time. I had engaged in a pig roast on Guam during the heavy flight schedule days when a "standown" was ordered. Guam has wild pigs that roam the base non-populated areas and were often hit by the weapons carriers on the back roads to the weapon storage area. They were often taken to the activity side of the base for any number of reasons. When killing a wild pig while driving to the weapons storage area, some notification will "leak" to various agencies on base. If asked they would bring the pig to the crew side of the base if asked to do so. On one occasion we were informed that a pig had been hit and was available in a break and a stand-down from our daily missions and the word went out to get the pig. Almost immediately the pig appeared.

There were enough experts on how to cook a pig to get the ball rolling and have a delicious dinner. Having participated in a "pig roast" I thought it would be a great thing to do for all the permanent party and the temporary crews. I used that experience to say we could do a pig roast right here at UT. It would mean finding a pig, but that should be easy as the markets in the local village of Sattaheep could surely supply one. There was an open air market right across the dirt road from the temple. We would need a roaster to cook it and we would need volunteers to turn the spit as it took hours to cook and baste a pig. We set everything in motion, assigning tasks for doing this. The market, about maybe a mile from the front gate was contacted. They said they could get us a good-sized pig and that they would butcher and gut the pig. Spices were plentiful so that was not a problem. The field maintenance squadron took responsibility to make an open roaster with a manual spit to cook the pig and volunteers were everywhere to turn it overnight. The maintenance guys took an engine casing, cleaned it out, put a lower rack and pan to catch the juices and welded bars on both end to hold a spit which they had already created out of some left over metal pieces, then formed a crank and attached it to the spit. We were in business!

The pig was ordered and a group of us took a motor pool truck to the front gate, took a left turn out of the base and walked in the blazing sun about a mile to the market, procured the pig and placed it in some sail cloth, used to cover parachutes, tied it to two poles and carried this large pig, stretched out on the poles, taking turns with the pole on our shoulders back to the gate. We were a popular show on the trip back to the main gate. The natives loved seeing four Americans and an accompanying crowd of kids and some adults walking down the dirt road to the base. We couldn't understand what they were saying, but it appeared we must have been entertaining and everyone seemed to be in a complimentary and happy mood.

The process began after we had dumped the pig in the back of the small truck we borrowed from motor-pool and brought it to our roasting spot in the fenced in yard around my trailer. The fire had already been started and was ready for the pig. Initial accoutrements were applied to the pig and it was placed on the long rod and then the loaded spit was lifted into place to begin cooking. Based on the size of the pig it was estimated it would take twelve to fourteen hours to cook it. The party would start when the pig was thoroughly ready to be consumed, of course some of the spit turners were finished early as refreshments were supplied all night. Promptly at 1000 hours the next morning, a sunny day, it was felt our pig was ready to be eaten and the feast began. It was a wild end to a beautiful pig, but an excellent party totally enjoyable for all. It was a memorable respite from everything!

THE COMBAT SUPPORT GROUP

The inner workings of the 307th seemed to be on a high level of efficiency; however, the 635th Combat Support Group was not as Howard asked me to attend a meeting about the base environment and the various serious incursions onto the base. He confessed to feeling he had some weak links in his staff and that too many unilateral decisions were being made by some weak staff members, especially in the area of base security. These constant incursions were having a debilitating, effect on the stability of the base. A nightly recurring problem had arisen on the perimeter sections of the base. The fence surrounding the base was being victimized by thieves who would come to the outer fence of the two-parallel-fence structure, (the fence was a twin fence, separated by a ten yard section between them, where mines are placed to deter entry into the confines of the base) and cut sections of the chain link, roll them up, throw them in the back of a "Baht Bus" and leave the scene before anyone could get to the area to apprehend them. This would leave vacant areas that marginalized the base interior.

The status-of-forces agreement between the US government and Thailand does not allow our US forces to shoot the thieves and the Thai marines will not fire on them. It is felt that certain on-base facilities will be next. The 307th utilizes many of the base major buildings. These buildings house the bulk of equipment that is prone to be lifted if not safeguarded. Howard can't supply constant security to those buildings as his security force is very thin and cannot keep a twenty-four-hour watch on them. He urged me to keep a watchful eye on these areas. I assured him that we would keep a caretaker staff in our work environments throughout the nights to avoid any incursions into their confines. He seemed to be relieved at my response, however it was a no-brainer as we were on an upswing in activity supporting up-country requests in some increased fighter activity and our work force had no choice but to be working in twenty-four-hour shifts. In addition, we are in the process of constantly getting replacement crews in, most of which are new to this operation. Our more experienced crews are redeploying home. Our level of training has increased three-fold, so our sortie level has ballooned in the last month. It seems that no sooner do we have a stable qualified force then we have more turn-over, but that's the price you pay with a temporary force, constantly in flux. Our in-house permanent party tanker pilot Instructor force is overworked, but they love it.

Within days of our conversation, I was informed by the command post that there was a burglary in progress in the base gym which due to the drawdown of permanent party was closed. An Air Police patrol had seen entry into the base gym by uniformed Thai marines. He alerted the AP command center and now had the gym surrounded. Slowly they convinced the perpetrators to come out and placed a small number of them under arrest. They had been in the process of stealing towels. It appeared this had been a planned event, utilizing a Thai marine vehicle and at least five marines. They would not make any statements of who had set them up for this adventure; however, it was clear to Howard and me that the source of our theft problem was Captain Vichit. When confronted with the fact that his military resources, in uniform were caught, he disavowed all knowledge of the event. Obviously, the frustration surrounding these current events was overpowering.

I decided I would ask General Aderholt to get involved. He was not surprised at the more egregious happenings and told me to set up an arrangement where the top officials could be together with my staff and Howard and his security chief. A meeting was arranged with Admiral Samut's office and it involved Howard and I, our Air Police commander, his top sergeant, General Aderholt, Admiral Samut, Captain Vichit and his chief of security. We gathered in a large meeting/conference room at Admiral Samut's headquarters in Samasut. General Aderholt opened the meeting with a simple statement, "the on-base thievery and incursions on our exterior had to stop". The Admiral and General Aderholt then digressed into a conversation and were discussing the situation in English to the assembled group. Included in this group at the long conference table was a staff-sergeant recorder, and other security personnel, both Thai and

Air Force. There were some beverages and fruit for those in attendance and while the discussion was getting a bit intense. I had noticed that Vichit and his security chief were in constant conversation during this time. General Aderholt suddenly raised his voice and started speaking in Thai and was addressing Vichit and his chief of security. Evidently the two (of them were speaking in Thai) said something they didn't expect anyone to hear or to understand. The general had lived here for years and spoke, according to the official releases, most of the dialects in the language. The tenure of his speech to the two officers was vehement to the extent that Admiral Samut rose and in some guttural words gestured to the captain and the security chief to leave, which they did as they bowed their way out of the room. Howard and I watched in amazement. A brief quiet among the assembled group ensued and then the meeting resumed back to everything in English. The Admiral was talking to Aderholt and nodding to Howard and I about measures he would take to secure our base and its contents. The meeting ended shortly afterwards, with Heinie and the admiral shaking hands and departing in different directions and the general as we exited, muttering a goodbye to us and drove back to the base for his U-21 flight back to Bangkok.

A sort of postscript, the night after the meeting, two Thais were seen by a security team cutting another section of the fence. The Thai Marine escorting our air-policeman raised his rifle and shot the two Thais dead. When a responding vehicle arrived at the scene outside of the fence area, they checked to make sure they were indeed dead and then departed the scene. The bodies were left as a message to anyone that the situation now was that you would be shot if you tried to remove any part of that fence. After two days, the only change at the location of the shooting was that the bodies were now nude, their clothes and shoes had been taken from their dead bodies. Eventually, the bodies disappeared, so did the Thai chief of security from the base, and a quiet Captain Vichit was hard to find. It was reported later that the local marine force had been subject to changes in their ranks as they had been supplemented with marines from Admiral Samut's own marines at Samasut.

PACAF suddenly became very interested in our security situation as General Rew and General Baxter arrived the day after the meeting and sat down with me and asked how they could help and I replied you needed to bulk up Howard's security force as he had indicated how thin it was. They seemed inclined to help, but I knew it would take time and the atmosphere was tenuous to say the least. The pipeline for assigning security police into a zone with only a few months of remaining presence would be very difficult, so I didn't hold out much hope that Howard would get any relief. I also discussed some unilateral decisions made by General Baxter's staff that were not done with any foresight in my opinion, nor were they even coordinated with me, but these edicts had a serious effect on the morale of my personnel. I had told General Rew of my opposition to these edicts and he agreed they were excessive and that they would have a debilitating effect on our enlisted personnel. After some discussion and with General Rew's urging, I was able to get General Baxter to agree and he took measures to rescind those directives the next day.

A new functional setup came down from SAC Headquarters placing the U-2 Operations and some more involved Intelligence nets under my authority. Having been on the outside and looking into the U-2 operations for the past five months it was a revelation to be included in their operation. What I had imagined was the center of their work was true. Intelligence-gathering is accomplished in different ways. Not only photography, but also radio and signal intelligence missions are flown to ascertain the intentions of an adversary. This also allows a more succinct operation as the 99th intelligence gathering will be working directly with our SSO for forwarding to other areas of interest. The previous procedure was the U-2 would be the second utilizer of this data, having gone through the downlink up-country. The changes in the military structure on base seemed to have a negative effect on Colonel O'Neill. Howard, our base commander seems to be having some difficulty coping with the stress of the increasing problems we are now experiencing. On-base and off-base incidents are more blatant, and It will take a watchful eye to make sure Howard can handle these problems as the 307th will be the object of most of any increase of hostile activity on base.

Colonel Dugard's Fence

Maintenance Building

Revetments and Tanker Tails

901ST AIR REFUELING SQUADRON

On October 1st, 1975 the 307thSW was re-designated as the 901st Air Refueling Squadron and Detachment 1 of the 43rd Strategic Wing. This designation would be an administrative nightmare as it would mean I would be going through the 43rd and Ray Horvath in Okinawa for any and all our activity. General Rew short-stopped this and made us administratively under him. This functionally doesn't change my procedures with the 3rd Air Division; I will be operating as a wing with reports directly to Guam. I will info the 43rd to keep SAC Headquarters happy. Coincident with that announcement, the Thai government announced that all US forces were to be out of the country by March 20th, 1976. This was a political gesture to alleviate the pressure that the government was getting from the new alliance of the three communist neighbors, Cambodia, Laos and Vietnam. I queried 3rd AD and asked about our status. Their reply was that we would start the preparations to vacate before that. A Retrograde Team was to be formed to develop a plan for a complete exit of forces, the disposition of material and the disestablishment of our unit in Thailand. You couldn't call it the beginning of the end, only the speed-up of our former plans. I am not sure how many fighters we have brought out of Thailand, but it was a significant number. The OV-10s, with Little Bobby Janka departed recently so how many units are left, a lot according to our reports.

My baseball instincts were aroused as the World Series was in progress between the Boston Red Sox and the Cincinnati Reds. It was very frustrating as we were getting a delayed television presentation on the smallest of television sets. But watch I did, the delay worked out to prime-time evening delivery. Our twelve-hour time difference means the games were played in our U-2 launch time, so it worked out fine as-long-as you didn't learn who won the game played that morning. Two important events were also in progress. Father Saulnier was reassigned to U-Dorn and we had a Sawadee for him. He had become an integral part of our group, not only for his spiritual contributions, but also for his caring attitude toward everyone, airman and officer alike. I was sorry to see him go as he would often stop to talk with me about life and faith and the tragedies enfolding around us. Also, OB, my Director of Operations had to take emergency leave as his wife was to undergo major surgery back home. I was now confined to only base activities and it also meant no flying, which was a bummer. I will also miss my golfing trips with Pat and Don Dallenback, (I was stationed with Don at SAC Headquarters, solid personnel guy) the base director of Personnel, who came on-board when the Buffs left and became a solid third member of the group. He was an intense competitor and source for easy money. I can still participate in the softball games, played on Saturdays. The softball league is in high gear and in a game yesterday I was in the batter's box when someone yelled out "who follows Colonel Dugard" and from the stands, Senior Master Sergeant Evans, our Wing Boomer stood up and yelled out, "everybody does". It was funny at the time and everybody seemed to enjoy the declaration.

I called the head of personnel in the Pentagon just to inquire about my future after UT. A former personnel friend at SAC on the other end said they had been trying to bring me there, but SAC had demurred, saying they had other immediate plans. Of all the places I didn't want to go the pentagon was high on that list. I was hopeful that it meant a wing somewhere, but knew I was being premature as there was still months before those assignments were made. there was too much left to do here at UT to worry about it now.

On a rainy Day 182, a tropical storm had evidently delayed what we thought would be the end of our monsoon season; a significantly humid and lingering rain poured to the extent that the klongs were like rivers. Our cloudless days were still ahead of us. You knew that with this kind of weather we would not experience relief from our need to support the withdrawl of forces. I was notified that there would be a general adjustment in the fighter forces with some going to Korea and others to CONUS bases. It was programmed to be a significant event. I would go to Guam and direct this move and become the airborne commander. The date had not been established, but soon. Our hope was that this period of heavy rain would finally come to an end, which would make things much easier.

Things were not improving on base. The Combat Support Group lost the last of their bulldozers today as someone drove it through both fences and last seen was going into the Bonchon area. Lum thien was being threatened because she would not leave the door open to my trailer. The thievery was indeed getting worse; this was despite an increase in security patrols. I asked Howard to send patrols through our trailer area during the day to alleviate some of Lum thien's concerns. The "steely boys" are not the Thai marines, but are from the village within the base confines. Tough to keep under control. There have been increased incidents of stabbings off base, mostly when there is resistance to a robbery. To make things worse, another new problem arose, and this was within our own ranks as we were alerted to the fact that there would be attempts to hide drugs on redeploying aircraft and smuggle them into the US. One attempt had already been uncovered and the individual has been apprehended. He will spend a lot of time in a federal prison. Hopefully, his apprehension will stem the tide and ward off others who might be trying to earn a quick buck!

To keep everyone's minds off the problems on and off base, I had asked people to come forward with ideas for the Bicentennial Celebration (1776-1976). The approaching new year will signify two-hundred years of existence for the United States. The results so far were incredible. There was a proposal to paint the entire front of the OMS building red, white and blue. Other themes are constantly being brought forward. Everyone is trying to outdo the next group. If only people back home were as patriotic and could see the spirit here, ten thousand miles from home, maybe it would be enough to turn the lack of patriotism around that seems to permeate our country.

General Aderholt and the Ambassador paid a surprise visit on my 185th day in-country. I was informed that they were coming in on the U-21 out of Bangkok as they were in the final approach. A quick meeting was arranged to be held in my office with only Howard being asked to attend. It seems that the Thai government, now surrounded by adversarial countries, is trying to rediscover who their friends are. It seems that there is some thought about a more limited with-drawl from the country and maintaining some sort of a presence. What that could mean for UT is not clear, but if it includes a fighter unit remaining there would have to be a tanker presence. I was told that the redistribution of fighter event was still on, but the date was still not determined. It is a strange conundrum; they don't want us, but they need us as we are the only safeguard from a military incursion they have. We were told this information was not to be shared. After the meeting the two of them departed on the U-21 back to Bangkok. Strange they personally came here to give that type of sensitive message. I thought a secure communication would have been enough.

Things continued to change, not only within the US military, but on the Thai side. The now very quiet Captain Vichit is no longer a part of our community as he was replaced by a Captain Khan. A sedate Sawadee party was held for him last night. It was not one of his typical parties as there were no females and very few Thai military, not even the Admiral. We saluted our time with him, praising him for his "cooperative" attitude toward us. Howard and I both presented him with a gift in keeping our relationship with the Thai military as a needed one at least on surface. We all knew the guy is a crook and his minions are a great part of our problem both on and off the base. It's amazing that his party last night escaped the ravages of the weather as the departure of the monsoon season seems to have been delayed yet again. We are besieged with heavy rain to the point where it is hazardous to move about, but his party was without rain or wind. There was an inch of rain in less than an hour today, my 191st day. Flying operations are impossible as the runway has standing water and the klongs are overflowing onto the streets.

The Embassy informed me today that U-Dorn would be officially closed by the end of December, meaning we will have to move the fighter wing out of country in the next month. The good news came from stateside as OB called to let me know his wife has come through her surgery and that he will be back in early November. When he is back on station it means that if the weather ever improves, I can move about again. Fortunately, a change did come. The weather did improve to the point that three aircraft waiting at Clark in the Philippines, were able to return to UT. The third aircraft returning stayed in the pattern, shooting touch-and-gos. Upon taxiing in he called the tower and said the aircraft was shot at in the pattern. Upon inspection a bullet hole in the wing was indeed found, of course the crew wants "Combat Pay". I told them fat chance of that ever happening! We did fill out a report which went forward. Last heard the OSI (Office of Special Investigation) was handling the investigation.

With the feeling that we had seen it all, the next morning the now 901st ARS was hit with an Operational Readiness Inspection (ORI) on a Sunday morning. It incorporated the squadron into the designated parent wing as we are now a part of the 43rd Strategic Wing in Kadena. Of course, we just had a 3rd AD inspection just over two weeks ago. Now as the world was deteriorating around us, we would go through another one. This time we would be flying sorties, the first would be launching Monday morning at 0330 hours and the second, one hour later. All launches would be over by 1040 in the morning. They would be flying to Kadena and Guam in support of their activities. The actual SAC team (not the 3rd AD) that will carry out the inspection will not arrive for another week.

We discovered one factor that arose from this inspection. There was a total lack of a system to know and control the whereabouts of our troops. The Sunday start found most of our personnel somewhere other than in the barracks. If we were to use percentages, we would have less than ten percent of our personnel on base, many were living with "Teelocks" off-base and others were off to Pattya for a weekend. It's a good thing the "team" doesn't come for another week as availability of personnel would certainly have raised a red flag. Fortunately, our senior NCO staff and the Operational staff were easy to find and did report at the desired time. I was remiss in not putting a process into play to control our resources.

As it turned out our launch and recovery went like clockwork as the word slowly got off the base and the affected squadron people reported for duty in time to make it work. Even OB returned just in time to lend a hand. Not that I could now leave the base, but it was also nice to see his toothy grin again. He had even heard of our bi-centennial actions and brought back some thirteen-star American flags which will be used in strategic areas. That initiative has really caught fire and now everyone is trying to outdo the other, from squadron contests to individual ideas.

The SAC inspection team came and went without a trip to Bangkok. When the inspection team finally finished their work, we were given high marks and they even mentioned the start of the patriotic endeavor over the entire base. To celebrate I had an NCO-Officer party at my trailer, flew in steaks from Guam on an incoming aircraft and had beer from the NCO club. The resident Operations Staff did all the cooking and a great time was had by all. On another high note, I have been invited to the last "Red River Rats" reunion to be held outside of the CONUS. It will be held at Korat AB up-country and I will be the sole B-52 representative. It will be an historic event and it should be interesting interfacing with all those fighter jocks for a weekend.

It is becoming apparent that Howard is really beginning to feel the strain of the job trying to keep ahead of the problems he faces. I told him it was time for him to quit telling me he "can't" do something and to kick some butt. PACAF hasn't done him any favors, his staff is very weak, and I believe the fact that we are pushing through all the odds getting sorties into the air, meeting the demands of HHQ on all fronts and telling everybody we are a can-do outfit has worn thin on his psyche. The last straw in his depression was the painting of our B-52 revetments red, white and blue. These are one-hundred feet long and twenty-five feet high and they take up the last third of the ramp. On the top, the maintenance folks placed a sign starting out at one end with "1776", followed by the words, "Welcome to Thailand---SAC Bi-Centennial Country", and ending "1976". After he told me we shouldn't have done it and that the new captain, Thai base commander, Captain Khan on base was upset, I told him to quit worrying about our initiatives and to start on his own. I reminded him that the colors were those of Thailand too! He did agree that they were impressive! I don't think Howard is long for this Asian world!

THE RED RIVER RATS REUNION

It's an honor to be recognized as a "Red River" Rat. It's a designation given to those who have flown missions over Hanoi and its's environs during the Vietnam War. The invitation came out of the blue from members of the "Triple Nickle "Squadron, (555th Fighter Squadron). Somewhere in conversations putting together support for refueling on the many missions that have been flown there was a great deal of bantering back and forth between the fighter pilots at Korat and myself about life in the cockpit. The squadron was led by their wing commander, a former Thunderbird lead pilot, who I had many discussions about life in the combat arena. Of course, they were focused on my time in the B-52 and his in the F-4 J, a difference we both recognized. I accepted this opportunity to be indoctrinated into the fighter pilot's life, knowing that I would be the butt of many derisive jokes. They have no idea that I have beaucoup time in the fastest combat aircraft ever in the inventory, the Mach 2, B-58. Not having any other aircraft at my disposal, I was going to fly a KC-135 into this up-country base that still had an entire wing of F-4 Js. They were anxiously awaiting my entry into their domain as I told them I would land at their base using fighter tactics. That is I will fly an overhead pattern with an appropriate pitchout and a visual pattern to a full stop landing. It would be part of a normal refueling mission in support of some of the Korat fighter aircraft and then landing at Korat instead of UT. It would be an early morning sortie, so the briefing was held at 0600 hours, with takeoff at 0800 hours. I told the crew what my plans were on getting to the destination and they seemed excited about the approach. I also explained the meaning of the reunion itself was and they agreed that it could turn out to be a great event. They, of course, would be welcome to participate in the weekend, which I was told there would be many surprises.

Everything went as advertised, takeoff on time, rendezvous on time, refueling completed and now to Korat. I called the tower and told them the type of aircraft and the pattern I would fly. Now, a KC-135 doing a pitchout was not the normal fare for the residents of a fighter base tower, so my announcement got a great deal of attention and the response was "say again type of approach". I repeated my intentions and a surprised "Roger that", came back.

I set up my overhead approach at the required altitude and skirted in at 200 knots. I saw the end of the runway pass by underneath and gave a two-second delay on a very clear, no wind day and entered into a forty-five degree bank to the left, rolled out on a perfect downwind, dropped the gear, sighting the runway in a descending turn, I bled off excess airspeed, dropped the flaps to a hundred percent, turned base at eight-hundred feet, started my turn to final at a thirty degree angle of bank and realized I should not have rolled out on base and blew the turn to final and would overshoot the runway. I applied power and announced a go-around and accelerated along the right side of the runway. Looking down I could see the entire approach end of the right side of the runway was lined with people. I sucked up the gear then the flaps as I heard some comments from more than likely the wing commander about the turn to final and I muttered some response to him. I accelerated to the end of the runway, brought the bird back up to twelve hundred feet and turned to a tight downwind. Once again, I prepared the aircraft for landing, dropped the gear, crossed the end of the runway, counted down four seconds and turned base, bleeding flaps to one hundred again. Setting my airspeed and I turned to final at thirty degrees angle of bank, rolled out at four-hundred feet and 130 knots, runway straight ahead. I made a smooth round-out and even smoother landing in the first three hundred feet of the runway. As I passed the assembled group on the right side of the aircraft I could see, but not hear the applause. I taxied to the first turnoff and was met by a follow-me vehicle with a sign on the back that said, "Welcome SAC". We parked the aircraft and upon exiting, got a water bath from the group, drenching my flight suit. I did get some positive feedback on my pitchout and pattern. It was the beginning of a memorable two days.

The festivities started with a briefing and a follow-on discussion on the withdrawing process for the remainder of the fighters in country and our support for them. The commanders of all the affected fighter wings were present, and it was briefed that all of the fighter wings would be rotating out of the country by the twentieth of December. (I didn't tell them of the meeting I had with Aderholt and the Ambassador as I was told not to discuss that meeting). Some follow-on drags could happen due to aircraft holdovers after equipment and stores were all removed. The meeting was followed with an outdoor barbeque late that afternoon, plenty of beer and food. The war stories were rampant and very interesting, hairy might be a better word! Many wanted to hear my experiences during "Linebacker", flying at altitude and having to face SA-2 and SA-3 surface to air missles (SAMS). Their greatest problems at low level was the hundred-meter ack-ack. Some of those in a discussion about the Linebacker II raids said they were flying "Red Crown" during that time in F-4s and cited specific instances that made me recall my experiences. They were in awe and puzzled that the B-52s were flying the same altitude and heading into the target area, night after night, and some recounted seeing B-52s being hit by the multitude of SAMs being directed to our waves of bombers. There were a few A-7 pilots, who had experienced close air support for chaff aircraft down low. Their stories would raise the hair on the back of your head. The fact that those chaff dispensing missions were fruitless due to the heavy winds at the lower altitudes was a disaster for the high-altitude missions. It turned out that many of those in attendance were new to the aircraft and never flew over the Red River during the war and relished hearing from those who did. The consummate comments were of a great respect for the BUFF and what they did during that war. There was a lot of back and forth, fighter and bomber, but all in all it was an enjoyable evening.

The next day started early with a brunch and then the fun began. There were a series of rickshaw (I mean really, they were Samlars) races formed by teams of three, one driving the three wheeled bike which was pulling the rickshaw that held two riders. We would then switch after one turn around an area almost the size of a normal track, or four hundred yards. The race would have two rickshaw teams competing with the winners going against each other and then the losers racing until exhaustion took over. It was very uplifting to see these fellow warriors bonding as one and enjoying the moment.

While the rickshaw races were being contested, the tubs of beer were being consumed in preparation for the "carrier landings" that would take place after a respite from all activity. More stories were exchanged; I had exhausted my own, so I listened attentively. Some were truly harrowing; some included loss of an aircraft, bailouts and one even a recovery after leaving his burning aircraft and being picked up by a SAR (Search and Rescue) helicopter. Some were stories about instances that they observed about individuals who were in the group of pilots but weren't talking. It was a very reflective time and sort of a catharsis for most of us.

Before anyone felt the urge to rest everyone gathered in an area where a ping-pong table was set up, but not to play with little plastic balls. I was introduced to this event by three fighter jocks who demonstrated what I was supposed to do. I must describe what "carrier landings" are all about. Take a table tennis table and use that as a runway. Aircraft on carriers fly a very wide and low pattern, so the area around the table was clear so you could traverse it with arms extended like wings. Individuals would start a carrier pattern running (flying) a pattern around that table, mimicking the sound of an aircraft. You would trot a visual downwind, turn to final and final approach around the table, calling out the proper time to extend gear and flaps. Failure to do so would be a go-around. There would be an individual who had control of your approach and would let you know about your clearance to land; diving face first on to the Mazola oil, greased table, by waving his two miniature flags. If they were waved as you approached on final you had to go around for another approach; if the flags were placed down, you were cleared to land and dived onto the table for a landing. Also, you had to have your legs bent at the knees once on the table. Failure to bend your legs indicated you did not drop your arresting hook and could not hit the barrier to stop you (which two individuals, one on each side, would provide a stretched strap to arrest you, before you went off the end on a successful approach). You needed three successful landings to qualify as a "carrier pilot"! Needless-to-say, it was hilarious as you were at the mercy of the landing judge or the yelling going on by the chorus of the group urging him on. The price of not catching the barrier was a splash down into a pit of water, cushioned by a mattress. It took me seven or eight approaches to qualify. One was due to me forgetting to lift my legs, but the other wave-offs were for the entertainment of the group surrounding the landing pattern. It was great fun and was really an escape from the reality of the da and the current situation.

The day ended with a group dinner outside catered by the O Club. More beer and more stories. I became an avid listener! As fate would have it my departure time tomorrow was a late one, so sleep would be plentiful. The party ended due to exhaustion more than anything else. I found my temporary abode and crashed. Upon first station time the next day I was given a brief Sawadee party, garland and all, with coffee and a sweet role for the entire crew by a large contingent of my new-found friends. The departure and direct flight back to UT was full of new weekend memories and thoughts of new friends.

The Rickshaw Race

Carrier Landings Platform, Note the arresting hook

THE DWINDLING DAYS

Mid-November of 1975, now almost seven months after the fall of Saigon, the closing of the UT operation was in full swing. There were millions of dollars-worth, of equipment and supplies that must be identified, tagged and shipped out and the associated accounts closed for this former strategic base. Despite the concerns for completing inventories and cost estimates for base equipment and the manpower needed for this work and other items that must be sent out of country, we were involved in the very busy drawdown of aircraft from U-Dorn and dragging them to Korea and Japan. It was a blessing that the weather had cooperated for the onset of this activity, but all of a sudden" Typhoon June" became a factor, not only interrupting our flying activity but throwing a monkey wrench into a visit from the 15th Air Force Commander, General Byron Shotts. He was to arrive here on Friday at 1600 hours but was being delayed in Hawaii due to the Typhoon, so we rescheduled the events for his arrival. The next day, his aircraft took off for Guam, only to be diverted to Kadena due to the lingering of the Typhoon. When arriving at Kadena, the General decided to turn around the aircraft and come directly to UT, putting us back on the original schedule. Our original plans were put back in place which meant undoing all that had been changed. They arrived at 2100 hours local time on Friday and OB and I were going to take them to their quarters, but they informed us they were hungry, so we took them to the Thai Officers Club for dinner. After a good Thai meal, we hoped to say goodnight, but many wanted to shop, so the small "Nit Noy" Thai shops were still open, and we went with them to insure they were not cheated on price.

The next morning after breakfast at the O'Club (pre-arranged as the O'Club had stopped meals more than a month ago) General Shotts and General Melton, his deputy for operations, were given a visit to the U-2

Operations which would tie into our visit to U-Dorn by T-39 later that day to tour the highly secretive Ramassun intelligence gathering operation. Both were dazzling and eye-opening presentations that reaffirmed my assessment of the tenuous Thailand situation and of the deteriorating climate in Southeast Asia. We boarded the T-39 and continued with a trip to the Embassy in Bangkok for a situation analysis from the civilian officials there. This briefing was very much the same as those I had received from the Embassy staff, but the two generals had never heard their take on the situation in-country. We arrived back at UT and had a get-together in my enclosed backyard for cocktails for his party of twenty-one officers and four enlisted, then traveling by bus, we took them to the beach for a catered Thai meal. (It was Lum thien and her cleaning lady friends who did all the cooking).

The next day, Sunday morning was a 0400-hours briefing for a significant redeployment of up-country aircraft, mostly out of Korat. It would initially entail using two tankers which would be followed by a second launch of two tankers. In the middle of all that, I would get the General to breakfast and receive the Ambassador on his Army U-21. A meeting would take place between the Ambassador and General Shotts and then the Fifteenth Air Force group would depart. It was a tall task, but it went off without a hitch. In the meeting, the general told the Ambassador how informative the U-2 briefing given to him and his staff had been. His staff then asked me to enlighten the Ambassador with a tour of the facility. He was given the same briefing by Lieutenant colonel Sinclair. Four hours after arriving, the Ambassador having finished his tour was very impressed with what he had seen and heard. While he was in the briefing, I watched the Fifteenth Air Force group board their aircraft and depart on a perfect day for flying. I rushed back to join the Ambassador in the final stages of the tour. When placed upon his awaiting U-21, he confided in me he might want to send some of his civilian staff to UT to experience what he had heard and seen. That's all I need! Each day is a new surprise! Tomorrow, Monday, we will start our next series of redeployments to the standard destinations.

Our operations clerk Sergeant White has taken to writing historic notes on the back of the cover for the daily flying schedule and then applying it to recent activity; some in truth and some in jest. Today's comments included this, *"The duel between Aaron Burr and Alexander Hamilton was a direct result of an argument on the links, which leads one to ask; Why does the boss always carry a .38 in his golf bag"*? He does have a way with words!

Even at ten degrees above the equator there are changes in the weather. It has become very noticeable in the waning days of November. Of course, the monsoon season is over, but with the typhoon June rain lingered and sustained the high-pressure area to the north, but now suddenly the rain has disappeared, and the temperature has dropped into the eighties. The humidity is still here, but it is very tolerable. Even the nights are almost cool, high sixties or low seventies, not seasonal at all! For those who live here, this is not normal. The Thais are wearing sweaters and you can see fires at night, not for cooking, but warmth. It is absolutely, beautiful! Windows are open and air conditioners are off. There is a flip side to this because snakes come out and use the roads to absorb the heat. Our personnel problems continue and in fact are getting worse, as some are finishing their tour length and rotating to a new duty station and no one comes to replace them. At the same time, we are ramping up our sortie count and retro-grading equipment and sending material to other locations such as Korea and some to Okinawa. We are turning to longer shifts to meet our needs and most of our skilled airmen are working seven days. I was told we have the largest sortie count in the Air Force, and I believe it. In order to fend off the possibility of our limited personnel resources getting into off-base difficulty, I placed a curfew on them. The fact that an international hold would be placed on someone this late in our time in Thailand would place them in a Thai prison or under the jurisdiction of JUSMAG, something the Embassy wants us to avoid. It is not a popular move, but it is the only way we can safeguard our resources. During all the activity on-station there is a request for an accident medical team to fly to U-Dorn. As Pepi and his team were assembling we were notified the victim had died and they were cancelling the request. Shortly thereafter, I got a call from General Baxter, the 17th AD commander, telling me that the victim was my good friend from B-58 days, Walt Ray. He was a frequent opponent on the tennis court and paddleball court. Walt had frequently caught the army U-21 flying to UT just to spend time playing the racquet sports with me. He had accompanied General Baxter on a couple of his trips here, so the general was aware of our friendship. He would spend the night in the "Q" and fly back the next day. General Baxter had also learned from others of our background together and wanted to tell me personally. It seems that Walt was awakened during the night and discovered a Thai security guard going through his clothes and accosted him. They engaged in a struggle and the Thai fatally stabbed Walt and fled. He was caught a short time later with Walt's wallet in hand and was summarily executed the next morning. Justice in swift here, but it can't give me back my friend.

Sawadee Party for Captain Vichit

THE GROWING CONCERNS

It would be strange to spend a Thanksgiving someplace, other than in the United States, but the time has come, and we will celebrate. This is a holiday despite the furtive atmosphere surrounding this country, so a stand-down was declared, and this day had to be special. The mess hall was in full throttle with the standard Thanksgiving meal being prepared. It was a good time, actually, the only time I could introduce a Turkey dinner to the Thai military, so invitations were sent out to a number of those I had been dealing with all these months, Captain Khan, his staff and Admiral Samut. I came to all their parties and events and it would be an insult if they did not come, anyway that's what I hoped. I had a special table set up in the mess hall, all decked out in special plates and silver ware. There would not be any trays or going through the line. OB and I waited out front of the mess hall and at noon an entourage of cars came to a stop and out stepped the admiral, Captain Khan and three Thai Naval Officers. I had told the mess hall troops to prepare a family style tray, with cut up turkey, mashed potatoes, stuffing and green beans. OB and I would carry those to the table aided by my senior staff. It was very interesting as the Thais were a bit hesitant to eat the turkey. I finally told them it was a wild bird and they smiled and started eating. I explained that this was a great family day in the United States. I watched as they ate this very unfamiliar fare and they seemed to enjoy it. The mashed potatoes were a puzzle! It was a real treat to host them for that time and It was interesting as a couple of the Thai officers did not speak English, so they were asking for help from Captain Khan. The shaking of the heads and the subsequent smiles were fun to watch. It turned out fine and when I escorted them to their cars, I received genuine "Wais" before they left. They expressed that they were very pleased to have been invited and departed in a jovial mood.

At the same time, Kathy, my executive officer, and Billie decided they were going to prepare a dinner for the remaining operations staff. They used both OB's and my kitchen to prepare the meal for about twenty of us. OB and I enjoyed having a second meal, this one was with our U-Tapao family and it was served by the two females with smiles and laughter, plus some very good red wine.

Friday dawned with the reality that we were back in the business of moving aircraft and then the unthinkable happened. In the middle of our preparation for the departure of all aircraft from Thailand, we had a major accident on the ramp as a large crane called a "cherry-picker", used to wash parts of an airplane and work on the tall tail section of aircraft, had a hydraulic ram fail and collapsed on the tail of a nearby tanker doing major structural damage to the vertical stabilizer. (I was reminded of my days with then Major Gaughn as it was an unpredictable happening with no one really at fault.) The crane was parked on the outside of the DC hanger and collapsed with the tanker parked where it was supposed to be. The 307th/901st had a spotless record in safety, but really it was an unfortunate incident. I did convene an accident Investigation board, sent an OPREP to SAC Headquarters through 3rd AD and hoped there was a way we could repair it locally without higher headquarters help. If through some miracle we could do it locally and complete the work in thirty days, it would be downgraded from a major accident to an incident. To make matters worse some of our repair equipment had already been sent out of country. I wasn't sure if we had the equipment to not seek help from Okinawa. That would be very time consuming. We had a young captain, Ed Maduli, our Field Maintenance supervisor, who I named as the project officer in charge of the repair project. After an assessment, his original report was not encouraging! Our sortie rate in support of the fighter units up north was at a peak at this time and the loss of a tanker to support these efforts would have a serious effect on our capability. There were turn-around possibilities to keep the brothers in the fast movers happy!

Captain Meduli had come up with a plan on repairing the tanker aircraft and it was an ingenious one. He and his maintenance superintendent, explained that by jury rigging some of the available equipment still on station, since much of our major repair equipment had already been retrograded, they could do all the sheet metal work and form-fit the pieces to the damaged tail. A new hydraulic valve for the "cherry picker" was procured from Kadena AFB and was flown in on a returning tanker who had participated in a fighter drag. We needed the "cherry picker" to work on the vertical stabilizer. Using available material, he would establish a schedule to work on the reconstruction of the tail; the metal shop would take the lead on prefabricating segments of the tail which were irreparable. He had set up shifts with his maintenance supervisors and himself overseeing each shift to install the new parts and remove the damaged sections. He was confident he could finish the work in thirty days!

When reporting that we were going to do the repair locally and would not need any assistance it was met with great skepticism as SAC had already started to gather technical support from a manufacturer and command personnel to send to UT to work on the aircraft, stating that the process would take a couple of months. I asked that they hold off and that we were confident of our local capability and of our own technicians, crossing my fingers that Captain Meduli was not overly optimistic. General Rew called and asked if we were not limited in our present status and offered to send some help. I told him we were very confident in our remaining enlisted personnel and their capacity to complete this job. I could almost hear his smile though the phone, but he said he would ask SAC to back off and hesitated a moment saying, "for now". I thanked him and uttered a prayer that we could repair the extensive damage to this aircraft, and especially do it in thirty days. Oh well, it was only a career. As it turned out the work was completed in twenty-seven days and the bird was airborne in our last supporting efforts for the redeploying fighters. General Rew was giddy about the repair and personally sent a "Well-Done" to our Field Maintenance Squadron, specifically mentioning each member of the entire repair crew. I managed to get a keg of beer to the FMS squadron and joined in the party they had celebrating their "miracle".

OUTSIDE PRESSURE

I was leaving the officers club early one Saturday during a less than busy weekend and was drawn to two women selling incredible tapestry and other woven goods. I was taken in by the artistry and weaving mastery of the articles and picked out a few items to send home. I was joined by a group of individuals who had been told about these ladies and the items they had for sale. I asked the women where they came from and it turned out that they were from Laos, crossing the border into Thailand, just three days ago. Laos has been the object of many rumors in our morning intelligence briefings, so I was interested in what they were saying about crossing the border. According to them, when they crossed into this country, they saw many armored groups, including tanks and heavy military equipment along with troops massing on the fringe of Thailand. They were somewhat alarmed, but their livelihood drove them to continue into Thailand, as these woven goods were their only source of income and this was an annual trek to the military bases where they have always had success in selling their goods. They felt they would have to leave soon in order to get back before some form of action took place and didn't want to be caught up in the beginning of a war. From their detailed description of the scene at the border it sounded like more than just a threat.

There had been recent incursions into Thailand from Malaysian and Laotian groups, but this sounded like more than an incursion! I made a call to our chief of intelligence, Lieutenant Colonel Tom Reed, and asked him to meet me at the SSO. I entered the maze of paths to the door, showed my badge and entered. As it closed and locked, I was buzzed into the working area. Lt. Colonel Reed was already there so he must have been close by as I came directly from the O-club. I sat down with him and related what I had just heard, and he said they had been getting cryptic messages about a massive build up along Thailand's northern border. I asked how long this has been going on and what was the immediate threat. He countered that U-2s have been gathering information over the past week and have presented the latest information to the Thai Military who have been somewhat skeptical of the threat, but something woke them up in the last twenty-four hours as the Thai military has started to mobilize forces to counter the current threat. Asking why this was not part of our daily Intelligence updates, he said it had been protected information, not to be divulged to all, (many of those in our daily briefings did not have SSO clearance). He was somewhat amused that I got it from a pair of Laotian merchants. I told him to keep me updated and went to a secure line to call 3rd AD, knowing they had all the information I just got. I asked if SAC had given any indication that in the event of a major incursion into Thailand, would the US forces in-country become involved. The answer was that it would take approval above Air Force levels for any such action. I hung up wondering if this would be the beginning of another conflict in Southeast Asia.

I called and asked Jerry Sinclair to come to the SSO as the 99th had to be current on their input to the situation. I interrupted his tennis match, but he said they were finished anyway in more ways than one as it was back up to 94 degrees with similar humidity and rain seemed to be imminent. Once in the SSO he told me they had come across the buildup accidently during a routine recon flight. The pilots routinely left their camera on until just before descent back into the base. During the downlink to Ramisson the buildup was picked up. What really concerned the intelligence people was that they were attempting to camouflage the buildup, evidently not realizing the capability of the U-2's cameras. After the next few words he said, "I will give you pictures to look at later today". Knowing I was only operationally in-charge I knew he would have let me know as things transpired. The information went through all the intelligence channels to the JUSMAAG and then shared with the Thai military. He then indicated it took some rather dynamic pictures to convince the Thai military we were serious about the possible threat. In order to convince the Thai General that the photos were authentic and had the ability to discern objects from that very high altitude, they took a series of photos of the general's house in Bangkok from that altitude and blew them up to show features of his house and rose garden in the back yard to the degree you could see the color of the rose petals on a bush. He said the definition of those photos convinced the military leaders that there was a threat. He said the pictures taken by the U-2 aircraft of the Laotian Army showed a massive military force poised on the border using camouflage nets over the tanks and other heavy equipment. There was also a report that SAM sites are now along the border, a region that we use for our refueling tracks. Something everyone was aware of. Our tankers do not have any equipment to detect SAM activity, so adjustments would have to be made in our training activity.

Before any changes were made in our refueling tracks the Thai military responded to the threat and within two days the Laotian army backed away from the border. I'm sure the two Laotian women have no idea what effect their conversation with me had, and hopefully their trip back across the border was less stressful.

THE BEGINNING OF THE END

In the days after Thanksgiving, word was received that a major event in support of the remaining fighter wings would take place next week. That was verified on Sunday night as an order for tanker support came that would involve every tanker on station. Preparations for this significant launch were much the same as in previous launches except for one thing. We were going to have to turn around aircraft and crews. The alternative was to use crews from the 43rd in Okinawa. We wanted to avoid that if possible as the 43rd then could pick up the redeploying aircraft for the second refueling into Guam. On Tuesday we launched in phases, two to three hours apart in a major operation to move the remaining aircraft out of country. The tankers were to return to UT after their work was done and prepare to do it over again with another group of fighters on Friday through Monday. These drags had an international flair to them which would require some diplomatic procedures to be followed and would impact recovery of aircraft and crews. Segments of the departing aircraft were going to Australia and some others to South Korea. The tankers supporting those drags would return to UT for turn-around missions.

Every aircraft and individual in the aircraft had to be checked by security and dogs to insure we were not moving drugs out of the country. Throw in maintenance situations which required "red ball" maintenance response as they had to be sniffed by the dog. It had all the earmarks of a colossal "bucket of worms". Between the two launches, I was told to go to Bangkok and coordinate numbers of aircraft at JUSMAG with our ability to support the overall operation. It would entail an overnight stay Wednesday night and an early return on the Army U-21 the next morning. As I finished my business and returned to the military hotel downtown, I decided to take a walk through some of the market areas close by. I was discouraged by the number of downtrodden individuals, the obvious misery, poverty and the many beggars on street corners, most of who were physically handicapped or diseased. I was overcome by the mass of humanity crowding the sidewalks. I gave up looking for a restaurant and I returned to eat at the hotel. It seemed odd to me that in the areas outside of the city, food was plentiful. It's everywhere-- coconuts and bananas are on trees, bushes abound in fruit and berries. Rice and tapioca are planted everywhere and fish are in every stream and pond yet, in this large metropolis people are starving.

I returned early the next morning as preparations started for the second half of this massive drag and the problems attendant to it. Some of the aircraft used in the drag were to refuel in Okinawa at Kadena AFB, so we loaded them with some of our retrograde items like refrigerators and air-conditioners, saving enough to get by until we left for good. Despite the return of rain and high winds, the launches on the first day, Saturday, went well and on time and the recovery at Kadena was as advertised, but a weather system that was moving in was going to delay the return of the aircraft until the next day. Sunday was another matter as one of the tankers to be used was finishing a phase procedure and was late to the ramp for launch. We accelerated some of the later aircraft to earlier launches to fill the void and managed to complete a late launch to rendezvous with the fighters. The returning tankers from Okinawa were to be used for Monday's sorties and were programmed to return after the departure of today's launches. Fortunately, everything worked out as we were able to recover enough aircraft from today and, combined with the returning birds from yesterday, we would make the numbers needed for the drag tomorrow. Monday went like clockwork with only a small contingent returning to UT as one group of fighters was going to Korea and another would go to Guam on the first stop on the way back to the CONUS. It would take at least two more days to recover all our aircraft back here to UT. We will await further orders for future activity, but a stand-down for our maintenance troops is a welcome respite after a harrowing few days of intense and difficult working conditions.

The after-Thanksgiving rush was followed by the December doldrums, to include the weather which has undergone a dramatic change. No rain and none in sight with the temperature very livable and the humidity dropping into the seventies. No fighter drags since the push in late November, so we are flying training missions in support of the remaining fighters in-country, which surprisingly, the number is still significant. It is hard to imagine how many aircraft were in Thailand at the height of the Vietnam War.

The base thievery has intensified. They now see we are moving things out of buildings and warehouses and they have the feeling they must strike while there are still items of value still available. The opportunities for taking those items of value are rapidly dwindling. There have been no more instances of the base fence being taken since the killing of the two thieves last month, but some of the mobile items such as small trucks and utility vehicles are last seen speeding through the main gate. The Thai Marines are waving them through and the counterpart Air Force Security Policemen powerless to do anything about it as our agreement with the government doesn't allow our security force to shoot at the culprit.

There are a couple of items that must be taken care of that will require some doing. Pete, our Python, and Iron Mike, our Gorilla, (who would never survive in the wild) would be at the mercy of the Thai populous, so we need to find them a spot to call home. Feelers are being sent out to various agencies in order to find a place for them. Based on our Veterinarian's analysis Mike is at an age that we should find a local zoo for him as long travel will not be something he can handle. On the other hand, Pete would be an asset to a zoo back in the United States. I'm told if we left Pete he would become "snake steak"! I have to work on calling some zoos to see if I can find an interest level.

The week of 15-21 December would see our last great effort in support of the last withdrawal of combat forces from Thailand. Seventeen Tankers would launch for this effort, most would be recovering in Guam. I was to lead this effort in the mission control aircraft. Cell takeoff time would vary throughout the day and the aircraft would return from Guam over the following two days and then repeat the effort on Friday, the 19th, with ten more sorties and eight final missions on Saturday the 20th. It was the final push out of country and would end our large fighter support needs the week before Christmas. It was the single largest effort of the year and would signify the real end to the fighters in Thailand. Our added last flight schedule for the week stated FINAL and had a caption "Sawadee Young Tigers". It was dated 17-21 December 1975 and had no sorties printed on it.

Two poems graced the cover of this last published schedule. The first, entitled plainly, "Young Tigers" read *"The long haul now is over, and the Young Tigers must withdraw; but they stand ever ready to extend their mighty paw. Ask any fighter jock, as he was very aware—that when he hollered "Bingo", a tiger was always there---It's not the end of the story, merely the turning of the page. The Young Tigers will again get their glory—when they hear the furtive plea, "I'm down to almost zero and I'm hurting mightily. Have you a little extra gas, so I can make one more pass"? The answer is always the same, "Sure we can play that game." And the boomer, very steady, will call "Tanker Ready." And a dept to freedom is paid when he says contact made".* The poet: Colonel G. Alan Dugard.

The second poem on the cover was from Sergeant Tom White, the wing clerk and was titled "Sawadee". It read *"A billowing cloud, a bevy of Thuds..... Boiling Thunder, Phantoms appear... An Arc'd Light, thirsty Buffs waiting... Alleycat, Hillsboro, Moonbeam and Cricket... A glorious Tiger with boom as a tail... Meeting and saving them all without fail... Phnom Penh, Saigon, The Tiger was there... Mayaguez, again we paid our fare... Red, Hickory, Peach, Saffron their names... With cunning and skill playing the deadliest games... The Tiger came first and proved his skill... Departing last with Peace and Good Will..."* The first KC-135 had arrived in August 1966 in support of the Vietnam War. The end of this time in history was most certainly in sight.

This effort signaled the real end to the Vietnam War for the United States. The missions were flown professionally and there were few problems with weather or in the air. My lead flight of Tankers and the accompanying fighters recovered in Guam as did follow-on cells of aircraft. Of the seventeen tankers who participated in this exercise, eight would accompany the fighters to the CONUS. After a two day stay in Guam, I returned to UT. There are still aircraft in Thailand and there will be more drags, although not of the magnitude of the previous movements from this country. Christmas will come and go and the personnel here on base will celebrate.

THE DEPARTURES

The beginning of the New Year, 1976, the Bicentennial year, is evidenced by the many red, white and blue edifices throughout the base. The most obvious, the patriotic revetments on the now empty flight line, brilliant in their color stand out. Our remaining tankers and crews are standing by for any late needs for support, but the cupboard is bare. We are constantly getting end-of- tour assignments, some to critical people that need to be here for the last efforts, essential to totally close operations. Fortunately, the crews and their crew-chiefs stay with the airplanes, but the technicians are essential to any remaining launches. Sporadic small moves are taking place with drags going to Brisbane, Australia and New Zealand from Clark in the Philippines and adjustments are made in the status of forces throughout Asia. The entire KC-135 inventory of our support aircraft returned to UT. There is a sense of un-fulfillment throughout base, if not the entire country. The feeling of the end of all activity is trickling down, as if someone doesn't want to close the spigot for the last time.

General Baxter has nothing better to do than oversee Howard's hold on this base and has become a real pain in the neck. PACAF even sent an IG (Inspector General) to the base to conduct an inspection, which we all think is comical, but we will go along to save the CSG (Combat Support Group) from having to answer embarrassing questions. The first obligation on my part is to take the IG, General Payne, to the golf course for a round of golf. I said I would do it as a favor to Howard. It was a first as we went there in an Air Force vehicle, not a "Popeye Taxi". He was a talker and seemed to have an excuse for every bad shot. I was hoping he would venture into the jungle to find one of his misguided golf balls, however he did use some good common sense and stayed on the grassy side of the deep rough. I think after the inspection was over the team realized what a futile effort it was as many of the essential people in the Support Group were rotated weeks ago and Howard has had difficulty just keeping the base secure.

Late in January I received an invitation from the three-star Admiral Samut's office, scripted both in Thai and English, to attend a formal Navy graduation ceremony of the Thai "Ceremony of Taking the Oath before the Colors for the Royal Thai Armed Forces Recruits", at Sattahip. I was invited to sit in the command platform at the event, which was to occur a January 25th afternoon where fifteen hundred cadets were to graduate. The Dress was Class "A" Uniform which meant coat and tie. It would be my first use of that uniform, which I brought to Thailand almost ten months ago.

The day began with the still present U-2 taking off on time. General Aderholt was to arrive on a T-39 out of Bangkok at noon. He wanted to talk to Howard and then we would travel by Air Force vehicle to Sattahip. As advertised, it was hot and humid and my tie was truly binding. The event started at 1400 hours with the chairman's arrival and adjournment was at 1645 hours with the gathering of troops. On the reviewing stand were many civilian and military dignitaries, including General Aderholt and myself representing the USAF, the top Thai Navy Admiral, numerous others and even some Buddhist monks who blessed everything. I was introduced to many of the top military brass but couldn't remember their names.

The ceremony began with a "pass and review" of the entire corps of cadets, very impressive. There were intricate marching drills, one involving the use of loaded weapons in a manual of arms drill, where the rifles were exchanged, throwing them back and forth and finishing with a flourish with the firing of the weapons into the air. Planes did an over-fly of the grounds and spread flowers and popped rice. The ceremony ended but the event continued in the head outdoor, but covered pavilion where a dinner was served, hosted by Admiral Samut. Sweet wine and heavy liquor flowed liberally, and large platters of food was served to satisfy all those in attendance. There was not a female presence at the dinner other than servers. It was a very congenial and dignified gathering which I enjoyed very much. It occurred to me that I was the only one present who didn't speak Thai, but it didn't seem to matter as most spoke English around me, a very considerate group! I returned to the base afterwards with a different impression of the Thai military as they were impressive in their actions and professional in their performance and possessed an esprit that I very much admired. General Aderholt and I were treated very well throughout and were referred to as "neighbors". We departed in the air-conditioned car where the general and I both loosened our ties.

There have been a few of the "Black Pajama" intrusions in the last couple of weeks and we are now placing armed guards on our storage of goods to be retrograded. I've been told there was a shooting in one of these instances, but it must have involved a Thai as there was no report of it being one of our troops. A sort of final blow to our base security happened last night, the fourth day of February, when one of our Yellow Fire Trucks, yes, I said yellow fire truck, roared out of the base gate, turned right, and has totally disappeared into the nether world. Howard hasn't thrown in the towel, but I noticed he is more willing to join my remaining staff and I for a beer at the O'Club Bar.

BILLIE STRECKER AND KATHY MICHAEL

Billie Strecker and Captain Kathy Michael

Billie and Kathy were two of the most dynamic and capable individuals I have ever served with; they were also full of fun and incredibly intelligent. Kathy had arrived later in my tour and took over as my right-hand person. She was essential in the smooth operation of the command section, anticipating needs and accomplishing tasks without being asked to do so. She also became a person full of ideas about making life livable in a foreign nation. She was able to and took full advantage of traveling around the country in order to soak up all the knowledge she could about the country and its makeup. With Billie's help she learned how to navigate the language and the customs of Thailand, but she also was a feverish worker, who really belonged in the Intelligence area as a career field and one, with the help of a Headquarters SAC personnel friend and former co-worker, now at the Military Personnel Center (MPC), Lackland AFB in San Antonio was able to place her in the Intel career field and had her assigned to Mather AFB California.

Billie was the last of the office staff in the command section to leave Thailand. She loved U-Tapao and the people and its environs. She was fluent in the language and had made many friends in-country. During her tenure she had guided Strategic Air Command 307th Bomb Wing commanders including me, through difficult times while serving in Thailand. She had seen UT as a major base during the Vietnam War as sortie after sortie was flown in support of "Bulletshot", "Linebacker" and all the other "Reflex" actions. She had seen hundreds of crews pass through this historic launching point of the B-52 and the KC-135, not to mention the U-2 operations. Most important she was a trusted warrior. She knew the Thai military, the Thai people and they were comfortable with this beautiful in mind and body, American woman, who was charming and giving to everyone. She had a way with all hands and could elicit help for those in need and comfort those who seemed lost. There was never a day that she wasn't seen talking in whatever language to merchants, crewmembers, maintenance crew chiefs and assorted visiting generals, or even Thai military individuals. She knew everybody and they knew her. It's obvious that she was the counsel to every incoming SAC commander and without her the job would have been ever more difficult. When it became obvious that she could not stay in Thailand she asked for and assignment in the Government Service (GS) field to Alaska, a place she stayed for a complete tour and then was reassigned to an Air Force Base in Florida. She married an Air Force Chief Master Sergeant and last heard of was living in the Keys on a boat.

PETE AND IRON MIKE

Days became difficult to endure. The workload had slowed to a crawl. I had received my next assignment and it sounded like it could be a very good one as I would be going to Barksdale AFB in Louisiana as the 2nd Bomb Wing Vice Commander. The commander was rumored to be waiting for an assignment, so it very well be a good move for me professionally. That being finalized I could turn back to the business at hand. The final missions started a bit at a time with two sorties a day, then three, but spread out. These are one-way trips with the crews and aircraft continuing to their home bases after dropping the meager number of fighters off. We are down to three aircraft and crews and some C-130s loading up some of the last retrograde items. My operations people have for the most part departed; Lieutenant Colonel Jose Stuntz and my girl Friday, Kathy left yesterday. OB rotated a week ago and it is to the point that what is left of the staff meet to discuss retrograde and not flying. No one can fathom the tremendous effort it takes to close an operation of this magnitude. We have millions of dollars, worth of equipment and supplies which we must identify, tag and ship out of Thailand. Anything left will be confiscated by the Thais. Our top priority is getting disposition on everything and shipping it out on redeploying aircraft if possible. The staff is now down to eleven people. I have been informed that I will be the last to go and leave between the 22nd and 26th of February, but not before I find a place for "Pete" and Iron Mike. I have made contact with the zoo in Bangkok and it turns out that they are receptive to taking Mike and they would actually come and pick him up and cart him to their location. That was one major worry I had, now taken care of.

That left Pete! I called the San Diego Zoo last night and asked them if they had a "Burmese reticulated python" and they said they had the largest one in the world. I asked how big and they said it was twenty feet long. I told them I didn't want to bust their bubble, but "Pete" is three to four feet longer than that. Of Course, they didn't believe me, but undeterred, I called a zoo I was very familiar with, the "Henry Dooley Zoo" in Omaha Nebraska. I had been stationed there at Offutt AFB and often took my children to go through the children-friendly atmosphere of this easy to navigate place. When I asked about a python, they informed me that their reticulated python had escaped from its cage and was run over by a car. I told them about Pete, his length and his demeanor and he is free if they would like to have him. They would love to have "Pete"! It was perfect as I was going to a commander's conference in Omaha when I left UT the end of February or early March and I could deliver it myself as I was flying tankers the entire way stopping in Kadena, Guam and Hawaii before going to Omaha. I only asked that the zoo people meet our aircraft and take the snake to the zoo. They assured me they would be there to pick Pete up and take him to the Zoo. It was all arranged, and I would keep them advised to the exact time of arrival.

The task at hand is how to subdue and take Pete from his cage, put him in a crate and maneuver him airplane to airplane as there would be an aircraft change in Guam, when we would go from a tanker to the 3rd Air Division Commander's aircraft. One thing I would have to do was I had to get permission to take him out of country. I called the embassy and they said it was a no-brainer. They would start the paperwork and then a call to the Thai government would seal the deal. United States customs was another factor as I also had to get them to agree. Another call to the Embassy took care of that and they said I could put the snake on my customs form and declare it as my possession. Pete would go through customs when we reached Hawaii. In our morning briefing I brought up putting Pete in some sort of crate and maintenance said they would put one together. I asked the Vet, who fortunately was still on station, how to get Pete ready to travel and he said if we put him in some breathable material and closed it, Pete would go to sleep. We discovered "sail cloth" was the perfect fabric, so the parachute shop created a twenty-five-foot long bag that could be closed at the end once the snake was placed inside. The finished crate appeared outside the OMS hanger shortly thereafter; twenty-five-foot long, fourteen inches deep and the same width with a thick plastic, swinging cover with holes drilled in it. Two hasp locks would secure the crate. We had everything ready; now the snake capture was next. How to get a two-hundred-plus pound snake (that was an estimate reached by the Vet and Pete's fans) into a sail cloth bag was the question of the day?

Pete was always a docile snake, stretched out to his full length and resting in the cage, sometimes lounging in his water pan. When he was fed, he didn't get nervous or hostile since he was used to humans around him. When his cage was cleaned there was no problem for the Thai who cared for him when walking into the cage as Pete didn't seem interested. People used to take time out to watch Pete eat his one chicken a week so why didn't we just go in and pick him up and slip him in his bag? It sounded so reasonable we adopted that as the plan. So, six of us would go into the cage and lift him up and one person would start the process of placing his head in the sack and work it down until he was totally in the sail cloth bag. Then, all we had to do was close the bag and put him in the crate. The crate would be stored in the maintenance DC hanger until we loaded the plane with the last of our retrograde items, mostly refrigerators and window air conditioners. We would do it two days prior to my departure so he would be asleep for the trip. The trip was scheduled to take three days. UT to Kadena, stopping long enough to pick up the 43rd Commander, Ray Horvath, then to Guam for an overnight, picking up General Rew and departing the next day for Hawaii. We would have an overnight in Hawaii with a customs review there and then we would fly non-stop to Offutt the next day. We should land at Offutt early in the morning according to the present schedule and I would get the exact time of landing from Hawaii to the Zoo to set up our meeting.

THE BEST LAID PLANS

I had sent most of what I acquired in Thailand to my next duty station, Barksdale AFB in Louisiana, In a redeploying tanker to that location, so I would be traveling light back to the states, if you can call a crate loaded with a snake, light. I had some goodbyes I wanted to make, so ventured one last time to Bangkok to see, Johnny and Annie, nothing big, just an afternoon meeting and returned the same night in the Army U-21. Knowing the tenuous conditions in the country, I spent time trying to convince Johnny to safeguard his future by placing some of his money in a Swiss banking account. He seemed to feel he was okay and repeated that Thailand had never been really conquered and that any force invading would be assimilated into their culture. It was difficult to say goodbye as they took me to the airport and watched as I taxied away.

The next day was the day for Pete's preparation for leaving. The U-2 operation had left U-Tapao and was relocated to South Korea, so my routine was interrupted as that familiar sound was no longer there. I did make a customary run with my armed vehicle pacing me. (The Yellow VW never showed). After a shower I drove to the command center. Once inside I was told by my clerk that I was wanted at Pete's cage. Upon arriving I saw a crowd around one side of the cage off the road. They sighted my vehicle and the Vet approached and said we couldn't get near Pete as someone had spooked him early that morning and agitated him to the extent he had coiled as if ready to strike. I had to see that, walking toward the cage I could now see this immense snake coiled in the corner of the enclosure. There would be no attempt to corral Pete until he calmed down. How long? We would have to wait.

Finally, in the early afternoon I got a call from one of my six-man group, saying Pete appeared to be back to normal. The six of us and a small audience of curious onlookers stood outside and we approached the outer door. Pete was lounging mostly in his water tray. Our group opened the cage door armed with our long sack; entering did not arouse Pete at all. He lifted his head and resumed his bathing in the pan. We spaced ourselves and walked toward the end of the cage. The cowardly Vet had refused to take part in this exercise, which might tell you something. The first person, with the open end of the sack, had a wooden shield to place in front of him in the event there was a problem. Suddenly, as we edged to the end, crouching down, Pete rose up to eye level and peeked over the shield, in curiosity, rather than agitated. The shield dropped, the lead guy fell back, but had a piece of Pete behind his head. Stimulated, we all grabbed at Pete, picking up the section of him where we stood and lifted him off the ground. We had planned on putting the tail in first and the head last, but we saw that if we could get the head in, we could let him do the work and slide into the bag. Inserting the head was a problem, but after a multitude of attempts the head went in and we were able to slide the rest of the sailcloth over him. We closed the bag and placed him in the crate, closed and locked the lid, and carried him on our shoulders to the DC hanger around the corner. Maintenance had placed a sign on the door indicating that the facility was guarded by a "Snake", written in the Thai language. The hard part was over, at least I thought so.

The next morning the Bangkok Zoo truck appeared to pick up Mike. I was not there, but I was told that when Mike realized he was leaving, he cried real tears and was last seen in the departing truck, sitting down in his cage with his eyes covered. Sad goodbye for all!

THE LAST DAY

It's come down to this, the last day in my military time in Thailand! A KC-135 sits on the ramp, loaded with the last usable refrigerators, forty in all. Three-hundred and two days since my tour began and two-hundred and ninety-four days since the fall of Saigon. The real end of the Vietnam War is in that single aircraft and its cargo. On board will be the commanders of the last fighter wings from up-country---the 388th, the 432nd and the 13th AD commander, General Baxter and myself, the last commander of the 320th Strategic Wing/91St Air Refueling Squadron, Strategic Air Command Wing in Southeast Asia. It's taken almost a year to really end this war. It was a tumultuous time, full of intrigue and some terrible mishaps. It was a time to form friendships and make commitments, but it was over. The day started normally enough as Manas Manat stopped by to bid me farewell. He was sorry to see me (the USA), leave his country. We exchanged our goodbyes and I watched him shuffle away, his ponytail bobbing as he exited my enclosure on this steamy day. I had to say goodbye to my loyal, little housekeeper Lum thien. She said goodbye to "Bot" with tears in her eyes and I knew as I left my only house in Thailand that she was the glue that kept it safe. My affinity for her cannot be expressed in words. I left without looking back.

I drove my command vehicle to the flight line where it would be taken to a C-141 and taken to Kadena AFB along with the last drivable military vehicles at UT for use there. I walked to the last aircraft associated with the Vietnam War and along with the other departing commanders, said our "Sawadee" to Thailand. I noticed as I entered the cargo door, that a long crate had been placed on the top of the refrigerators. Pete was also leaving the country. In my hands I had a copy of Pete's orders—yes, we cut official orders for Pete, assigning Pete as an Instructor Snake to the Henry

Dorley Zoo in Omaha Nebraska. Of course, I had his pass to the United States on a customs declaration as one "Reticulated Burmese Python". I asked the aircraft commander if he minded if I took the controls of this last departing flight and he nicely sat in the jump seat. I took the left seat in the pilot's compartment, started four humming engines, taxied to and then took the active, applied the power to the four engines, powered down the football field width runway and launched over the familiar beach into the Gulf of Thailand, heading to Okinawa. Final destination--- Home!

EPILOGUE

Howard and the remaining support group personnel would leave with the C-141 that evening for their journey home along with the last of the retrograde items. Pete would have and survive the long journey to Omaha and the Henry Dorley Zoo. He had to change airplanes in Guam after spending the night and it was discovered that his cage could not be loaded into the new command aircraft due to the size of the cargo door and seats in the new aircraft. The crate had to be cut almost in half, leaving a fourteen-foot cramped, but livable set of quarters for Pete. After landing in Hawaii, the customs agent bordered the aircraft and his first question was, "who has the snake". I held up my hand and pointed to the crate lying in the pathway of the aircraft. He asked for my customs form, I handed it to him, he saw the single declaration indicating Pete, and said I was clear to go. I grabbed my overnight bag and deplaned as the rest of those on board were detained to go through a normal, lengthy customs process. Evidently, he felt I wasn't hiding anything and if I did, he wasn't checking Pete! I was asked by one of the commanders if they could have a part of my snake to avoid the Custom's procedures. The agent smiled as he shook his head. The next day Pete departed Hickam AFB on the tropical island of Oahu with the rest of the passengers for a very chilly March morning to Offutt AFB in Omaha Nebraska. Information had been passed to the Zoo of our early morning arrival time and upon landing, with the temperature at fifteen degrees, the Serpentarium truck awaited. The crate was gently offloaded into the truck on the snowy ramp and I asked if they minded if I went with them and they were happy to comply with my request. After arriving and unloading Pete, he was taken to a large room in the Zoo, where one of the individuals cut open the sailcloth and Pete, in all his glory slithered out to the awes and appraisal of all. In a brief examination, it was divulged they really didn't believe his length, also they told me that he was overweight and had been fed too often. A chicken every week was too much! The Zoo, especially the snake people, was very pleased with their new acquisition! Pete, the 307th Reticulated Python, was placed in the Children's Zoo at the Henry Dorley Zoo. Before my departure from Omaha a week later I dropped by to see Pete in his new quarters. A brass plaque was placed on the entrance to his sizable cage with the caption of "Pete, a Burmese Reticulated Python, Donated by the 307th Strategic Wing Personnel, U-Tapao AB Thailand".

POSTSCRIPT

This letter was written to my wife, Rosemary from Thailand and was the last of a series of my letters to her during my remote year tour in that country. The closing of U-Tapao, the termination of the United States military presence in Southeast Asia, and my departure on the last KC-135, the last mission aircraft in country, would take place in a matter of days. It was not included as part of the "Sawadee Buffs" novel as it is a reflection on my personal feelings about this proud country and its people and the effect it had on my life. It has not been edited or changed in any way.

My Dear Rosemary,   20 February 1976

This is the last of my letters from Thailand, a time of great emotions, funny experiences and a great personal maturation has transpired, and I feel good about it. I'm very confused in many ways. I've learned an awful lot about people, their strengths and weaknesses. I'm amazed sometimes about my own attitudes, which border on live and let live, when I watch the social antics (not military) of others. I'm convinced that I have formed over here will never change and that I will always be critical, more so than ever, toward people, places and things.

I have learned also that men and women respond to leadership and that running an organization takes a cool head and a lot of respect for the feelings of others. Also, they return that respect in dedication if you show the slightest amount of care.

I have watched others "lead" and find that they are really being led and I've heard too much conversation on why things cannot be done. I know that in any situation into which I am thrust in the future I better never hear the words "we can't", as I will be quick to find someone else to do the job. I also pity the guy who "retires" on me while actively receiving a salary or takes advantage of me. I may be slow to recognize it, but when I do, I will be merciless. I'm more convinced than ever that the Air Force is a great way of life and I'm pleased with my profession and the people that I'm associated with. I'm sometimes appalled with the lack of guts of our leaders. The dedication of most deserves the best from leaders and that means not turning your back when a decision must be made.

I've never been as proud of my heritage as an American as I am now. I feel strongly about my country an its meaning to most people. You have to live somewhere else to realize what freedom means and what law and order means. I now know why immigrants are so imbued with the United States. I only wish those who condemn our system are secure, because our freedom guarantees it, be made to live in a totalitarian country for a few months. This includes of course, some of our representatives, who spout drivel and self-righteous indignation at our attempts to help others around the world but see nothing wrong with the USSR doing the same thing. I take great exception to other countries who are quick to condemn us, but are the first to ask for aid, whether it is because of catastrophic happenstance or financial distress. I'm really, tired of people in high positions saying what they think people want to hear in order to push their own agenda and I'm sick to death of people hiding behind "freedom of the press" and academic freedom. It's amazing that the words they are quick to use represents that which they are destroying.

I only hope that our children and their generation will bring about a new sense of pride in country and God. It's sorely needed! I know I sound like a zealot, but I've seen and heard a lot this last year and as I say I'm on the outside looking in and I know people don't realize what a great country we have and what a high standard of living we enjoy. I will never forget my experiences over here. I know it has made me a better person, a better officer and a patriotic American.

It has also made me realize how precious my family is, and what love is all about. Maybe others should endure what we had to as I'm sure they would cherish what we have. I hope I can convey my feelings to more people, and I hope my actions in the future will display my attitudes, not through cohesion, but example.

Well I guess this is what Thailand has done to me. I have many stories I could tell and maybe someday I will. I'm sure, we as a unit over here were one of the finest, most efficient, happiest ever assembled. We had a common bond, we enjoyed one another and outside of combat units, we were more cohesive than any group I've ever seen. The "farewells" to friends here as they leave have been tearful, man to man and very sincere. It's not often you receive things from an individual who served with you, but I received a plaque from on of my NCO's and he signed it merely, "Hector", I was touched as I have been throughout this time by people. They can be and are beautiful.

Love you and see you soon,
Alan

Note: This letter was an expression of my personal feelings at the end of a very arduous and trying ten and a half months. The official SAC "End of Tour" report will show the accomplishments of the 307th Strategic Wing and it can be found in the history of the wing in command archives.

GLOSSARY OF TERMS

Sawadee	Hello and Goodbye in the Thai Language
UT	U-Tapao Royal Thai Navy Base, used by the US Air Force as a strategic base during the Vietnam War.
B-52 D/G	Classification of the type of Strategic Bomber used during the Vietnam War
Buff	Big Ugly Fat F------The endearing term for the B-52
KC-135	Air Force "Refueling" aircraft used by Strategic Bomber and Tactical Fighter aircraft to extend flight operations
C-141	Military Airlift Aircraft, used to move men and material
F-4/F-111/ OV-10/F-105/B-66	Tactical Aircraft used in the Vietnam War
F-5/C-47/C-119/DC-3/A-1-E/C-45/C-130	Other Aircraft used during the Vietnam War
AB	Afterburner Increased power state beyond full throttle
SA-6/7	Soviet Shoulder mounted Missiles
SAM	Surface to Air Missile SA-2--- SA-3 Ground Controlled
CC	Commander
VC	Vice Commander-second in command
DO	Director of Operations
LG	Director of Maintenance

NCO	Non-Commissioned Officer
HHQ	Higher Headquarters
AD	Air Division
CSG	Combat Support Group
AC	Aircraft Commander
CP	Co-Pilot
NAV	Navigator
Sortie	Aircraft numbers for mission and/or Target designation
Frag	Mission Directive for Sortie Development
BOQ	Bachelor Officers Quarters
GS	Government Service
JUSMAG	Joint United States Military Advisory Group
MAAG	Military Allied Advisory Group
SSO	Sensitive Security Operations/ High Security clearance area
POW	Prisoner of War
AFB	Air Force Base
Zulu (Z)Time	The worldwide common time based on time in Greenwich England
TDY	Temporary Duty
PCS	Permanent Change of Station
RTB	Return to Base
APU	Auxiliary Power Unit
OER	Officer Effectiveness Report
IG	Inspector General
Red Crown	A point where fighters orbited ready to support aircraft in need
SAR	Search and Rescue
Klong	Any body of water to include drainage paths
Typhoon	Clockwise Movement of a storm center in the Pacific Ocean
Monsoon	Twice yearly movement of a strong and deep frontal rain in Asia

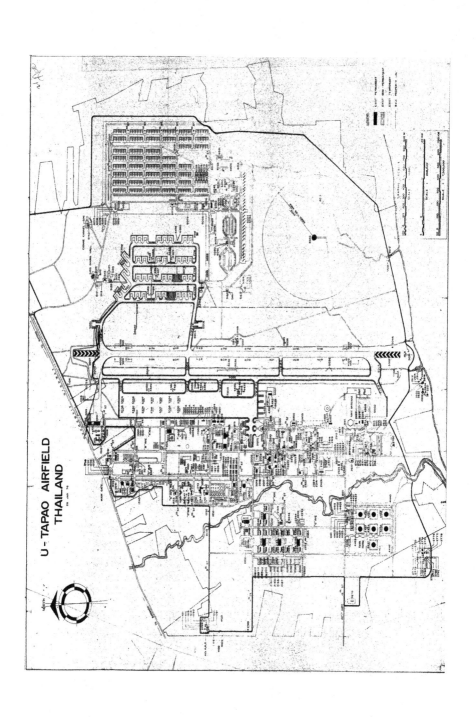

U - TAPAO AIRFIELD
THAILAND

Printed in the United States
By Bookmasters